Regulatory Model for Digital Rights Management

Cong Xu

Regulatory Model for Digital Rights Management

Analysis of U.S., Europe and China

Springer

Cong Xu
Law School
Shanghai University
Shanghai, China

ISBN 978-981-15-1994-9 ISBN 978-981-15-1995-6 (eBook)
https://doi.org/10.1007/978-981-15-1995-6

This Springer imprint is published by the registered company Springer Nature Singapore Pte Ltd.
The registered company address is: 152 Beach Road, #21-01/04 Gateway East, Singapore 189721, Singapore

Acknowledgement

30 July 2015

It is a task that could never have been completed without the generous support, assistance, and friendship of many friends and colleagues in China, Italy, Lithuania, Netherlands and other countries.

First of all, I have to acknowledge the recommendation of Prof. Graham Dutfield at University of Leeds. His encouragement was one of my motivation for being a PhD member of Last-JD.

This book was supervised by Professor Mindaugas Kiskis at Mykolas Romeris University and Professor Maria Timoteo at Bologna University. I would like to express my gratitude to them for carrying the weight of a long-lasting supervision. It was very kind of the whole team in Tilburg Institute for Law, Technology, and Society (TILT) to provide a series of intensive but comprehensive training on my research. With their encouragement, I derived inspiring ideas and overcame the difficulties I faced in my study. I have to admit that during that time in the Netherlands, I received a grounding in both practical and theoretical aspects of regulation that has influenced my approach ever since. I also want to thank my friends who are doing their doctor research in Tilburg University, as well when I needed support and help on my PhD career.

My special thanks go to Professor Monica Pamirani (University of Bologna, Director of Last-JD program) and Professor Guido Boella (University of Turin, Vice Director of Last-JD program), who constantly remind me that my research life just started when I was enrolled as a PhD candidate in the Last-JD program. I will never forget the impressive greetings of caring I received from them during my difficult times, which means a lot to me and my family. I must however specifically acknowledge the support and advices of Li Luo (Senior Lecturer in Coventry University), Jian Zhang (PhD in Tilburg University) and Dr. Giorgio Spedicato (Adjunct Professor in Bologna University).

It is acknowledged that some of the original material contained in this dissertation has previously been published, although not in its present form, in various international conference and peer-reviewed journals. These are indicated in the selected bibliography at the end of my book. There are others who have read parts or the whole of the manuscript and have generously offered their constructive comments and criticisms. I owe them a lot of thanks.

The unprecedented growth and the rapid development of the Internet have prompted new forms of regulation in digital environment. The present volume is inspired by the array of perspectives represented at the workshop, and draws on the paper presentations and roundtable discussions held in different places. I dedicate the work I put into this book to my parents, Bin Xu and Guihua Lu, who loved me very much and taught me to be strong, independent and open-minded when I was a child. I could not imagine where I would be without your love and unconditional support over these years. In this winter, the sudden death of my grandfather subjected me a great blow, which stimulated me to devote myself to my beloved research career.

Contributors

Alberto Sgarzi	CIRSFID, University of Bologna, Italy
Alessandra Malerba	PhD. Research Fellow (2013–2016), Erasmus Mundus Joint International Doctoral Degree in Law, Science and Technology
Arif Jamil	PhD Research Fellow (2012–2015), Erasmus Mundus Joint International Doctoral Degree in Law, Science and Technology
Benoit Misonne	Team Leader of IP Key-EU-China New Intellectual Property Cooperation
Bert-Jaap Koops	PhD Research Fellow, Tilburg Institute for Law, Technology, and Society (TILT).
Bin Wang	PhD Research Fellow, Leeds University, U.K
Bing-Wan Xiong	Assistant Professor, Law School, Renmin University, China
Chih-Ping Chang	PhD Research Fellow (2013–2016), Erasmus Mundus Joint International Doctoral Degree in Law, Science and Technology
Chun-Tian Liu	Professor, Head of Intellectual Property Academy, Renmin University, China
Davide Follador	Technical Expert of IP Key-EU-China New Intellectual Property Cooperation
Denard Veshi	PhD Research Fellow (2012–2015), Erasmus Mundus Joint International Doctoral Degree in Law, Science and Technology
Dusan Pavlovic	PhD Research Fellow (2013–2016), Erasmus Mundus Joint International Doctoral Degree in Law, Science and Technology
Dr. C.M.K.C. Cuijpers	Associate Professor, Tilburg Institute for Law, Technology, and Society (TILT)
Dr. Danny Friedmann	Lecturer Intellectual Property and the Law Course at Faculty of Law, Chinese University of Hong Kong.
Dr. Dina Ferrari	Research Assistant, CIRSFID, University of Bologna, Italy
Dr. Eleni Kosta	Associate Professor, Tilburg Institute for Law, Technology, and Society (TILT)

(continued)

Dr. Giorgio Spedicato	Adjunct Professor of Intellectual Property Law, University of Bologna, Italy
Dr. Tadas Limba	Associate Professor, Head of Institute of Digital Technologies, Faculty of Social Technologies, Mykolas Romeris University, Vilnius, Lithuania
Dusko Martic	PhD Research Fellow (2012–2015), Erasmus Mundus Joint International Doctoral Degree in Law, Science and Technology
Eduard Fosch Villaronga	PhD Research Fellow (2013–2016), Erasmus Mundus Joint International Doctoral Degree in Law, Science and Technology
Eniafe Festus Ayetiran	PhD Research Fellow (2012–2015), Erasmus Mundus Joint International Doctoral Degree in Law, Science and Technology
Graham Dutfield	Professor, Law School, Leeds University, U.K
Hai-Jun Jin	Associate Professor, Intellectual Property Academy, Renmin University, China
Ji Huang	PhD, Professor, Intellectual Property Academy, Renmin University, China
Jian Zhang	PhD Research Fellow, Law School, Tilburg University.
Jun-Ping Zheng	PhD Research Fellow, Law School, University of Bologna, Italy
L.M.H. (Leonie) de Jong	General Manager, Tilburg Institute for Law, Technology, and Society (TILT)
Li-Zhou Wei	PhD Research Fellow, Max-Plank Institute for Innovation and Competition, Munich, Germany
Lulu Wei	PhD Research Fellow, Tilburg Institute for Law, Technology, and Society (TILT).
M.A. Dizon	PhD Research Fellow, Tilburg Institute for Law, Technology, and Society (TILT)
Maartje Niezen	Senior Lecturer, Tilburg Institute for Law, Technology, and Society (TILT).
Martynas Mockus	PhD Research Fellow (2012–2015), Erasmus Mundus Joint International Doctoral Degree in Law, Science and Technology
Maurice Schellekens	Senior Lecturer, Tilburg Institute for Law, Technology, and Society (TILT).
Mohamed Hegazy	Head of Intellectual Property Office at Information Technology Industry Development Agency (ITIDA), Egypt.
Mohammad Bagher Asghariaghamashhadi	PhD Research Fellow (2013–2016), Erasmus Mundus Joint International Doctoral Degree in Law, Science and Technology
Prof. Cees Stuurman	Tilburg Institute for Law, Technology, and Society (TILT)
Prof. Dr. Guido Boella	Institute of Informatics, University of Turin, Italy
Prof. Dr. Maria Timoteo	Professor of Comparative Law, Law School, University of Bologna, Italy
Prof. Dr. Massimo Durante	University of Turin, Italy
Prof. Dr. MindaugasKiškis	Faculty of Social Policy, Institute of Communication and Informatics, MykolasRomeris University, Vilnius, Lithuania
Prof. Dr. Monica Palmirani	University of Bologna, Italy

(continued)

Prof. Dr. R.E. Leenes	Head of Tilburg Institute for Law, Technology, and Society (TILT)
Prof. Dr. Reto M. Hilty	Director of Max-Plank Institute for Innovation and Competition, Munich, Germany
Prof. Dr. Ugo Pagallo	University of Turin, Italy
Prof. Giuseppe Mazziotti	Assistant Professor at Trinity College Dublin, Attorney at-law, Intellectual Property & IT Law Consultant, EU Affairs; CEPS, Université de Versailles St. Quentin-en-Yvelines, International Federation of the Phonographic Industry.
Prof. Jonas Juškevičius	Mykolas Romeris University, Vilnius, Lithuania
Prof. Ryo Shimanami	Graduate School of Law, Kobe University, Japan
Qian Wang	Professor, Intellectual Property Academy, East China University of Political Science and Law, China.
Qing Wang	Professor, School of information Management, Wuhan University, China.
Robert Muthuri	PhD Research Fellow (2013–2016), Erasmus Mundus Joint International Doctoral Degree in Law, Science and Technology
Shao-Ling Chen	Researcher, Academy of Legal Science, East China University of Political Science and Law, China.
Shi-Yu Wang	PhD Research Fellow, Intellectual Property Academy, Renmin University, China
Tazia Bianchi	CIRSFID, University of Bologna, Italy
Vaida Kavaliukaite	Editing and publishing assistant at European Institute for Gender Equality & Senior Coordinator of Doctoral Studies, MykolasRomeris University (April 2013–October 2014), Vilnius, Lithuania.
Xian-Zhi Ao	Legal Counsel, Legal Counsel at Chrysler Group LLC Shanghai, China.
Xiao-Qing Zhou	Lawyer, Chinainlaw Partners Law Firm.
Yi-An Sun	PhD Research Fellow (2012–2015), Erasmus Mundus Joint International Doctoral Degree in Law, Science and Technology
Zhan Li	Project Officer of IP Key-EU-China New Intellectual Property Cooperation
and	
All the respondents of the study	

The exact contribution of all the persons mentioned above is not fully stated

Cong Xu

Contents

Chapter 1
Introduction

1.1 Statement of Problem

Prompt progress in the development of information and communication technologies (ICTs) across the globe during the past two decades has brought us to the information society from the purely traditional copyright society with a hundreds of years of history. What is notably different from the traditional copyright society is that the atmosphere (cyber sphere), which constitutes the main part of the information society, has no fixed boundary across the different states or peoples. As the traditional copyright industry in physical world developed and evolved in early information age, its potential destiny in cyber sphere has drawn more attention than before.

Technology is the other crucial element under digital copyright world. On the one hand, technology provides a new protection approach to copyrighted work in network. On the other hand, it widely prohibits the public's access, which leads to the abuse of copyright holder's right. Digital rights management was initiated with the popular will as a digital-based copyright safeguard measure. Gradually, it aroused controversy with the rapid technology development by both the general public and the right holders. Relevant regulatory models on digital rights management in different countries are struggling to seek the positive point for furthering digital copyright sustainability.

In China, traditional copyright regulatory mechanism devotes considerable efforts to combat the thriving digital copyright industry. With the rapid progress of technology, the obvious and rather intuitive pressure of the regulatory model is the diversity of regulative environment in digital era between nations. How the grim situation that digital rights management regulatory model has encountered will be in the future especially in China? This research is based on the situation that occurred in China, which has attracted more increasing discussion on what kind of regulatory model is better for China.

C. Xu, *Regulatory Model for Digital Rights Management*,
https://doi.org/10.1007/978-981-15-1995-6_1

Under the external pressure of being required to establish a fast copyright system in line with international standards, the formulation and revision of the Copyright Law in China considerably use international treaties and the relevant regulations in overseas legislation for reference (like the US and the EU).However, this approach to legislation on digital rights management regulatory model brings about some side effects: (1) logic conflicts between articles; (2) legislation out of date or too rough; (3) leading to the failure of legislative objectives. However, ultimately, international treaties and the relevant regulations in overseas legislation are against local legal context in China. In other words, China needs to establish a better digital rights management regulatory model, which is in line with international requirements, and also in conformity with China's actual conditions.

In this book, as the creative section, with regard to digital rights management regulatory model establishment in China, the following approaches to using international treaties and overseas legislation for reference are suggested: (1) taking a major country in one legal system as a sample for reference; (2) changing from copying the regulations under international treaties without revision to drawing up new precise rules by using native legislative language and according to national circumstances; (3) no hasty alterations to the general international regulations without ample reasons.

1.2 Research Questions

A: Under the external pressure of being required to establish a fast copyright system in line with international standards, the formulation and revision of the Copyright Law and digital rights management model in China considerably use international treaties and the relevant regulations in overseas for reference. Even China has adopted almost the same outer regulatory architecture as Western countries, why does it not work in China?

B: This approach to legislation has been proven to bring about some side effects: (1) learning widely from others' strong points leading to logic conflicts between articles; (2) copying international treaties without revision making the legislation out of date or too rough; (3) altering the general international regulations leading to the failure of legislative objectives. Based on the first research question, the current digital rights management regulatory model is against China's local context, the second research question would be "what kind of regulatory model should be used in China?"

1.3 Overview of Methodology

Many scholars across the globe have begun their research in the comparison between China's regulatory model and the western regulatory pattern. In particular, some scholars from Europe and America have made some preliminary achievements, which have laid out a significant foundation for further research in this area. However, it is also worth mentioning that the more systematic research in this area is becoming pressing and there is gap between the workshop research and the implementation in practice, especially in digital times.

Copyright seems not that new to us, while digital copyright issues, like DRM, may trigger even subsequent social impact. From my perspectives, any academic research shall focus on providing viable and tangible solutions to the problems in practice. The academic research shall be more than staying within the workshop. As such, an empirical approach will be adopted in my research. In doing so, I will try to find out what differences have been figured out in relation to the current digital rights management regulatory models between China, the US and Europe in our informational society, what problems have been brought out regarding China's digital rights management regulatory model, and what solutions are available to tackle those problems. Besides, I will try to use the scientific methodologies in my forthcoming research, including but not limited to the quantitative methodology. Finally, the comparative methodology will also be implemented in my research, including the comparison of the different legal and cultural system of different countries in the world, and I will focus on how such differences will affect the regulatory model of digital rights management architecture.

With regard to the comparative analysis of my research, the main research methods used will be the Functionalism and the Contextualism.[1]

Functionalism The definition will be narrowed down in this research paper. It could be acquainted as one vital analytical aspect of digital rights management regulatory model in China, the US and Europe.

(1) Social needs (C) + Social Mechanism (C) = Social Function (C)
(2) Social needs (W) + Social Mechanism (W) = Social Function (W)
C: China; W: Western Countries

Modelling speaking, the social response can be developed or formulated as the result of the social needs and social mechanism. The dissertation tries to explicitly explain how this formula could work in diverse digital rights management regulatory backgrounds. It would be articulated in the following chapters that the social needs on digital works and digital copyright protection in China, the US and Europe are the same. In other words, the characters of digital copyright played in different countries

[1] "'[C]ontextualism' refers to the position that the truth-conditions of knowledge ascribing and knowledge denying sentences. . .vary in certain ways according to the context in which they are uttered" (Schaffer [1], p. 73).

and regions are the same. "The protection of original creative works" stands the equivalent position to "cultural knowledge dissemination" in digital society, whether in developed countries or developing nations. For copyright in China, at least intellectual property matter, it was acknowledged and recognised much later than that in the Western countries.

In this regard, the method of Functionalism is on the same basis of "social needs". Social function, if transposed as the factor to be considered, is not merely deemed as the final result of both formulas. Alternatively, social function is the common goal that in practice most countries will probe or chase. It seeks to explore the eventual harmonisation in digital copyright world. Briefly speaking, social functions of digital rights management regulatory model, or we might say, the intellectual property regulatory system in different environments, comes to be approximate rather than be born the same by nature.

In the course of certain social function formation, or to fulfil the same common social function in relation to digital copyright regulatory architecture, it seems to those countries that social mechanism should be the same or at least similar. What the social mechanisms are expected to be formed is the regulatory models.

As argued by some intellects, it is impossible for Functionalism and Contextualism to exist in the same sphere because they conflict with each other, theoretically speaking. Notwithstanding, the battle between Functionalism and Contextualism is not caused by the research methods themselves, but by the research flow or the results.

Contextualism Contextualism will primarily discuss the role of the contexts in which the regulatory model adopted and also the differences and the influence brought by the various regulatory model contexts. As stated in the research, the basic formulas expressed below, in general, could be regarded as the chief train of thoughts on contextualism perspective. The research interpretation of Contextualism follows the identical way of Functionalism.

(1) Social needs (C) + Social Mechanism (C) = Social Response (C)
(2) Social needs (W) + Social Mechanism (W) = Social Response (W)
C: China; W: Western Countries

Like components in Functionalism formula, "social needs" are assumed the same, as the demand to intellectual creation protection and knowledge spreading in the society does not change under Contextualism.

The social mechanisms can be drawn up from two aspects: legislative mechanisms and non-legislative mechanisms. However, as mentioned above, social mechanism would be the same if we would like to achieve the same social function. Further, the social mechanisms in terms of digital rights management regulatory models in different areas, based on my research, are similar as well. For instance, China established its copyright regulatory system, which almost cites the whole legislative and practical architecture of Western countries. In short, there is little difference between the first components and the second components in formula 1 and 2.

Social Response has been supposed to be the social acceptance and the practical enforcement of the tentative regulatory model on digital rights management in different countries. However, the sums (social response) in the two equations above are hardly approximate, which can be treated as the incentive of the contextualism exploration. What promotes the comparative outcomes with regard to the digital copyright system in particular situations? Context matters.

Functionalism could be thought of as the research premise of Contextualism, otherwise the research components are constant. The research methodology cannot be interpreted in a variable atmosphere so as to ensure the analysis outcome acceptable and convincing.

Reference

1. Schaffer J (2004) From contextualism to contrastivism. Philos Stud 1999, 119:73–103

Part I
Theoretical Perspective of Digital Rights Management Systems

Chapter 2
Panorama of Digital Rights Management Systems

2.1 How Digital Rights Management Got Here

In the progress of human civilization, the emergence and development of copyright system stay closely with advanced technologies, especially the replica technique and communication technology. Each significant technology evolution, as it were, all remained historically recognizable imprints in the blossom of copyright scheme. Inherently, unique value existing in copyright law system has to be challenged by constant technologies development. Fortunately, they get along with each other well in the overwhelming majority of cases to promote copyright system's value and technologies' progress. Generally speaking, this harmony between copyright and technologies existed commonly in the past, at least, in the analogue technique times. The smoothing interaction of copyright system and technologies is not merely in favor of new techniques growth and the public's interest, but also helpful to the development of copyright derivatives market.

Digital technologies was developed first in America in the middle of the twentieth century. The technical basis of digital technology was the binary algorithm, which was created by German Mathematician Gottfried Wilhelm Leibniz in the seventeenth century. "0" and "1" are consist of binary coding, which records massive information and keep as the expression of sound, images and text. Compared with analogue technique, digital technologies made vast information communication come true through small mediums compression technology. Digital technologies pose a revolutionary influence on information storage, reproduction and communication. Briefly, the technical challenges that copyright system met in digital environment are mainly centered on two aspects: one is the novel communication routes, the other one is the large amount of piracy problem.

C. Xu, *Regulatory Model for Digital Rights Management*,
https://doi.org/10.1007/978-981-15-1995-6_2

2.1.1 Background of Digital Rights Management

When American Mauchly and Echert invented the first "ENIAC" (Electronic Numerical Integrator and Computer) in 1945,[1] it already indicated that digital technologies had proceeded on its way. In 1946, "EDVAC" (Electronic Discrete Variable Auto Computer) scheme proposed by Mathematician Von Neumann thereupon became the computer prototype in the world. Along with the classification of "software" and "hardware" in 1969 by International Business Machines Corporation (IBM),[2] the computer products had been increasingly sophisticated from then on. In those days, computers were not popular consumable, however, they were captured by the attention of legal universe. In 1960s, American people objected the proposal. Nevertheless, the software of computers was accepted to be copyright registration finally.[3] Computer technologies, as the core element of digital technologies, made speedy development under the circumstance where copyright barely intervened.

The spat on digital rights management never stops. The fighting campaign in Great Britain, led by Cambridge University professor Ross Anderson intends to prevent digital rights management.[4] If John Walker was not treated as one of the representative opponents on digital rights management in digital environment by the public, then it would be preposterous when he was ranting "How big brother and big media can put the internet genie back in the bottle"?[5] Another famous dissenter on digital rights management technologies and its economic strategy, Cory Doctorow, who is also the blogger of the popular technology blog "BoingBoing".

> Digital rights Management is an example of a malicious feature - a feature designed to hurt the user of the software, and therefore, it's something for which there can never be toleration.......[6]

When the famous software freedom activist Richard Matthew Stallman shows his concern and anger on digital rights management in his article "The Rights to Read", "should the digital rights management exist" seemed a continuous controversy since digital rights management appeared.

> As the majority of hobbyists must be aware, most of you steal your software. Hardware must be paid for, but software is something to share. Who cares if the people who worked on it get paid? Is this fair?[7] (Bill, Gates)

It was an open letter that was issued in 1976 when Bill Gates' company was "Micro-Soft" though.[8] This letter was regarded to be a letter for those who made

---

[1]http://history-computer.com/ModernComputer/Electronic/ENIAC.html.

[2]http://history-computer.com/ModernComputer/Electronic/ENIAC.html.

[3]Lam [1].

[4]Roemer [2].

[5]Walker [3], pp. 24–77. Also see http://en.wikipedia.org/wiki/Digital_rights_management.

[6]Stallman [4], pp. 85–87.

[7]Whitehead [5].

[8]Ibid 8.

piracies of Altair BASIC. "The fact that Altair BASIC came on a reel of analogue paper tape clearly demonstrates that the whole history of commercial software can be thought of as an ongoing technological war between those offering the codes for sale and those determined to take it for free."[9]

To a vast majority computer gamers in the UK, it was in the late twentieth century that copy protection appeared to arresting concern along with "Jet Set Willy" published. This "Jet Set Willy" was a computer game that was developed for home computers (ZX Spectrum) by game programmer Matthew Smith. It was said by some people that the simple setting of ZX Spectrum's data storage, to a certain degree, facilitate the piracy.[10] Any person could record and made a game copy with a blank tape when double tape recorders used.

In 1977, Apple Computer Incorporation promoted its new product Apple II, which astonished computer world. The sales volume of Apple Company even increased yearly 700% and it brought the real "PC" (personal computer) times.[11] In fact, sole development of electronic computing technologies has been far from the power of digital technologies. Indeed, the most stirring thing was the combination of computing technologies and communication technologies. In 1969, to deal with the "communication" issue between computers, the Advanced Research Projects Agency of the U.S. Department of Defense (DARPA) created the earliest network in the world, which is named "ARPANET". Distributed Networks, instead of Centralized Networks, were applied by "ARPANET" for safer networks establishment. "ARPANET", in a certain degree, formed the features of current internet.[12]

If we cannot agree more with this concise description about "science", which is "trust, but verify",[13] we might also accept the simple saying on "technology", which conclude as "evolution, but paradox". As people concerned that modern science brought vast uncertain "theory" for laboratory research, technology, as it were, has been doubted by the public, even the inventors or creators themselves, for its multi-faces. Its designed goals and features had been changed rapidly, or more than that, both of them deviated from technologies' essence. Ideally, technologies merely highlight its creators' desire for facilitating or changing our life. There are no good or bad boys in technologies value system. In this regard, "neutrality" is regarded as nothing, but the exact expression for technologies' character,[14] no matter whether this discipline has been swayed or not.

---

[9]Ibid 8.

[10]Ibid 8.

[11]http://www.vintageisthenewold.com/apple/.

[12]Aditya Kapoor's Blog, "Technology and Learning—The prehistory of the Internet", https://adityakapoor1.wordpress.com/2010/11/12/the-prehistory-of-the-internet/.

[13]"How Science Goes Wrong", The Economist. Available at: http://www.economist.com/news/leaders/21588069-scientific-research-has-changed-world-now-it-needs-change-itself-how-science-goes-wrong. October/19th/2013, p. 11.

[14]Will [6].

Since human beings stepped into digital times, it already indicated that numerous traditional matters had to be subverted by digital elements. Certainly, traditional communication approaches were also included, as communication mediums and its ways were treated as the revolutionary change. The communication channels in physical circumstance encountered its misfortune, which was either desolated, or replaced by digital means. Copyright regime, as this kind of industry that develops and promotes itself relying on communication spreading, reflects the value of its existence on the communication progress as well under digital environment.

Updated digital communication mediums seemed to be the active actor for making traditional copyright still alive when it met technologies. The combination of technologies and copyright showed the inevitable trend in digital surrounding. Admittedly, this connection between copyright and technologies also presented the requirement of copyright holders. How to survive in digital times? Or, in other words, how to keep the interest of copyright holders and comply with the characteristic and development of digital era, which is the main concern in nowadays.

The approach that accessing to information and knowledge is more regarded as unique method for solving the current dilemma of copyright system in digital context. Copyright law system has proved that it owns potential ability for getting with the increasingly rapid development of technology in former days and definitely has its special measure to further its function in digital world in the future. It is acceptable and essential that the complementary feature of copyright makes up the defect in terms of the so called access right that may emphasize the interest of the public not the right holders'.[15]

During the last two hundred years, the law on copyright has allowed the public to get a wealth of concepts, ideas, information or expressions described in the works by differently way because the final goal of copyright is for the sake of the public.[16] Nevertheless, internet changed the situation of copyright, which is challenging the present law on copyright and copyright practice. Additionally, the copyright protection under this circumstance also poses challenges to the system of copyright.[17] At present, the development of digital technology may violate the right of the copyright owners. The copyright architecture should be increasingly advanced to accommodate itself to the new environment, whereas, the over-protection of copyright may hinder the development of digital technology and thus harm the interests of the public.

The whole copyrights system has been primarily and gradually changed by the novel technology that embarrasses the exploitation of copyright works and makes it hard to manage in networks environment. In digital context, the massive

[15]Samuelson [7], p. 519.

[16]Steering Committee on the Role of Scientific and Technical Data and Information in the Public Domain, Office of International Scientific and Technical Information Programs, National Research Council, and National Academy of Sciences, 'The Role of Scientific and Technical Data and Information in the Public Domain: Proceedings of a Symposium', Aug, 2003.

[17]Summer [8], p. 31.

reproduction and distribution based on the new information development and technology innovation has increasingly spread dramatically. However, the technical progress at the same time initiates some potential issues like illegal piracy and unlawful commercial exploitation. The commercial profit gradually went into the general public's vision. A certain amount of examples with regard to the economic interest balance have risked the established commercial modules that absorbed the element of both the normal use of copyright works and the competitive market.[18]

Technological protection measures are more than proposed schemes, which have become important significant components of current copyright system and profoundly changed the copyright system. When the digital technology was not developed, copyright holders are not afraid of private copying because it cannot significantly affect the commercial profits of copyright owners. Even when the internet is introduced in 1992, the enormous capacity of documents makes reciprocal interchange impossible. Private copying has little impact on the benefits of copyright holders. However, the constantly innovative technology has led to an earth-shaking impact on the communication and exchange mode while the benefits of copyright owners have been greatly damaged. In this context, copyright owners began to realize the threat caused by private copying and as a result, a dazzling array of Technological Measures is being developed. While the priest climbs a post, the devil climbs ten, and any technological protection measures shall be cracked without the protection of laws. Besides, 'a few hackers are able to overturn the business mode', so copyright holders begin to 'seek to amend the laws, and try unremitting efforts to set more legal provisions for new-developed encryption technology.' After going through endless obstacles, the World Intellectual Property Organization finally regulates anti-circumvention provisions into international protection system. Afterwards, anti-circumvention provisions are gradually brought into copyright laws in various countries,[19] and technological protection measures finally establish a position in the copyright law world.

At present, primary electronic databases all adopt encryption technology to control users' access and copying. Online music shop iTunes launched by Apple Computer is regarded as an online international implementation modality of copyright based on the contract, copyright rules, and technology adopted by management media. Some scholars believe that technological protection measures have become indispensable parts of copyright law in the network era so we have to construct access right based on technological protection measures to perfect economic right regime. Then, what is the legal nature and essence of technological protection measures? Can they be regarded as the basis of copyright protection system in the digital era? These questions should be carefully answered whether to correctly comment on the technological protection measures or scientifically planning for the future of copyright. However, the academic circle intends to prefer the

[18]McEwan [9].

[19]Amen et al. [10].

technological protection measures without rational analysis and positioning.[20] This paper starts from the legal nature and essence of technological protection measures to analyze their passive influences and carry out positioning under the macro environment of the future mode construction of copyright system in the digital era.

The legislation and implementation systems of copyright protection aim to protect the legitimate rights and interests of authors, coordinate the relationship between author and users, and encourage authors to carry out creations as well as widespread promotions of creations so as to promote the development of scientific culture. Copyright System emerges along with the issuance of The Statute of Anne, and the recent development history shows an ever-present contradiction between private right of author and public benefits. The balance of interest of various parties is the main issue remaining to be considered while it can be said that the copyright aims to show balance. However, the development of network technology has brought unprecedented challenges for the original balanced system. Both the circumvention of digitalization and technologically protective measures of copyright demonstrate the characteristics of the network, free information flow and information sharing, which are unprecedented challenges for the right of copyright monopoly.[21] Besides, some people even vow that the copyright shall be overturned in the network era. On the one hand, there is about the precarious benefit of copyright holders; on the other hand, there are unprecedented requirements of information sharing. Network technology does not only provide powerful information and convenient communication approach, but also tools and channels for people to probe into other people's privacy, steal other's commercial secrets, carry out illegal transaction, obtain improper interests, and evade liability, etc. Accordingly, some copyright holders have to set up protective measures for their information and rights. However, some hackers try unremitting efforts, aiming to crack the protection technologies. In the network era, the development of digital technique and internet has brought with unprecedented challenges for the interest of copyright holders while traditional afterwards relief measures seem powerless when facing modern infringement activities. Therefore, preventive copyright protection measures emerge as times require. At present, popular measures refer to digital right management technology.

2.1.2 Why We Need Digital Right Management

Along with the development of digital technology, internet does not merely provide convenience while getting information but also profoundly affect the management mode of traditional intellectual property,[22] which present a challenge for current

[20]Purnhagen and Rott [11], pp. 439–458.

[21]Geiger [12], pp. 1–14.

[22]Anderson and Rainie [13].

copyright system. In this context, how to create, manage, protect and apply intellectual property so as to promote a healthy development of internet industry through effective use of copyright protection regime is an issue of common interest in the intellectual property circle and in the internet industry. At present, the copyright protection problem under the network environment has become a matter of general concern in the copyright protection field throughout the world. The copyright has the following features under the background of internet communication:

The rapid increase on types and quantities of copyright work continuously swells the ranks of the creative team, communication and consumption team. The application of digital technology and the diffusion of the internet enable sky-rocketing people to participate in the creation of copyright work and to spread to the public on their own. Second, their rapid development makes it become difficult. With the increase of networking broadband and improvement in transmission quality, it becomes easier for people to copy, spread and use others' works. Further, anyone could be granted with the access to certain works while clicking the mouse and spread out. Furthermore, digitalized works is easily violated comparing to traditional works. Finally, there is a glittering array of violation approaches in the network era.[23] Meanwhile, some websites illegally duplicate, upload and disseminate others' works without approved authorization, which does not only violate the legal right of the right holder but also disturb the disseminative order of network normal operation, affect the healthy development of internet industry and bring along with devastating shock on traditional industries such as books, music, film and television industry, etc. Internet service providers, internet content providers, internet content customers all carry out these unlawful practices and all of them shall bear relevant tort liabilities. The development of internet industry cannot be separated from product and content innovation, which should be protected by sophisticated copyright protection regime. Therefore, it is of vital importance to further perfect the copyright protection regime, effectively protect copyright protection, and fight online piracy behaviors.[24] In fact, online infringement approaches and channels are too numerous to enumerate. The following reasons are responsible for this phenomenon: pursuit for grand financial interest, lagging legal protection laws and regulations, dislocated moral evaluation and imbalanced recognition on the principle of balance of interest. The above conditions show that the development of internet is calling for legal norms, which face severe challenges brought by Internet Infringement.

There are both inheritances and differences between copyright protection in traditional copyright protection system and the network era, which possess the same theoretical origin, legal philosophy greatly emphasizes on the fairness and justice principle, elaborating balance of interest, namely to continually resolve

[23]Liu et al. [14], pp. 49–58.

[24]Limitations and Exceptions to Copyright and Neighbouring Rights in the Digital Environment: An International Library Perspective, IFLA CLM September, 2002, http://www.ifla.org/publications/limitations-and-exceptions-to-copyright-and-neighbouring-rights-in-the-digital-environm, 2004, access date: 11/08/2015.

frictions between interest of authors and public interest. The core concept of legal economics is benefit. To the creators, exclusive right helps creators to get compensation; to the society, all consumers obtain the benefit satisfaction based on voluntary payments to acquire products and services. In the network environment, copyright has jumped from printing copyright to digital copyright. Copyright protection can be carried out based on public means or implementations conducted by individuals, namely technological measures and right management, which shall be protected by law. At the same time, the copyright needs both protection and management. However, copyright holders feel powerless while facing massive authorization in the network environment, and they have to ask for the help of technologically protective measures connected with copyright.[25] There are two approaches for copyright protection: the first is using public means, which protects the copyright based on legislation and law enforcement. However, this kind of protection belongs to "compensation type". The right of copyright holders has been violated, so the law punishment and legal remedies cannot completely heal the wounds; the second is adopting individual means, which refers to the precautionary measure and forewarning measures conducted by copyright holders so as to maintain their interests and meanwhile prevent the occurrence of infringement act. Technological Measures and right management both belong to the second means range.

Implementations conducted by individuals, namely technological measures and right management, shall be protected by law. At the same time, the copyright needs both protection and management. However, copyright holders feel powerless while facing massive authorization in the network environment, and they have to ask for the help of technological protection measures of copyright. To conclude, the emergence of internet has changed people's thinking mode, expression way and behavior type, which affected the social relations from various perspectives.[26] The copyright under the network environment has changed a lot from copy genre to communication mode. The internet development with digital element as the basis has profoundly affected the publishing industry. Moreover, the emergence of online publishing not only changes the traditional publishing form, process and management variety; the publishing transformation, which has been ignited, shall become the inevitable trend in the publishing industry. Implementations acted by folks, namely technological measures and right management, shall be protected by law.

Many scholars considered that laws were weak once wide-range violation of laws appeared. Since the effect of enforcement against large-scale unlawful practices was very limited, the cost was high. As the "Gatekeeper Liability" concept introduced by Prof. Kraakman, it was regarded as the supplement of direct law enforcement that the service/products providers' liability was affirmed by the government.[27] In such way, illegal doings would be probably stopped in advance. Like prescription drugs system, it made doctors to be responsible for preventing the patients from medicine

[25]Gordon and Bahls [15], p. 619.

[26]Vathitphund [16], pp. 9–10.

[27]Tuch [17], p. 107.

abuse. Copyright regulatory system, has been virtually based on this similar "gate-keepers" model, which intermediary agencies would finitely undertake due tort liability. Those intermediaries are the "gatekeepers" under copyright scheme.[28]

A large number of artists or creators are able to communicate with the public via internet, where the cost of recording devices decreases dramatically and large Records Group is not the only option in digital music industry. These songs created in the circumstance were so-called "internet music", and also the consequent music players came up. The public's consumption habit has been changed along with the emerging business model. In 2002, the congressman Howard Berman made a speech in the meeting of the Computer and Communications Industry Association (CCIA), which expressed felicitously, "There is no justification for internet piracy. There is no difference between pocketing a CD in a Tower Records and downloading copyrighted songs from Morpheus. Theft is theft".[29]

Berman also pointed out that "internet piracy threatens to undermine the symbiosis between the technology and media industries. The widespread availability of pirate works online makes it difficult for copyright owners to develop viable internet business models. No matter what bells and whistles they add, copyright owners cannot compete with unauthorized internet services that make their works available for free".[30]

2.1.2.1 Not Just A Copy Protection Fortress

Copyrights can be defined as a right for the source to not allow anybody else copy the way or the method of something that is performed.[31] In other words, the uniqueness of the method or the product is now acquired by the maker only, and nobody under the legal jurisdiction would have the authority to remake that product or to use that method without the permission of the source.

If you understood digital rights management architecture merely as an important magic weapon against digital piracy at internet surroundings, you might be not that absurd from technical perspective.[32] However, the unilateral conclusion on digital rights management would be challenged by its partial and imbalanced acknowledgement. It can refer to what has been stated or mentioned as the foregoing, digital rights management cannot be described or defined by a unique technological component, but a comprehensive organism, which has been employed by modern copyright regulatory system in digital circumstance.

[28]Fisher [18], p. 134.

[29]"Music Industry News - as it happens", http://www.musicdish.com/mag/print.php3?id=6337, access date: 26/01/2014.

[30]Ibid.

[31]Bonne [19].

[32]Layton [20].

In other words, whether the position of digital rights management just on copy protection, in essence, is a question on "whether digital rights management system only concerns technologies?" Digital rights management itself, in general, plays an active role in digital copyright protection, as technological solutions effectively hold up digital copyright infringements and regulate digital works markets. Digital rights management, to a certain degree, achieved the maximum involvement of the content creators. We might say the main function of digital rights management is to protect authorized works and stop the access to copyrighted works without permission. Moreover, technologies embedded in digital rights management scheme also design the digital industry business models or usage patterns of consumers. Another part of digital rights management system is regulation, which intends to build the mutual restriction of content creators and the end-users.

In this regard, digital rights management has been not only focusing on technologies, which are deemed as the sole elements of digital copy protection.[33] On one side, as the comprehensiveness of its feature, digital rights management system has combined the technologies and regulation as the sword into digital copyright infringement war. On the other side, what has discussed above on the characters of digital rights management also reflects that digital piracy has not been eradicated at network environment although its technologies updated rapidly. It is unreasonable to query the effectiveness of digital rights management because of the current lawful practices, which indirectly makes sense that technologies are not the whole of digital rights management. Thus, in terms of copy protection, it is merely the tip of digital rights management iceberg.

2.1.2.2 Enable Content Creators to Get Paid

The intellectual property right and other rights are not the same. To a certain extent, however, intellectual property right is more close to a special monopoly right, which we have to without question admit that the kind of monopoly is a justified monopoly. As John-Locke's has demonstrated in the well-known statement of property as labor's 'just desert', intellectual property is deemed as "a suitable reward for intellectual labour".[34]

If the digital copyright protection is titled by "defensive warfare", then digital rights management system would be one of the defence lines. Digital rights management construction, technically speaking, based on its distribution and usage mechanism, provides various profit-earning channels between content creators and the end-users. Digital rights management strategy helps the content creators to obtain the profit directly through different interactive models, which are based on digital

---

[33]Bates [21].

[34]Rooney et al. [22]. During the same period, Georg Hegel argues that intellectual property is recognition of individual's sovereignty over their thoughts, while these two arguments are based on ethical concerns.

rights management standards. Moreover, about the economic benefit, digital rights management architecture guarantees content creators' earnings from two sides.

What I touched upon above regarding the designed inner structure of digital rights management is the first aspect, which gives these right holders one chance for direct profit collection. As a matter of fact, the existence of digital rights management scheme indeed prevents the digital copyright infringements that lessen the economic loss of content creators, which is called "indirect benefit". Generally, the necessity of digital rights management is not only out of money consideration, but also for anti-piracy purpose. Likewise, this is the reason why digital rights management system was created and praised in digital environment.[35]

2.1.2.3 New Business Methods

Traditional copyright has been thought of as mediums-leaning copyright regime.[36] Various copyright types are expressed and represented by different mediums. With technologies integration, namely digitalization, all mediums turned into digitalized types in information communication. Simply put, books, movies, musical works, paintings and audiovisual contents have been diffused by the ultimate pattern "0" and "1", which are the digital outputs of computing technique. It was pointedly described that one of the most remarkable differences between traditional copyright law and digital copyright law is regarding mediums.

In physical world, traditional copyright ordinarily regulates replication and distribution concerning physical mediums, while in digital environment, copyright law more stresses the using and acquisition of digital data regulation. It seems that there is little regulatory similarity between techniques included in traditional copyright law and digital technologies covered by digital copyright law.

Digital technologies in digital rights management system, to a certain degree, could provide a more rapid, integrated channel to satisfy consumers. Take digital music industry as an example, internet consumers may obtain music not in a CD shop, but through on-line service. Customers could either purchase sole song on internet, not a CD collection. The improvement of internet bandwidth even brought "celestial jukebox" in digital world, which offers a platform to internet users for accessing the music anytime and anywhere without downloading or storing into the computers.[37] Profits also can be earned by creators through digital technologies.

If the biggest contribution of digital rights management was deemed as the solid shield against copy protection in digital circumstance, the change of mediums tremendously boost the development of digital works wrapped by digital rights management technologies. In the meantime, digital industry transaction flourishes with digital rights management system.

---

[35]Ibid.

[36]Ibid 16.

[37]Ibid 23, pp. 25–26.

2.1.2.4 Be Taken, But Still Work

We have to admit that digital rights management framework has not been promoted to the unassailable solution against the digital copyright infringement nowadays. However, it seems that this is not the most impeccable approach for digital copyright protection in the world yet.[38] After all, digital rights management scheme includes technologies. Those sophisticated techniques could be replaced by advanced or improved technology. Much more worse, digital rights management could be broken gradually with new creaking tools or techniques.

As the digital rights management technologies defenses are designed by specific computing algorithm and programming rules. However, the essence of the logic language in computing science can be expressed by "sequence", "option" and "logic loop". Each component of the inner structure of digital rights management system might be operated. There is no "endless loop" allowed to be existed. The whole system can be edited by the coding program, which seems flexibly switched.

Tentatively, digital rights management should be treated as the piracy-controlled tools in digital world, which actually is the suboptimal satisfaction currently,[39] as the computing programs' features signify that digital rights management technologies, which are encoded by various functional computing languages. In this regard, digital rights management technologies programming can definitely be cracked or bypassed by solvable computing codes input. What is controversial and hotly discussed nowadays would fully express why the effect of digital rights management system is questionable.

Still, digital rights management has been regarded as the most resultful approach against digital copyright infringement in digital copyright environment. It does/ cannot necessarily restrict the whole society for impairing the copyright holders' benefit, though. However, to the general public, this system indeed has reached its anti-piracy goal, since it has been used. Moreover, you cannot expect each person in the world to be an expert of computing science or even a cracker. To a certain degree, the core commercial market of digital rights management architecture is focusing on the general public, or the end-users. Thus, it is obvious that it is easy to break this technology, which does still work.

Summary From active economic aspect, digital rights management architecture offers a platform for network users' consumption. Some officers from U.S. Federal Trade Commission adhere to it is pretty obvious that digital rights management is beneficial for the users in that it offers more choices to purchase or download digital works.[40]

It is understandable that the foremost advantage of digital rights management system is protection of reproducing digital works in line with what the original

[38]Melendez-Ortiz and Roffe [23].

[39]Haskin [24].

[40]Kerr [25], p. 13.

intention of digital rights management establishment. Although the consensus that copyright works protection could be broken both in physical world and in digital environment, digital rights management is deemed as a groundbreaking and effective attempt against digital copyright piracy.[41]

2.2 Digital Rights Management Technological Protection Measures

2.2.1 Digital Watermarking

Watermarks emerged in paper making industry around several hundred years ago.[42] With the rapid development of technology, especially digital technology, watermarks gradually were applied in the digital world after their popular usage in banknotes or stamps at the beginning of the nineteenth century.[43] Although digital watermarking has many uses in digital context, however, one paramount of these uses is this technology nowadays has been widely used for digital copyright protection. Digital multimedia content' copyright protection that digital watermarking technology deal with mainly centers on still image, audio document and video files.

From the application aspect, digital watermarking is one of the constituent parts of DRM.[44] "Digital watermarking is a process that embeds or inserts extra information, named the watermark or mark, into the original data to generate the output, which is called a *watermarked* or *marked* data".[45] A basic digital watermarking structure can be divided into two sections: (1) **Embedding Part;** is a system that contains an embedded imperceptible watermark into protected source. Original copyright authentication data, tamper detection information or other confidential messages for restricting access are all possibly embodied the watermark.[46] (2) **Extraction Part;** based on specific decoding algorithm, watermarking system also can display the cryptic watermarks to users.[47] This process merely distinguish correct key for embedded information extraction, which obstructs invalid access effectively (Fig. 2.1).

Digital watermarking, as an indispensable technique tool for copyright protection, is characterized by several traits as follows:

[41]Cope and Freeman [26].

[42]Kutter and Hartung [27], p. 98.

[43]Petitcolas [28], p. 91.

[44]Guo [29], p. 1.

[45]Wang et al. [30], pp. 3–4.

[46]Ibid 33.

[47]Ibid 35, p. 4. Wang et al. [30], p. 4.

Fig. 2.1 Structure of digital watermarks-based systems

- **Robustness;** It has been accepted as one of characteristic features of digital watermarking. What robustness focuses is the integrity or partial integrity that the embedded watermarks after digital processing (including inter-channel noise/filtering operations/transforming, etc.).
- **Imperceptibility;** Digital watermarking is the technology that watermarks embedded in host data cannot be perceptible by visual sense or auditory sense. In other words, scarcely any modification or distortion to the watermarked content would occur after watermarks inserted.
- **Security;** as I mentioned above in digital watermarking extraction section that, the system requires the users to cryptographically provide the right keys to reach the watermarked information. This is the vital character of digital watermarking, which is regarded as the effective way to protect digital copyrighted content.

IBM released a visible watermarking technologies several years ago, which was different from the indiscernible watermarking technology discussed above.[48] It allows copyright holders or distributors to embed their marks or logos in the image as visible watermarks. This kind of watermarks would not be erased only if "decryption" software applications or some watermarking-remover programs were used.[49]

2.2.2 Fingerprinting

Technicians who have acquaintance with digital copyright protection technologies might comprehend that technically, there is some difference between digital watermarking technique and digital fingerprinting approach. Both digital watermarking system and digital fingerprinting technique are content-based identification technologies. Digital watermarking embedding system normally contains identification information of copyright holders; however, digital fingerprinting system embodies identification of users and distributors (Fig. 2.2).

Digital fingerprinting system consists of two subsystems, one is to embody digital fingerprints into copyrighted resource and distribute these files, known as "distribution system"; the other one aims to track and identify these distributors that distribute

[48]Morimoto [31], p. 108.

[49]Ibid 37.

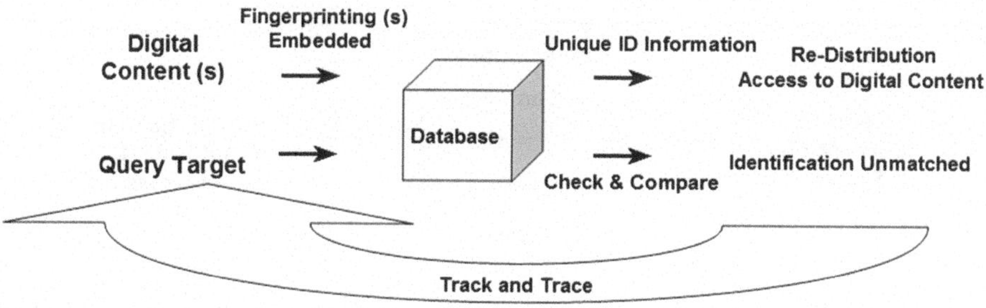

Fig. 2.2 Basic principle of digital fingerprinting technology

digital content without unique signatures delivered by the developers, known as "tracking or identification system". These two sections interwork in coordination and a series of licenses between distributors and users can provide digital fingerprinting technology a good way to achieve its function. The main duty of digital fingerprinting technology intends to differentiate between the authorized users and those false ones. Usually, original issuers embed various user's sequence numbers and identification information as different types of digital fingerprinting into digital copyrighted works to prevent copyright infringement. Otherwise, the original distributors could track the unauthorized distribution based on "tracking system". For these points, digital fingerprinting technology pleased copyright owners.

Moreover, digital fingerprinting is characteristic of robustness, which is comparable to the similar feature in the watermarking technology, as robustness is the essential requirement for content-based identification system, which ought to be against any distorted query signals.[50] In contrast, one character of fingerprinting differs from digital watermarking technique, which is "*compact signature*" or "*signature compactness*".[51] This specialty is justifiable on the grounds of a great deal of content's identification and distribution that digital fingerprinting scheme has to handle. Compact signatures would be convenient and unambiguous for dealing with corresponding information in copyright protection and transaction.

In 2001, one on-line music file sharing company, known as "Napster", subscribed no other than fingerprinting technology from Luodeye.[52] It distributed exclusive signatures for millions of songs. These digital signatures helped Napster Company to track and filter the dishonest users or distributors who were supposed to re-distribute the original copyrighted content without any permission from record labels.[53]

Music identification is one of audio fingerprinting technology practical applications. A few products adopted this technology have been wielded widespread

[50]Ibid 32.

[51]Liu et al. [32], p. 134.

[52]Staff [33].

[53]"Napster strikes filtering partnership with Loudeye", San Francisco Business Times, 7, Jun, 2001. http://www.bizjournals.com/sanfrancisco/stories/2001/06/04/daily29.html.Access date: 21/11/2013.

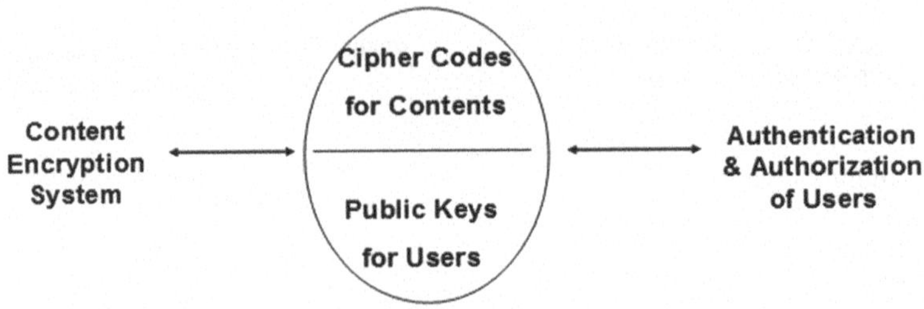

Fig. 2.3 Encryption-based cipher codes management and content distribution

currently. "Gracenote Mobile" software, developed by Gracenote Inc. (U.S.A) and Philips Research (the Netherlands) in 2004, can be applied on mobile phone for music/song's identification. 'Gracenote Mobile' application was integrated with Audio fingerprinting identification technology from Philips and Wave fingerprinting database from Gracenote. For example, when subscribers would like to get the music's detailed information, they are encouraged to dial the Gracenote's service number for inquiry. Users normally collected the sound data of the songs around and sent a piece of 5–10 s music to the Gracenote's server for matching feedback. If successfully done with matching, the servers would send singers, artists' image or other information to these subscribers through the text messages. Amena, a Spanish network carrier, employed a music identification service named "Music Wave", which was also based on audio fingerprinting technology.[54] Besides, a British startup "Shazam", had provided this similar service as well since 2002, but its service was based on the different audio fingerprinting technology from Philips.[55]

2.2.3 *Encryption*

Among technologies for digital rights management, encryption undoubtedly is treated as the most direct and strongest way to protect digital copyright.

Encryption is such a technology that it restricts unauthorized users to get the encrypted contents based on encryption algorithm, which encrypts multi-media information files to cryptographs. Copyright holders and distributors are increasingly aware of the importance of encryption technology for copyright protection in digital environment. Although encryption method has been wildly applied in current digital copyright defending, it is seldom used solely. Namely, encryption technique frequently combines with other technologies to be a compositive system for digital rights management (Fig. 2.3).

[54]Shuyu [34], p. 20.

[55]Ramona and Peeters [35].

Encryption nowadays has been regarded to be increasingly useful for devices identification and safe transmission of signals from original distributor to the end-users. Digital rights management system, with the data encryption and copy prevention at its core, technologically speaking, is founded largely on cryptology theory. The tradition way of encryption technology for protected copyrighted works is to encrypting these works. Only authorized users could obtain the cipher code, which is binding with users' hardware information, for deciphering these encrypted contents. For enhancing copyright protection, encryption technology also can be improved by extending the length of cipher code constantly. Encrypting and hardware binding combination technology restrains illegal reproduction in digital world effectively from right holders' perspective.

McAfee, Inc., a famous computer security software company in America issued its proposed digital rights management solution, known as McAfee Endpoint Encryption.

McAfee Endpoint Encryption scheme adopts the industry-leading encryption algorithm, provides multi-layers data protection against specific risks. Its encryption solution management involved PCs, laptops, net documents, network shared folders, mobile storage mediums, USB storage devices, etc.[56] Users relied on McAfee Endpoint Encryption for safeguarding various confidential information (including clients data, intellectual property rights, legal or financial records and employee communication) transparently along with system function's stability. McAfee Endpoint Encryption solution fulfilled refined control, automatic security report and monitoring based on McAfee ePolicy Orchestrator (ePO) platform.[57] Moreover, the flexible encryption settings can be customized by administrators in the light of particular circumstances. Any individual or users groups can be authorized or deprived the right to access the resource.

Nowadays, people have been apt to watch movie on smart phones or tablet PCs, which has triggered the daunting situation of DVD sales. The film studios, technical corporations and retailers launched "Ultra-Violet" standard for increasing DVD sales and remedying poor home-cinema returns Ultra-Violet was created by the Digital Entertainment Content Ecosystem (DECE LLC). The service provided by Ultra-Violet facilitates these subscribers of DVDs or Blu ray Discs to watch movies via internet or cell phones. Movies are be stored in the "digital lock", DVD or Blu ray Discs users are able to enjoy the films through various mobile devices with activated Ultra-Violet. Although Ultra-Violet service seems somewhat inconvenient to its users, it has been regarded as one of the most popular way of digital rights management nowadays. Buyers of Ultra-Violet have to create an Ultra-Violet account after they obtain the twelve electronic codes. Afterwards, users need to

[56]https://community.mcafee.com/community/business/data/blog/tags/usb, access date: 10/12/2013.

[57]IPS Administration Guide McAfee® Network Security Platform 8.0. http://kb.mcafee.com/resources/sites/MCAFEE/content/live/PRODUCT_DOCUMENTATION/24000/PD24730/en_US/NSP_8.0_IPS_Administration_revA_en-us.pdf, p. 277. Access date: 10/12/2013.

get another account from an independent internet service platform (like Flixster) for watching videos.[58]

Ultra-Violet standard has been supported by the majority of Hollywood and Silicon Valley enterprises, which indicates the potential development orientation of digital movies. UltraViolet allows legal users to transmit or download the content that has been purchased to multi platforms or devices. Ultra-Violet's practice encourages "buy once, play everywhere"[59] because UltraViolet adopted the basic encryption technology, which ensures the subscribers can play the digital works with the same version of the digital rights management all over the world. It also established a digital rights management platform between cooperative partners of UltraViolet service for international content compatibility.

2.2.4 Access Control

It is incorrect to digital rights management that technological protection measures are the whole digital rights management system. Technological protection measures the important components of digital rights management system. According to some scholars that technological protection measures actually are technological approaches that aim to encourage the authorized use of digital works.[60] These promotions are fulfilled through controlling access to these contents or restricting to employ these works from specific aspects, which include reproduction, distribution, etc.[61] However, digital rights managements actually are "technology systems facilitating the trusted, dynamic management of rights in any kind of digital information, throughout its lifecycle and wherever and however it is distributed."[62]

In the light of different functions, technological protection measures are usually sorted to "access control" technology and "use control" technology. For access control method, it is a technological way to restrict unauthorized users to access to digital content. Passwords and cryptography are the approaches to identify whether ones are authorized.[63] Access control technology prevents users' access to digital works unless these users get the authorization to employ them or the devices are authorized to display or play them.[64]

Technologically, access control technology contains Content Scramble System (CSS) and the Advanced Access Content System (AACS), and regional DVD

---

[58]http://rental.signals.co.za/blogcomment.aspx?bid=14. Access date: 10/12/2013.

[59]http://maliksadiq13.wordpress.com/2013/09/11/ultraviolet-outlier-in-the-telcos-online-video-ambitions/, access date: 10/12/2013.

[60]Kerr et al. [25], p. 13. (Ibid).

[61]Meléndez-Jubarbe [36], p. 192.

[62]Ibid 49; Original source from Garnett [37].

[63]Ibid 49, p. 14.

[64]Meléndez-Jubarbe [36], p. 195.

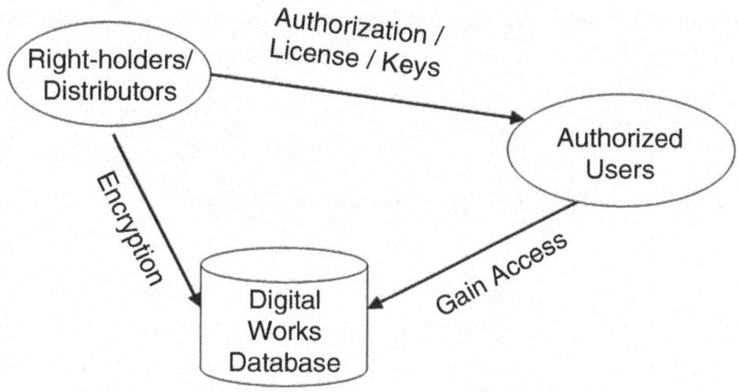

Fig. 2.4 Encryption-based access control method structure

coding.[65] CSS contains scrambling, key encryption and conditional access three parts.[66] Take CSS as an example for explanation. In physical world, CSS is helpful to block users' access to the content in DVD format. The content of disks and the keys for accessing the content are both encrypted. The only way for lawfully decrypting the content is getting the compliant CSS license and play/display the content on a particular protected disk. With regard to regional DVD coding, it means that DVD play devices purchased in specific regions could merely play the disks authorized for play at this region (Fig. 2.4).[67]

Access control technology, for the right holders, seems as most effective method to protect their copyright. The current access control technology does not work alone. It runs along with other technologies, which probably arises a series of problems on digital rights management system. At times, even the users were authorized lawfully for accessing the digital content, they would still encounter the embarrassing situation that these works could not be used. In this regard, use control method, which I will introduce at ensuing paragraph, and access control technology become the controversial issue in digital rights management area.

Granted, as technology developed rapidly, seldom one technique was used for digital rights management or copyright protection. McAfee Endpoint Encryption solution scheme, mentioned above, mainly used the encryption technology on specific algorithm. However, an access prohibiting effect somehow also was reached with the combination of encryption and access control technology under this solution.[68] Encryption algorithm are embedded in both McAfee Endpoint Encryption for PC and McAfee Endpoint Encryption for Files and Folders or full disk encryption. In fact, if PCs were lost or stolen, the explicit solution for PC would initiate identification authorization for formidable access control, while for McAfee Endpoint Encryption for Files and Folders, it would extend the access limitation to almost

[65]Ibid 53, p. 16.

[66]Digital Rights Background, Systems, Assessment, Commission Staff Working Paper. http://www.umic.pt/images/stories/publicacoes/drm_workingdoc.pdf. p. 18. Access date: 03/12/2013.

[67]Ibid 49, p. 17.

[68]Ibid.

unlimited amount of internet users in case PCs, laptops, internet servers or other mobile storage mediums were visited without permission.

2.2.5 Use Control (Copy Control)

Use control technology is also called "copy control" (anti-copy) technology. This method is controlling the subsequent use of works, even once access has been permitted.[69] Compare "use access" technology's function with access control technology, "use access" technology in fact restricts the way of works usage. Since "use" involves quite a few of specific conducts (like copy/distribution/performance, etc.) in copyright protection, use control method is not merely control "copy", but also many "uses". As the most widely adopted approach in digital rights management or copyright protection, use control is a technological synthesis more than a kind of technology. Just as Jacques de Werra refers:

> these technologies can protect not only against the mere copying of the work, but also against acts infringing other exclusive rights of copyright owners. . .A technological protection measure for audio (and video) content could also be developed in order to prevent the streaming of these works on the Internet. Because streaming 'does not copy the music onto the listener's hard drive', but 'merely allows her to hear it', such a technology would mainly prevent the infringement of the right of public performance and the right of distribution, and not the right of reproduction.[70]

Here, CSS is also an example of use control method in practice. CSS and Region Protected Codes (RPC) embedded in the DVD effectively made restrictions on regional usage of DVD playback, while Serial Copy Management System (SCMS), based on watermarking technology, prohibits multiple generations of digital copies from copyrighted originals without permission.[71] Watermarks can be embedded in the digital works under SCMS, and these watermarks resource also can be applied as an identification of original material or track copies,[72] otherwise to help actualize copy-control function.[73] The watermark details in SCMS can be applied to identify if CDs can be copied without control, and the copy times if ones were supposed to employ the corresponding recording equipment under SCMS for reproducing CD without SCMS watermarks, the trial would be frustrated (Fig. 2.5).

Digital Transmission Content Protection (DTCP) is another comprehensive use control technology, which was issued by Digital Transmission Licensing Administration (DTLA). The aim of DTCP technique is to restrict unauthorized distribution of digitalized audiovisual material, which is received at home once it has been

[69]Ibid 49, p. 19. 2003.

[70]Ibid 49, p. 14. 2003. Original from de Werra [38].

[71]Ibid 49, p. 20. 2003.

[72]Ibid 49, p. 21. 2003.

[73]Cunard [39].

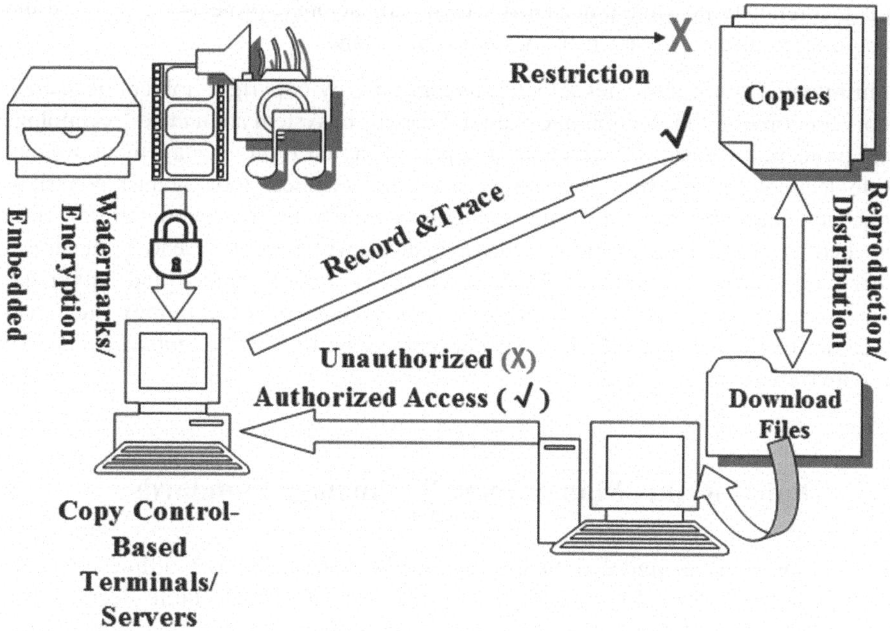

Fig. 2.5 SCMS-based use control architecture

decoded or deciphered.[74] DTCP builds encryption technology between digital information and sink equipment.[75] DTCP contains a "usage rules" ("copy control information") that signal the sink devices for the conditions under which they can received the copies of resource through DTCP.[76] Further, DTCP allows devices revocation when personal device certificates have been rescinded in the case that private key embedded has been decrypted, or has been pirated into another device.[77] These revoked devices could not receive the information via DTCP.

In Secure Digital Music Initiative (SDMI), music would have been safeguarded not merely by watermarking technology, but also by secure.[78] SDMI organization was established by the music industry for digital music protection. SDMI suggests digital watermarking technology should be encoded in CDs and digital music data distributed at internet. Similarly, the SDMI-compatible devices or software could collect the information on times of reproduction like SCMS. If the copy times exceeded the limited frequencies, the CDs or digital music cannot be played. Indeed,

[74]Ibid 49, p. 22.

[75]Ibid 49, p. 22.

[76]Ibid 49, p. 22.

[77]Digital Transmission Content Protection (DTCP), Technical and Licensing Overview. http://www.dtcp.com/documents/dtcp/dtcp-overview.pdf.

[78]Ibid 49, p. 23.

it is theoretically possible that SDMI scheme efficaciously protects the profit of the recording industry. However, it does not well instead.

Summary The technologies adopted increasingly by copyright holders or distributors for copyright protection under digital copyright system are named "technological protection measures", which are the part of digital rights management system. Solo technology has been seldom used as the technical tool against copyright infringements. The only fate which technology system has been combating with is cracked by much more advanced technology along with specific research time draws near based on the complexity. More significantly, digital content and authorized works secured by technology system would spread once their technology shield had been destroyed or wrecked, which also brought about irreversible impact and losses to copyright owners.

2.3 Digital Rights Management Technology Standards

The comprehensive digital right management system includes multiple elements such as licence, technology and regulations.[79] Prof. Stefan Bechtold deemed that "Digital Right Management systems are not only technological phenomena: they pose complex legal, business, organizational and economic problems".[80] How does digital rights management coordinate these various factors? Digital rights management operates based on instruction that relates to licenses, obligations constrains and transactions between copyright holders and end-users.

The tool that digital rights management relies on for precise definition of the rights is "Right Expression Languages" (RELs). RELs under digital rights management system communicate the information on what kinds of authorities belong to whom and what types of licenses or transactions would be taken before granted authorities obtained, etc. REL is at present treated as the most effective way to handle the deficiencies of current technological devices for digital rights management. Essentially, REL is a XML (Extensible Markup Language)-based language, which meets the requirements of digital rights management system for a trusted platform service.[81]

[79]ICT Regulation Toolkit, "New Technologies and Their Impact on Regulation", http://www.ictregulationtoolkit.org/1.7.

[80]Bechtold [40].

[81]Iannella [41], p. 47.

Fig. 2.6 XrML primary structure (Xiaobin and Shaokuan [43], p. 49)

```
< XrML>
  < BODY>
      ( ISSUED) ?
      ( TIME) ?
      ( DESCRIPTOR) ?
      ( ISSUER) ?
      ( ISSUEDPRINCIPALS) ?
      ( WORK) ?
      < / BODY>
      ( SIGNATURE) ?
```

2.3.1 *Extensible Rights Markup Language (XrML)*

XrML originally came from Digital Property Rights Language (DPRL), which issued by Xerox PARC (Palo Alto Research Center) in 1996.[82] DPRL developed to XrML after its meta language and programming language transformed from LISP to XML in 1999. In 2000, ContentGuard, a unit operated by Microsoft and Xerox, issued XrML. This company has been focusing on digital rights management technologies development. Its digital Rights Language and the basic patent portfolio were first developed at the Xerox Palo Alto Research Center (PARC).[83]

XrML is also a XML-based language, which provides a simple and effective method for permission or authority's marking up and management on digital files. Creators and distributors of digital resource (digital content/digital service) can identify the users who employ these resource and the authorized right they obtained. The comprehensiveness of XrML showed in various phases and workflow through providing digital rights expression structures (Fig. 2.6).

The XrML contains four main components, known as "Principals", "Resource", "Rights" and "Condition". (Presented in the figure above). "Principal parts" are individuals or organizations that can be identified, and also the entities that are granted by the righter holders. Each principal merely marks up one single authorized target; "Right" under XrML means the authorized principals under some circumstances can operate the digital resource, like reproduction or distribution, etc.; "Resource" is the objects that the right holders endue their permission. "Resource" can be digital video/audio files, e-books and images, or a certain kind of service; "Condition" in XrML intends to define the qualifications of end-users, requirements or terms under which right holders or distributors would grant their authorization or permission (Fig. 2.7).

[82]Guo [42], p. 6.

[83]"Content Guard, Inc. Marks Its Spinoff from Xerox with Microsoft Alliance", *Information Today*, Volume 17, Number 6, June 2000, http://www.infotoday.com/it/jun00/news7.htm. Access date: 09/12/2013.

Fig. 2.7 XrML data model

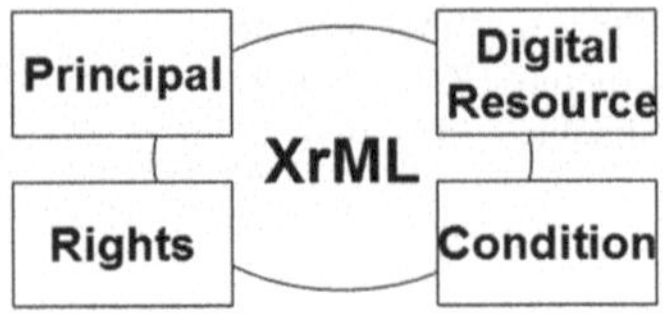

XrML has been regarded as the most commonly used and relatively mature expression language in digital rights management system.[84] XrML aims to build a universal standard for demarcating usage condition and protected content under digital rights management scheme. The specialties of XrML are well-received by skilled personnel in digital rights management technology area.

- First, XrML is a fully open-ended and extensible language. It provides digital resource suppliers a flexible approach to make full use of the material on the principle of utility maximization.
- Second, well-organized documents and highly structured data in XrML makes it readable to both humans and machines. Clear described right scope and other issues could be specified at multi-platforms identically.[85]
- Furthermore, XrML's strong semantic characteristics facilitate browsers and digitalized copyright management systems to identify and manage the information involved in copyright protection.
- Finally, XrML is unified, which is the demand of e-content market. In addition, digital rights management needs to solve its interoperability issue through standards consolidation. XrML is such a protection mechanism with a standard right expression language and instructions description to promote computers to identify and implement automatically.

XrML nowadays has been widely adopted in digital issues, especially in e-commerce. Microsoft applied XrML for digital rights definition and metadata specification in its e-books business. Metadata expressions of XrML helped Microsoft to create or update relevant the catalogues of its e-books.[86] ContentGuard company, mentioned above, released its version 2.0 of XrML several years ago for allowing developers to expediently build a system, which specified the rights and conditions for accessing digital resource.[87]

[84] "Survey on XML-Based Policy Languages for Open Environments", http://www.academia.edu/6269692/Survey_on_XML-Based_Policy_Languages_for_Open_Environments, access date: 15/08/2015.

[85] Waupotitsch et al. [44].

[86] Ibid 71.

[87] Alvear [45].

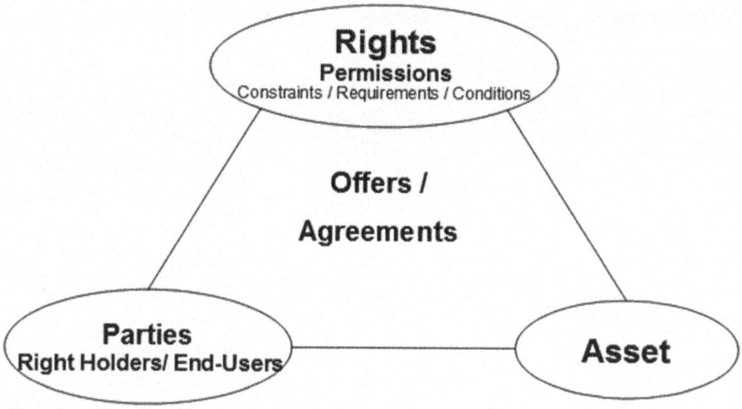

Fig. 2.8 ODRL model

2.3.2 Open Digital Rights Language (ODRL)

ODRL was issued in 2000 by IPR systems company and adopted by W3C. ODRL is also a XML-based digital rights expression language, which comprises some core entities and nexus of these entities. In the basic model of ODRL, it defines three kernel entities: (1) Asset; (2) Rights; and (3) Parties (Fig. 2.8).

For the "Asset", it contains both physical and digital content (Video/Audio/E-books/Software and other resource); The "Assets" have to be defined by explicit identifier.[88] The "Rights" of ODRL includes permission, in which constraints, requirements and conditions are all defined by contracts or licenses. "Rights" somehow express the permission details. The end-users and right holders will be described in "Parties" under ODRL. It is understandable that end-users here are users who employ the asset, while the right holders are those who play the roles on creation, production and distribution, and the entities that own the material or the permission of resource usage. ODRL model could express the relationship of "Offer" and "Agreements" through three core elements. "Offers" are provided by the asset owners, and "Agreements" are made by various parties for specific "Offer", when they are doing transactions.

ODRL is also extensible, which aims to provide electronic publications, digital image and other works an interoperability right expression mechanism for publication, distribution and consumption. Users can add their copyright data dictionary to ODRL extensive approach. Data dictionary under ODRL is the gathering of vocabularies for the expression of permissions, constrains, requirements and conditions (Fig. 2.9).[89]

[88]Guth [46], p. 103.

[89]Ibid 69, p. 48.

Fig. 2.9 ODRL structure model

```
<rights>
  <offer>
    <asset id="ASSET-001">
        <context>...<context>
    </asset>
    <asset id="ASSET-002">
        <context>...<context>
    </asset>
    <permission>
        <asset id="ASSET-001">
        <sell/>
    </permission>
    </permission>
        <asset id="ASSET-001">
        <asset id="ASSET-002">
    </permission>
  </offer>
</rights>
```

Adobe, as the supporter of ODRL framework, it provides digital rights management settlements for pdf format documents exchange based on the ODRL initiative.[90] Documents are made by Adobe Content Server software. Related reader can do interpretation or implementation with their material through secure reading devices.[91]

Electronic Media Management System, issued by IBM, is compatible with many resource formats. This system relies on a particular REL, which was affected by ODRL. ODRL was used by the Open mobile Alliance (OMA) as part of its international criteria of mobile Digital rights management. OMA 2.0, compared with previous version 1.0, is much higher degree of ODRL utilization. Version 2.0 extended its rights expressions semantically for more demand of mobile area.[92]

XrML and ODRL are both XML-based rights expression languages. It is obvious that their semantic design of inner structures is similar seemingly, and they are congruent with digital rights management's requirements. However, from the perspective of specific description methods, ODRL differs greatly from XrML in essence. ODRL merely defines a few key terms, which provides more extensive space for parties. In this regard, XrML's superiority reflects on its high manoeuvrability. Detailed expression facilitates the users to adopt this language.

Currently, XrML and ODRL are both faced with following problems: First, XrML and ODRL merely support the rights that are explicit granted, not any others, even existing specific rights obtained under the law; second is the issue of exceptions

[90]Guth [46], p. 112.

[91]Ibid.

[92]Ibid 69, p. 51.

and limitations description of copyright protection has not been solved. The third one is that XrML and ODRL are rights expression languages for restrictive and limited usage, it would not be expected for the both to be commonly adopted among various digital resource.

2.3.3 Extensible Access Control Markup Language (XACML)

In 2003, eXtensible Access Control Markup Language (XACML) was approved as a standard by the Organization for the Advancement of Structured Information Standards (OASIS). XACML defines an expression language, which intends to protect digital resource as a policy language and an access policy decision language.[93] XACML policy model language is based on a model that provides a *formal* expression of the access control policy and how it works.

Policy language in XACML allows administrators to define the access control requirement to get application resource. Policy language supports combinational logic that formulates data types, functions and simple/complex rules.

Access control decision languages provided by XACML are used to describe the requirements when the digital resource is under operation process. When the policy for digital resource protection is made, properties in requirements and properties included in policy rules will be compared through functions. It finally generates a policy decision for permissions or denials.

Besides, XACML also defines the policy request system and response format,[94] which makes users to formulate an "inquiry" for their actions' permission or denial. However, policy request system and response format both define the interface between Policy Decision Point (PDP) and Policy Enforcement Point (PEP). PEP issues requests and manages the responses, while PDP evaluates requests based on access policies, requester' properties and circumstances' properties, then returns the evaluation decisions to PEP (Fig. 2.10).

Policy languages and access decision languages, defined by XACML, mainly consist of three high-layer policy elements: "Rule", "Policy", and "Policy Set".[95] Each "Rule" is constituted by "Condition", "Effect" and "Target". "Policy" also can be divided into three parts, "Target", "Rule" and "Combining Algorithm". Target is contained in each layer and it is comprised by "Subject", "Resource" and "Action".

Target Each policy can make only one target. The target is helpful to identify if policies were relevant with requirements. The relevance between policies and requirements determines to evaluate the policies. The evaluation will be completed

---

[93]De Capitani di Vimercatil et al. [47], p. 37.

[94]Lorch et al. [48].

[95]Ibid 81, p. 37.

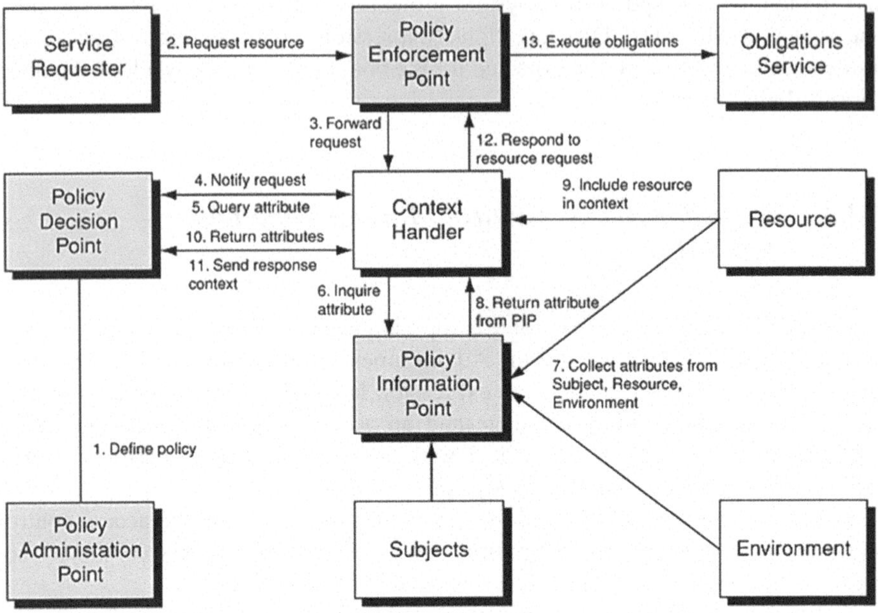

Fig. 2.10 Overview of XACML architecture (Steel et al. [49])

through description of three entities (subject, resource action) contained in target. If the target's conditions are satisfied, its corresponding policies will apply to the request.[96]

Rule One policy can be relevant with many rules. Every rule contains "Conditions", "Effects" and "Targets".

(1) Conditions: are the statement of properties. The evaluation effects are "True", "False" or "Indeterminate". (Indeterminate means there is not enough information for making a right effect)
(2) Effects: they are the expected consequences that accord with rules. The value of the effects can be "Permit" or "Deny";
(3) Targets: Here targets are similar to the targets in policies. Both of them are conducive to estimate the relevance between rules and requests. The implementation mechanism of this target also resembles the policy targets.

Combining Algorithm As mentioned above, a policy could comprise different rules. However, various rules are likely to conflicting effects, which is exactly combining algorithm has to deal with. Every policy and request will get one effect, while each policy can merely employ one combining algorithm.

[96]Ardagna et al. [50], p. 41.

Obligations One aim of XACML is offering a higher-level access control, not merely a permission or denial policy. Obligations are optional mechanism for the access-control languages.

Axiomatic develops and produces massive electronic controls for global applications. One of these manufactures is "eXtensible Authorization". eXtensible Authorization supports the acquisition of context-related resource such as the location and the users' ID, the types of technical data interrelated "regulations and purpose of use both in terms of the current access request with regard to the end-use of an exported item for which an export license or agreement is applicable and verification that the user is not black-listed by authorities."[97] Axiomatic eXtensible Authorization adopted XACML approach to communicate authorization solutions. Further, XACML can be made to order and used to particular aspects by various XACML profiles.[98] The XACML Technical Committee of OASIS issues profiles for digital rights management and Export Control that facilitate application.[99]

2.3.4 MPEG Rights Expression Language

MPEG stands for Moving Picture Experts Group, which was set up by International Standard Organization (ISO) and International Electronic Committee (IEC) in 1988. Members of MPEG are technicians or experts in video, audio or other system areas. MPEG devotes itself for standardization of moving pictures (MPEG Video) and sound codes (MPEG Audio). Since MPEG-3 was abandoned on the development process, there were only three versions (MPEG-1, MPEG-2, MPEG-4) at the first phase of its outcome.

At the beginning stage, MPEG orientated itself to be an international standardization level. Thus, MPEG is well compatible with others, and MPEG can provide the better compression ratio than other algorithms, which maximizes at 200:1.[100] More important thing is, it hardly damages the data when MPEG compresses the data at a high compression ratio.

MPEG-21 is a multi-media framework research project that was carried out by MPEG standardization group. MPEG-21 is a combination of images, technologies, policies and digital units definition, identification/description of digital units, digital rights managements, RELs, rights data dictionary, document formats and other parts. The sections, which are related to digital rights management, mainly contain part 3 "digital units identification and description", part 4 "digital rights management",

[97]https://www.axiomatics.com/manufacturing.html, access date: 02/12/2013.

[98]Han and Lei [51], p. 479.

[99]https://www.axiomatics.com/manufacturing.html, access date: 02/12/2013.

[100]Gell [52].

part 5 "rights expression languages" and part 6 "rights data dictionary", etc. The main MPEG versions are known as:

MPEG-1 MPEG-1 was designed for industry standards, which had been proverbially adopted on different devices with various bandwidths (CD-ROM, Video-CD). It is a criteria for lossy compression of video/audio data. It is designed to compress raw digital video and CD audio of Video Home System criteria under 1.5 Mbit/s without undue feature damage. MPEG-1 can be operated under its optimization model, using Standard Interchange Format (SIF) standard for image compression.

MPEG-2 Similar to MPEG1's structure, MPEG 2 was added with some supplements. MPEG 2 is capable to support a wider range of compression ratio for various high-quality images and storage capacity than MPEG 1. MPEG 2 was made the specific standards of VCD and DVD, besides, it also can be used for broadcast-quality digital videos of broadcastings, cable television networks (CATV network) and cable networks.

MPEG-4 MPEG 4 specification was formalized as SO/IEC 14496: Information Technology- Coding of Audio-Visual Objects. MPEG 4 compression ratio, based on its updated function, is nine times higher than MPEG 2 for taking audio/video quality under low bandwidth. In MPEG 4, one merit is that optimal image can be obtained with least data. The arithmetic complexity of MPEG 4 is more higher than MPEG 1 and MPEG 2. MPEG 4 is commonly used in the video games, internet video broadcasting, wireless communication, videophones, etc.

MPEG-7 Unlike the methods how MPEG 1–MPEG 4 deal with the compression of images and sounds. MPEG 7 focuses on the description standard of multimedia content. Based on this approach, MPEG 7 can build its database, which is quite helpful to search for relevant images. MPEG 7 was set up based on XML, which was treated as a convenient method for using digital information or images. In this regard, MPEG 7 was also named as "Multimedia Content Description Interface" (MCDI).

MPEG21 (ISO/IEC 21000) was defined as a multimedia framework, which was constituted of several elements.[101] They are as follows:

(1) **Digital Item Declaration:** which provides a flexible and unified digital item declaration format.
(2) **Digital Item Identification and Description:** it offers unified digital item format for identification and description.
(3) **Content Handling and Usage:** this section supplies a standard interface and license, which deal with digital content production, storage, processing, etc. between various internets and platforms.
(4) **Intellectual Property Management and Protection:** a framework of digital multi-media rights management.

[101]Thomas-Kerr et al. [53], p. 73.

Versions	Characters	Advantages	Disadvantages	Practical Application
MPEG 2	1.Simply Constructed 2. Scalability 3. 4~6 Mbps/ S	1.Producets/Market-ripe 2.Peripheral Assistance/ Products Integrity	Poor Compressibility	DVD; (H)DTV
MPEG 4	1.Well Compressibility 2. High Resolution / Quality of DVD / Video Tape Recorder （VTR） 3. Scalability 4. Object-based, 3D	Audio/Video Transmission with Low Bandwidth	1. Higher Licence Fee 2. Complex Specifications	Portable Devices; Interactive Equipments
MPEG 7	Video Database	——	——	——
MPEG 21	Common Media Platform	——	——	——

Fig. 2.11 Comparison of different MPEG standards

(5) **Terminals and Networks:** Compatible circumstance and environment will be provided for cross-networks or cross-platforms.
(6) **Content Representation:** It is the method for content presentation.
(7) **Event Reporting:** Immediate and appropriate report for system performance (Fig. 2.11).

MPEG-A MPEG A (ISO/IEC 23000) is another standard of MPEG. MPEG A is based on a combination of current technologies selected by MPEG standards which has been issued. This combination is named "Multimedia Application Formats" (MAFs). The goal of MAFs is to promote innovations and rapid development of multimedia application and service to meet the market demand.

Summary The first generation of digital rights management technology mainly commits itself to the development of safe settings and encrypted techniques related to the digital content. So the digital rights management system is able to prevent unlawful copy of digital material based on different technical standards. Following improved generation of digital rights management technology extends its protection to description, identification and other parts concerning digital copyright.[102]

Digital rights management has been branded by special features in digital information times. The digital environment full of multi-digital works indicates that without specific regulations and approaches, those controversial issues cannot be solved merely on technical improvement.

[102]Sander [54].

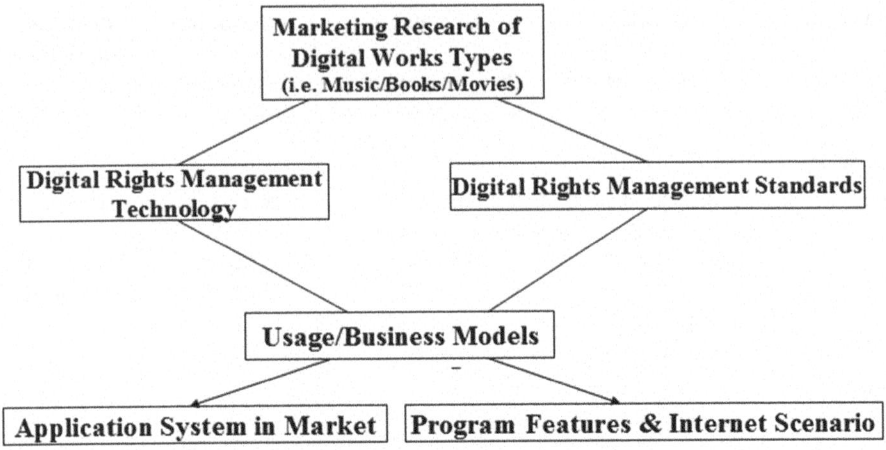

Fig. 2.12 The role of usage model under the digital rights management-based business system

2.4 Digital Rights Management Usage Models

Digital rights management system is increasingly deployed by combined techniques. However, as a popular tool for copyright protection, it has to be evaluated by the commercial factors for a good market prospect. Digital rights management operators would promptly improve the business models if any usage feedback from the consumers (Fig. 2.12).[103]

Digital rights management based business types provides diverse ways for consumers to access to (temporarily obtain)/get (permanently obtain) and use the digital works. Musical industry and publishing field are two main areas in which digital resources are protected by digital rights management technology. Therefore, the usage models mentioned afterwards, which are commonly deployed, have four major molds as follow: Prepaid model, Rental service, Subscription business and Peer-to-Peer genre (Fig. 2.13).

2.4.1 Prepaid

A prepaid credit card released by a specific institution is "preloaded with funds and is used like a plain credit card".[104] As far as we know, the prepaid credit card works differently from a common credit card, since the card holders are not allowed to obtain any products without deposit. In other words, payment has to be done before purchasers get the products or service.

[103]Ibid.

[104]Prepaid Credit Card [55].

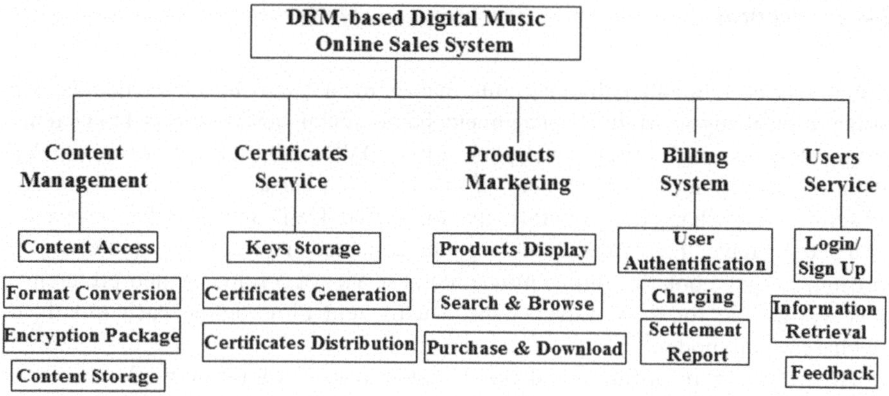

Fig. 2.13 Classic digital music sales scheme under digital rights management system

It is adopted by digital rights management system usage architecture, which is prepaid model. Prepaid service under digital rights management-based business models, interpreted literally, is a usage type of digital works, which requires consumers to pay via prepaid card or other similar mediums in advance. Users normally have to submit prepayment with specific cards provided by the service providers or their own credit cards. Consumption lasts until money runs out, then consumers will be charged for renewal after service expired. Prepaid model, under digital rights management scheme, merits convenient maintenance and low cost distinctly to its users.[105]

Content or service suppliers even offer personalized products or services to users, which are based on the prepaid system record concerning consumers' behavior (i.e., frequency of usage). It is difficult for consumers to obtain their account balance or other information, which has been one of the weak points of prepaid model. Another disadvantage comes from the prepayment system. Prepayment system collects consumers' fee beforehand based on usage duration or amount of information. Consequently, only when the prepaid system kept the records in this respect, dealers hardly associate the content or material that users dip into with their revenue.

Moreover, there is another prepaid way, which applies prepaid tokens to replace the prepaid card. According to Sai Ho Kwok, users have to be enrolled by the external digital rights management service center for tokens buy.[106] Tokens would be distributed to the consumers a particular local digital right management services center from a tokens database.[107] Tokens play the similar role of 'full bodied' money here for digital works purchase or subscription. Tokens are exchanged for the specific service selected by users, such as pay-per-play, pay-per-view pay-per-download, pay-as-you-play, time-limited control, etc.

---

[105]Cooperm [56].

[106]Kwok [57], p. 23.

[107]Ibid, p. 24.

2.4.2 Rental

Rental service is another digital rights management based business models. The earlier typical digital rights management based rental business was DVD rental service. Pay less each DVD, watch more films. DVD rental service or online DVD rental model provides more choices of movies, even latest issued ones. Basically, subscribers are charged a monthly fee for postal DVD rental order. Users are arranged to have their bank debit account deducted automatically (autopay).[108] Consumers may book this online movie rental service according to their preference. It is worthwhile for those buyers who usually rent films online each month, to purchase rental model.[109]

The frequency regarding broadcasted content (especially music works) has been defined by the digital rights management licenses for rental service. For example, one store, operating online video business, may provide video rental service to its consumers. Once users "rent" the digital content and downloaded the license issued by digital rights management system, the license would expire until it accomplished the rental service. Normally, the license had been overdue 30 days later since the date of issuance or expiry of 24 hours from first broadcasting (whichever is earlier).

Although Netflix has been hesitating to drop out from the DVD rental business market,[110] however, this service, which seems old-fashioned, as a matter of fact, has contributed to its profitable revenue. Still about seven million subscribers pay for Netflix's rental business. Once fees were paid, Netflix would send consumers DVDs of films or TV shows by post.

Amazon.com was supposed to launch an on-line rental service of its e-books, alike Netflix's business model of panel computers and e-books to the consumers in 2011.[111] To compete with Apple's iPad, Amazon had issued an electronic reader Kindle to the e-books market. Users were encouraged to submit an annual payment for accessing the digital resource from its media library.[112] Actually a certain amount of publishers were in suboptimal satisfaction with Amazon's promotion, since what Amazon intended to do worried these publishers that this online rental business would reduce the books' value.

---

[108] Jeeny [58].

[109] Ibid.

[110] Roettgers [59].

[111] Damouni [60].

[112] Ibid.

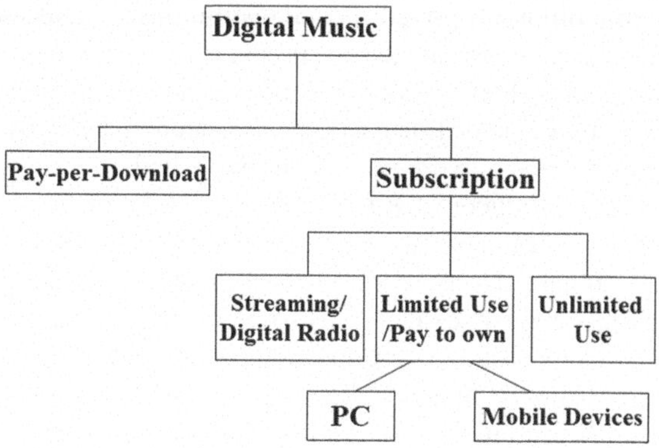

Fig. 2.14 Digital music business models (Bohn [63])

2.4.3 Subscription

Digital rights management-based subscription model is regarded as a low-cost payment approach for obtaining digital works.[113] The main approaches for purchasing digital music on line are two types: Pay-per-download and Subscription. Subscription model, compared with Pay-per-download, has showed more economic advantages on its operation principle (Fig. 2.14).

Before the operators ran this digital rights management-based and value-added subscription business on line, they found what the consumers truly minded was not digital rights management technology embedded this model, but simply how conveniently they are able to access to digital resource. Subscription model rightly accords with the owners' crucial benefit on copyright protection, as well as user's demand for models' conveniences.[114]

For other digital content companies, the reasons why subscription model are favored seemed nothing new but two aspects. On the one hand, subscription business under digital rights management offers a new market to digital works, in which the consumers have a fresh appetite for knowledge distribution experience. On the other hand, besides the copyright holders, subscription model service providers also will be paid via this novel usage-based channel.

Unlike those predecessors who made digital music subscription service, the startup, Safari books online website provides its users ten days free trial before the following subscription service. For its subscription model, "7 cents per page viewed--this means that if a 400-page book is read, the publisher receives $28",[115] said by Andrew Savikas, the CEO of Safari Books Online. Savikas also mentioned that most of its subscription consumptions are from agencies, such as libraries,

[113]Buhse [61], p. 209. Original from Picot et al. [62], p. 272.

[114]Ibid.

[115]"E-book Subscription Model: Is the Time Right?", Comment from Publisher Weekly, 29/04/2013, http://www.publishersweekly.com/pw/by-topic/digital/content-and-e-books/article/56989-e-book-subscription-model-is-the-time-right.html, access date: 20/12/2013.

communities or governmental institutions.[116] Especially libraries, a majority of them purchased constant subscription service from Safari after their first usage. It appeared that even older books could be bought on the subscription-based website. Savikas said that books titles would be obtained by subscribers at its backlist, and half popular books were previously published.

The producer of RealPlayer, RealNetwork issued Rhapsody for songs subscription service several years ago. Four kinds of usage service were offered to its consumers. Users were allowed to access 25 songs per month for free under the basic service package.[117] The real music subscription service supplied by Rhapsody charged consumers around $10, letting the subscribers to enjoy as many tracks as they want on their PC. In addition, consumers were also allowed to transfer these tracks to mobile devices with a higher subscription payment.[118] Users are certainly permitted to unsubscribe this subscription business at any time they want.[119]

Subscription model is the direct method to be against copyrighted works piracy, whereas more restrictive protection of copyrighted works would be a potential damage to the previous balance in physical copyright world.[120] It is understandable that the benefit on revenue comes from consumers to both record companies and distributors directly for sharing. Moreover, subscription method will be more profitable to content industry on account of constant streaming income from subscribers ("Potential Profit" or "Indirect Profit").[121]

2.4.4 Peer-to-Peer

> In the larger EU countries, between 15% -30% of broadband Internet subscribers use at least one Peer-to-Peer application and most Peer-to-Peer households use two.[122]

Peer-to-Peer model, also known as "P2P", is an internet work type that relies on information exchange among peers without any central servers. P2P has been regarded as a classic and popular model for file sharing in digital environment nowadays. In P2P structure, each peer can be both the roles of information user and information provider. Each peer is treated as a node for information communication, and they enjoy the equal status. Every user also plays the character of server, which supports the on-line communication. The emergence of P2P model has

[116]Ibid.

[117]Ibid 99.

[118]Ibid 99.

[119]Subscription model is also named "specific limited purchase model" under digital rights management based usage business.

[120]Lucchi [64], p. 79.

[121]Ibid 99.

[122]Andrea Gavosto, Bruno Lamborghini, Stefano Lamborghini, *Peer-to-Peer Network and the Distribution in the EU*, See Noam and Pupillo [65], p. 289.

brought a profound change on the digital rights management in the network era. As a new type of distributed computing model, in which the information would be exchanged among different nodes, P2P supports multipoint to multipoint digital resource transmission. P2P also provides a flexible communication way for files sharing, which is depended on its function superiority.

In the early stage, P2P was designed for exploring potential computing capability of internet, while Napster's promotion of its P2P made this model penetrated among users in 1999.[123] The first generation of software issued by Napster was to exchange MP3 files. Users cannot find any documents on Napster server, which merely provided a software for file sharing. Napster users activated the information exchange system for logging on after they installed Napster software. The core of P2P is based on technical design. Individuals are able to download musical resource and meanwhile the files downloaded will be stored in users' own hard drive archives. P2P software identifies if one downloaded files with it, they definitely would change another identity—network content providers to other users.

"What seemingly a mega creative intention to internet users in digital world actually is a potential trouble to Napster and other internet service providers who provide the similar business".[124] Generally, platforms offered by Napster facilitated internet users to share digital works on internet. Although Napster was brought into court by some recording companies afterwards, Napster P2P technology showed its extensive use potential on copyrighted resource protection.

In the usage model of digital rights management, admittedly, P2P has been used as the significant revolutionary business model for digital copyright development. However, P2P technology was regularly used by people who were supposed to reproduce or distribute copyrighted multi-media documents without copyright holders' authorization before.[125] Previous P2P model were deployed by most internet users mainly to locate the digital files, which had been "torn" and shared with others for free through networks.[126] Digital rights management operators seemed not accustomed to the unpleasant situation that P2P technology precipitated. A bearish result, which digital rights management system encountered with, was from double-whammy, consumers decline and decreasing turnovers. Namely, from the economic perspective, it is impossible for digital rights management scheme to merely prohibit the massive illegal reproductions or distributions regardless of the profits. To alleviate the pressure from marketing, digital rights management attempted to integrate with P2P.

Digital rights management has been somehow accepted to be the supplement of P2P technology for copyright protection.[127] How digital rights management system cooperates with P2P has turned out an urgent issue to the copyright owners and

[123] A&M Records, Inc. v. Napster, Inc., 239 F.3d 1004, 2001.

[124] Lackman [66], p. 1161.

[125] Einhorn and Rosenblatt [67], p. 1.

[126] Ibid, p. 2.

[127] Ibid.

distributors. It has been acknowledged that P2P platform is helpful for searching an unauthorized digital work. However, it is also useful for locating a legal file or other resources in the public domain. A lot of copyright owners already recognized in P2P a novel medium that provides new opportunities for the economic beneficial.[128]

> Films on Digital Versatile Disks (DVD) are also very popular. Here, Peer-to-Peer acts like a video-on-demand service, and a substitute for rental. When compared to physically renting a film, the appeal of Peer-to-Peer lies in the fact of not having to go to the video shop or distributing machine. Compared to VoD [Video on Demand], Peer-to-Peer's main appeal is that the films can be kept once they are downloaded, burned, transferred, and so on.[129]

Super-distribution is the trait of P2P technology, which allows copyrighted works to be distributed repeatedly.[130] Brad Cox elucidated the feature of software that it can indicate whether it is being used.[131] While the principle of super-distribution is to establish a payment mechanism for per usage to consumers, it is based on the software distribution. Superdistribution of P2P makes it possible that it allows digital works to be purchased by consumers on line and an individual account to be obtained for reselling these resources simultaneously (Fig. 2.15).

"P2P Streaming" has been one of the popular P2P business models that supports superdistribution under digital rights management system so far.[132] Similar to Napster, Mercora is such a website for P2P streaming service, which is connected with cyber radio. Unlike other P2P platform, Mercora only provides streaming service to the users on the web when its parent company is done with songs royalty.[133] Users are permitted to install its software for free and meanwhile the digital albums or songs stored in their PC hard drives are also scanned to be a private collection database.[134] Moreover, musical works found on this website are allowed to be added or deleted from users' own play lists as they want. Users are able to search for a keyword of songs, a list of songs available for broadcasting. However, its service prohibits any users to stream more than 4 pieces of songs from one artist or over three from the same album during their course.[135] Certainly, songs provided by Mercora's at the play list are selectable, which is different from traditional radio stations/platforms.

> ......[It]make its money by letting you buy the music that you're listening to through Amazon, as well as posting unobtrusive Google-supplied ads to the application.[136]

---

[128]Noam and Pupillo [65], p. 15.

[129]Andrea Gavosto, Bruno Lamborghini, Stefano Lamborghini, "Peer-to-Peer Network and the Distribution in the EU", See Noam and Pupillo [65], p. 275.

[130]Ibid 111, p. 10.

[131]Cox [68].

[132]Ibid 111, p. 10.

[133]Metz [70].

[134]http://buzzsonic.com/category/online-radio/. Access date: 15/12/2013.

[135]Ibid 120.

[136]Ibid 120.

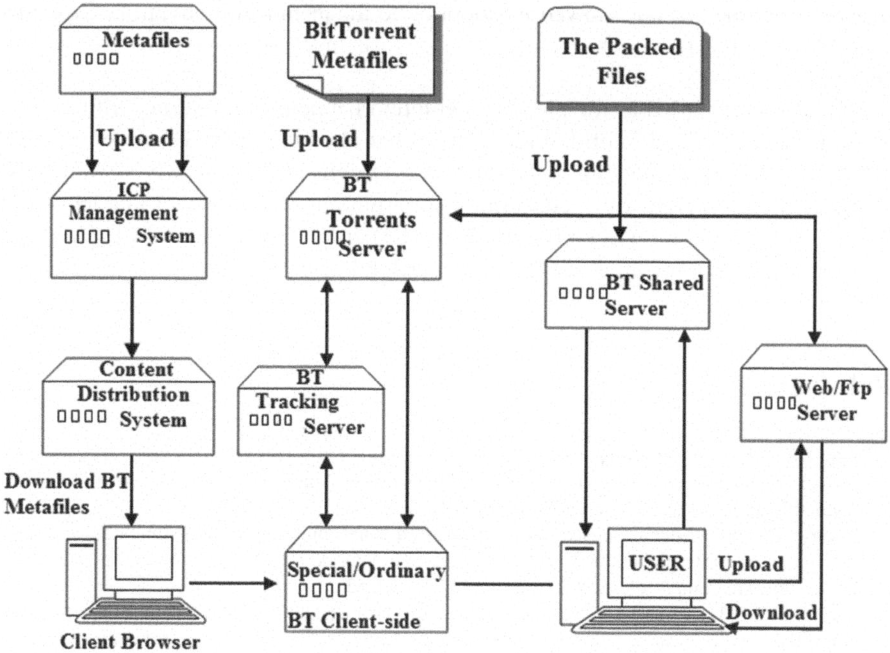

Fig. 2.15 Distribution mechanism of content products at BitTorrent platform (Xingdong [69], p. 38)

The kernel of integration between digital rights management and P2P technology focuses on a more adaptable method for copyrighted material exchange. Superdistribution implies the information-oriented development of digital rights management and the way in which the society is moving forward. Under the digital rights management usage models, P2P actualizes more users/consumers interactively involved, greater amount of copyrighted works transaction, and a reduction of illegal decrypted actions. The breakthrough made by P2P model, in a manner, has satisfied both sides of users and copyright owners. Win-win prospect will at utmost achieve the balance of copyright holders'/distributors' economic interest and the public's benefit. P2P scheme showed that advanced technique design for a digital rights management solution was no better than an interaction synthesis of technological innovation and users' participation.

Summary When copyright independently exists under the intellectual property regime, it merely regulates the issues happened in the physical world. With the rapid development of new technology, the problems with regard to copyright gradually spread into the digital context.[137] It is understandable that copyright system has been challenged by the novel technology and sometimes the current

[137]Tehranian [71], p. 45.

copyright regime has not showed its adoption to the technical innovation. Growing concern from the public is deemed as a control mechanism on the information dissemination.[138]

P2P also is regarded as the greatest revolution happened on internet with expectation to the email and World Wide Web. When the emergence of dispersed P2P technology software challenged the current copyright protection, we have already recognized the previous rules concerning copyright protection have to be adjusted. Therefore, the legislation of copyright should be perspective towards the technology evolution to accommodate itself to various technologies.[139]

References

1. Lam PH (1995) Copyright protection of foreign computer software in the People's Republic of China: significant progress in two years. Loyola Los Angeles Int Comp Law Rev: 861. Available at: http://digitalcommons.lmu.edu/ilr/vol17/iss4/6
2. Roemer R (2003) Locking down loose bits: trusted computing, digital rights management, and the fight for copyright control on your computer. UCLA J Law Technol (8). http://www.lawtechjournal.com/articles/2003/08_040223_roemer.pdf
3. Walker J (2003) The Digital Imprimatur: how big brother and big media can put the Internet genie back in the bottle. Knowl Technol Policy 16(3):24–77. http://www.fourmilab.ch/documents/digital-imprimatur/
4. Stallman RM (1997) The right to read. Commun ACM 40(2):85–87
5. Whitehead D (2013) Banging the DRM, the history of anti-piracy. http://www.eurogamer.net/articles/banging-the-drm-article, 14/04/2013
6. Will H (2014) Understanding net neutrality: we need a better analogy. The National Memo, November 17, 2014. Available at: http://www.nationalmemo.com/net-neutrality-better-analogy/
7. Samuelson P (1999) Intellectual property and the digital economy: why the anti-circumvention regulations need to be revised. Berkeley Technol Law J 14:519. Available at: http://heinonline.org/HOL/LandingPage?collection=journals&handle=hein.journals/berktech14&div=35&id=&page=. Accessed 14 Aug 2015
8. Summer S (1999) Music on the Internet: can the present laws and treaties protect music copyright in cyberspace? Curr: Int Trade Law J 8:31. Available at: https://litigation-essentials.lexisnexis.com/webcd/app?action=DocumentDisplay&crawlid=1&crawlid=1&doctype=cite&docid=8+Currents+Int'l+Trade+L.J.+31&srctype=smi&srcid=3B15&key=990a1ea8c1eebf0c89d434e991010b0a. Accessed 14 Aug 2015
9. McEwan T (2001) Managing values and beliefs in organisations. Financial Times Management May, 2001
10. Amen K, Keogh T, Wolff N (2013) Digital copyright: a tale of domestic discord, presented in three acts. http://www.infotoday.com/cilmag/may02/Amen_Keogh_Wolff.htm. Accessed 14 Aug 2013
11. Purnhagen K, Rott P (eds) (2014) Varieties of European economic law and regulation. In: Studies in European economic law and regulation, vol 3, pp 439–458. Competition law and consumer law: why we need a common consumer model, July, 2014

[138]Geiger [72], p. 366.

[139]Katz [73], pp. 245–284.

12. Geiger C (2010) The future of copyright in Europe: striking a fair balance between protection and access to information. Intellect Prop Q 14(1):1–14
13. Anderson A, Rainie L (2014) Digital Life in 2025. http://www.pewinternet.org/2014/03/11/digital-life-in-2025/, March 11, 2014. Accessed 26 Sep 2015
14. Liu Q, Safavi-Naini R, Sheppard NP (2003) Digital rights management for content distribution. Conferences in Research and Practice in Information Technology Series, vol 34, pp 49–58
15. Gordon WJ, Bahls D (2007) Public's right to fair use: amending Section 107 to avoid the fared use fallacy. Utah Law Rev: 619. Available at: http://heinonline.org/HOL/LandingPage?collection=journals&handle=hein.journals/utahlr2007&div=26&id=&page=. Accessed 14 Aug 2014
16. Vathitphund T (2010) Access to knowledge difficulties in developing countries: a balanced access to copyrighted works in the digital environment. Int Rev Law Comput Technol 24 (1):9–10
17. Tuch A (2010) "Multiple Gatekeepers" John M. Olin Fellow and Fellow of the Program on Corporate Governance, Harvard Law School. Va Law Rev 96:107. http://www.law.harvard.edu/programs/olin_center/fellows_papers/pdf/Tuch_33.pdf
18. Fisher WW III (2004) Promises to keep, technology, law and the future of entertainment. Stanford Law and Politics, p 134
19. Bonne P (2003) Copyright protection and copy control when distributing and publishing digital information, GSEC Practical Version 1.4b, Option 1, 2003
20. Layton J (2014) How digital rights management works. Available at: http://computer.howstuffworks.com/drm.htm. Accessed 14 Aug 2014
21. Bates BJ (2015) Value and digital rights management: a social economics approach. Paper to be presented to the Communication Technology division, Association for Education in Journalism & Mass Communication, for the 2006 annual convention, San Francisco, CA. Available at: http://www.cci.utk.edu/files/aej2006-DRMSocEcon.pdf. Accessed 16 Aug 2015
22. Rooney D, Hearn G, Mandeville T, Joseph R (2003) Public policy in knowledge-based economies: foundations and frameworks-new horizons in public policy series. Elgar, Cheltenham [u.a.]
23. Melendez-Ortiz R, Roffe P (2009) Intellectual property and sustainable development: development agendas in a changing world. Edward Elgar Publishing Ltd
24. Haskin D (2007) Will DRM-free music threaten iTunes? Computerworld, Apr 30, 2007. http://www.infoworld.com/article/2663702/applications/will-drm-free-music-threaten-itunes-.html
25. Kerr I, Maurushat A, Tacit C (2003) Technological protection measures: tilting at copyright's windmill. Ottawa Law Rev 34(7):13. http://heinonline.org/HOL/LandingPage?collection=journals&handle=hein.journals/ottlr34&div=8&id=&page=. Accessed 15 Aug 2010
26. Cope B, Freeman R (2001) Digital rights management and content development: technology drivers across the book production supply chain, from creator to consumer. Oct 2001
27. Kutter M, Hartung F (1999) Introduction to watermarking techniques. In: Katzenbeisser S, Petitcolas FAP (eds) Chapter 5. Information hiding techniques for steganography and digital watermarking, p 98
28. Petitcolas FAP (2003) Digital watermarking. In: Becker E, Buhse W, Gunnewig D, Rump N (eds) Digital rights management: technological, economic, legal and political aspects. Springer, p 91
29. Guo XC (2008) Methodologies in digital watermarking: robust and reversible watermarking techniques for authentication, security and privacy protection. University of Toronto, p 1
30. Wang F-H, Pan J-S, Jain LC (2009) Innovations in digital watermarking techniques. Springer, pp 3–4
31. Morimoto N (1999) Digital watermarking technology with practical applications. Information Science, Special Issue on Multimedia Informing Technologies, vol 2(4), p 108

32. Liu Y, Sadeghi A-R, Ghosal D, Mukherjee B (2011) Video streaming forensic – content identification with traffic snooping. Information Security, Lecture Notes in Computer Science, vol 6531, p 134
33. Staff M (2001) Napster, Loudeye Strike Digital Fingerprinting Deal. http://www.macworld.com/article/1017876/napster.html. Jun 7, 2001. Accessed 21 Nov 2013
34. Shuyu F (2007) Efficient and Robust Audio Fingerprinting. http://scholarbank.nus.edu.sg/bitstream/handle/10635/13438/FengSY.pdf?...1, p 20
35. Ramona M, Peeters G (2013) Audioprint: an efficient audio fingerprint system based on a novel cost-less synchronization scheme. http://recherche.ircam.fr/anasyn/peeters/ARTICLES/Ramona_2013_ICASSP_AudioPrint.pdf. Accessed 21 Nov 2013
36. Meléndez-Jubarbe H (2009) DRM interoperability. Boston Univ J Sci Technol Law 15:192
37. Garnett N (2001) Technological protection of copyright works, and copyright management systems (Paper presented to the ALAI Congress, June 2001) [unpublished], online: ALAI 2001 Congress Program and Presentation. http://www.law.columbia.edu/conferencesI2001/program_en.htm
38. de Werra J (2001) The legal system of technological protection measures under the WIPO treaties, the *DMCA*, the European Union Directives and other National Laws (Japan, Australia). online: ALAI 2001 Congress Program and Presentation, http://www.law.columbia.edu/conferences/2001/program_en.htm
39. Cunard JP (2001) Technological protection of copyrighted works and copyright management systems: a brief survey of the landscape. ALAI 2001 Congress Program and Presentation, http://www.law.columbia.edu/conferences/2001/program_en.htm. Accessed 03 Dec 2013
40. Bechtold S (2001) From copyright to information law—implications of digital rights management. Available at: http://www.ip.ethz.ch/people/bechtold/publications/2002_DRM.pdf. Digital Rights Management Workshop
41. Iannella R (2004) The open digital rights language: XML for digital rights management. Information Security Technical Report, vol 9(3), p 47
42. Guo H (2014) Digital Rights Management (DRM) Using XrML. http://www.tml.tkk.fi/Studies/Tik-110.501/2001/papers/guo.heng.pdf, p 6
43. Xiaobin H, Shaokuan H (2003) Digital Rights Management and XrmL. Document, Information and Knowledge 4:49
44. Waupotitsch R, Eidenbenz S, Smith JP, Kroc L (2006) Multi-scale integrated information and telecommunications system (MIITS): first results from a large-scale end-to-end network simulator. Winter Simulation Conference 06, Proceedings of the 38th conference
45. Alvear J (2001) ContentGuard Speaks Digital Rights Language. http://www.streamingmedia.com/Articles/Editorial/Featured-Articles/ContentGuard-Speaks-Digital-Rights-Language-64450.aspx. November 28, 2001. Accessed 09 Dec 2014
46. Guth S (2003) Rights Expression Languages. In: Becker E, Buhse W, Gunnewig D, Rump N (eds) Digital rights management: technological, economic, legal and political aspects. Springer, p 103
47. De Capitani di Vimercatil S, Foresti S, Jajodia S, Samarati P (2007) Access control policies and languages in open environments. "Secure Data Management in Decentralized Systems". Springer, p 37
48. Lorch M, Kafura D, Shah S (2015) An XACML-based policy management and authorization service for Globus resources. Proceedings of the Fourth International Workshop on Grid Computing, http://www.computer.org/csdl/proceedings/grid/2003/2026/00/20260208.pdf. 2003. Accessed 15 Aug 2015
49. Steel C, Lai R, Nagappan R (2012) Core security patterns: identity management standards and technologies. Prentice Hall, Dec 14, 2012. http://www.informit.com/articles/article.aspx?p=1398625&seqNum=12. Accessed 06 Dec 2013
50. Ardagna CA, Damiani E, De Capitani di Vimercati S, Samarati P (2004) XML-based access control languages. Information Security Technical Report, vol 9(3), p 41

51. Han W, Lei C (2012) A survey on policy languages in network and security management. Comput Netw 56:479
52. Gell R (2014) How to play MPEG video with MPEG Player software? http://www.anymp4.com/blu-ray-player/play-mpeg-video-with-mpeg-player-software.html. Accessed 06 Dec 2014
53. Thomas-Kerr J, Burnett I, Ritz CH, Devillers S, de Schrijever D, Van de Walle R (2007) Is that a fish in your ear? A universal metalanguage for multimedia. IEEE Multimedia 14(2): 73. http://ro.uow.edu.au/cgi/viewcontent.cgi?article=1522&context=infopapers. Accessed 09 Dec 2013
54. Sander T (2002) Golden times for digital rights management? Financial Cryptography, Springer
55. Prepaid Credit Card: "Definition of 'Prepaid Credit Card'". http://www.investopedia.com/terms/p/prepaid-credit-card.asp. Accessed 23 Dec 2013
56. Cooperm MN (2005) Time for the recording industry to face the music: the political, social and economic benefits of peer-to-peer communications networks. Consumer Federation of America, Consumers Union, Free Press, U.S. Public Interest Research Groups, March, 2005
57. Kwok SH (2002) Digital rights management for the online music business. ACM SIGecom Exchanges 3(3):23. http://www.sigecom.org/exchanges/volume_3/3.3-Kwok.pdf
58. Jeeny (2012) Cheap DVD Rental. http://www.moneysavingexpert.com/shopping/cheap-dvd-rental. 28/08/2012. Accessed 23 Dec 2013
59. Roettgers J (2013) Netflix may ditch DVDs sooner rather than later. Available at http://www.businessweek.com/articles/2013-10-21/netflix-may-ditch-dvds-sooner-rather-than-later#r=nav-r-story
60. Damouni N (2011) In: Adler L (ed) Amazon in talks to launch digital book library: report. http://www.reuters.com/article/2011/09/12/us-amazon-media-library-idUSTRE78A3RL20110912. 12/09/2011
61. Buhse W (2002) Implications of digital rights management for online music–a business perspective. Security and Privacy in Digital Rights Management, Lecture Notes in Computer Science, vol 2320. Springer, p 209
62. Picot A, Reichwald R, Wigand R (2001) Die grenzenlose Unternehmung, Wiesbaden, p 272
63. Bohn P (2005) Rent-A-Star: do you subscribe to digital music? Berlecon Research, 22/06/2005. http://www.indicare.org/tiki-read_article.php?articleId=112. Accessed 19 Dec 2013
64. Lucchi N (2006) Digital media & intellectual property, management of rights and consumer protection in a comparative analysis. Springer, p 79
65. Noam EM, Pupillo LM (eds) (2008) Peer-to-peer video the economics, policy, and culture of today's new mass medium. Springer
66. Lackman EM (2002–2003) Slowing down the speed of sound: a transatlantic race to head off digital copyright infringement. Fordham Intellect Prop Media Entertain Law J 13:1161. Available at: http://heinonline.org/HOL/LandingPage?collection=journals&handle=hein.journals/frdipm13&div=38&id=&page=. Accessed 14 Aug 2010
67. Einhorn MA, Rosenblatt B (2005) Peer-to-peer networking and digital rights management, how market tools can solve copyright problems. Policy Analysis, No. 534. February 17, 2005, p 1
68. Cox B (1995) Superdistribution: objects as property on the electronic frontier. Addison-Wesley
69. Xingdong Z (2006) The study and design of digital rights management system based on P2P technology, p 38
70. Metz C (2013) Mercora P2P Radio. http://www.pcmag.com/article2/0,2817,1755278,00.asp. Accessed 15 Dec 2013
71. Tehranian J (2003–2004) All rights reserved - reassessing copyright and patent enforcement in the digital age. Univ Cincinnati Law Rev 72:45. Available at: http://heinonline.org/HOL/LandingPage?collection=journals&handle=hein.journals/ucinlr72&div=9&id=&page=. Accessed 14 Aug 2013
72. Geiger C (2006) Copyright and free access to information, for a fair balance of interests in a globalised world. Eur Intellect Prop Rev 7(28):366
73. Katz A (2006) The potential demise of another natural monopoly: new technologies and the administration of performing rights. J Competition Law Econ 2(2):245–284. http://jcle.oxfordjournals.org/cgi/content/abstract/2/2/245. Accessed 14 Aug 2015

Chapter 3
Digital Rights Management Dilemma: Theoretical Context

3.1 Culture Perspective

Since the emergence of human beings, it is proved that their life has been changed gently from every single aspect. Humans' wisdom witnesses the rapid development of the whole society that provides a platform for people's evergreen concern about the relationship between their intellectual output and economic income. The increasingly growing focus upon the private property interest first appeared with its original intention of safeguarding feudal hierarchy. At the beginning of intellectual property system development, the nobles spared no efforts to strive for their private benefit in all fields, especially in culture and knowledge area, which is accepted by the general public to be the origin of intellectual property regime.

"Culture", as an elusive word, has been regarded as "one of the two or three most complicated words in the English language".[1] According to scholar's observation,[2] previous studies from various scholars with disciplinary background in the past decades have observed that the interrelationship between intellectual property and culture has been characteristic of increasing frequency and emphasis in a large number of fields. Intellectual property protection is the accompaniment of intellectual property acculturation, which accordingly flourished intellectual property legal system. If culture in intellectual property, or copyright had been in retrospect, it might be discovered by historical data that copyright culture underwent primarily oral culture, literal culture and networks copyright culture.

A certain number of created works improvised by bards and other artists became the main resource of oral culture,[3] which was occasioned by the primitive idea for

[1]Williams [1]. Patent, Trade-mark, and Copyright Foundation of the George Washington University, and also see *Proceedings of the annual public conference of the George Washington University*. Vols. 1–7. 1958.

[2]Yu [2].

[3]Geller [3], p. 211. Original resource comes from Havelock [4], pp. 93–94.

C. Xu, *Regulatory Model for Digital Rights Management*,
https://doi.org/10.1007/978-981-15-1995-6_3

recording historic habit and customs in extenso. Moreover, elements in oral culture can "vary flexibly in response to an open-ended scope of social variables",[4] unlike written culture. Literal culture, introduced into copyright culture area, was deemed as a contribution to categorized objects system under copyright culture. It is at this literal culture period that copyright shaped its traditional and classic architecture that novel copyright culture relied on. While when copyright met technologies, a new culture base on allied elements came out, this was acknowledged as "networks copyright culture". This type of copyright culture came along with novel technical evolution and three kinds of copyright culture are also divided by their mediums types. Networks copyright culture developed itself based on literal culture, which created a copyright scheme with intermarriage of technology and culture.

Compared with the traditional means of communication, networks, along with the revolution of its technical means and dissemination of the information, on the one hand are to achieve rapid spread of knowledge, establish extensive web technology background to the emergence of Knowledge-Economy era upon the proliferation of speed and density, profoundly the knowledge and technological innovations changed. Intellectual property rights, regional, timeliness and other traditional features, give rise to an enormous impact and overall innovation.[5]

Culture progress has driven copyright industry prosperous development and copyright mediums innovation as well. Similarly, technologies on copyright protection improvement or mediums advances either accelerated copyright culture step forward. What both of them have been in response to each other, in essence, reflects the veritable relationship mapping of technologies and culture. Cultural analysis on copyright issue, especially in digital world, has been thought of an indispensable method for copyright matters research.

3.1.1 Culture Background

Admittedly, digital rights management technology is simply thought of as a response to the emerging features of digital copyright architecture. Technology itself under digital rights management system has no admissibility of copyright law. As has already been suggested, however, the whole scheme of digital rights management acts as part of comprehensive copyright protection system, and especially a crucial element in digital copyright world. If we have to explore the nexus of copyright and culture, whether apparent or elusive, aspects could be summed up as follows:

Above all, the fundamental purpose of copyright law, which aims to spread and encourage knowledge or culture communication, has been acknowledged. Prosperous development of "culture" is regarded as one of typical incentives of copyright law. The Statute of Anne in Britain in 1710, treated as the first modern copyright

---

[4]Ibid, p. 211.

[5]David Rooney, etc., Hearn et al. [5].

statute in the world, incited "learning" as its goal.[6] The French copyright laws in Revolutionary times [*French Playwrights Decree*], issued in 1791, made the classic article has ever usually cited in Europe[7]: "[T]he most sacred, the most legitimate, the most unassailable, and, if I may say so, the most personal of all the properties is the work, fruit of the thought of the writer."[8]

Second, the object of copyright law is the "work". Works are basically the outcomes that authors or creators devote their intellectual effort in, while the source material of intellectual creation is mainly from culture knowledge. What knowledge creation constitutes reflects various cultural elements. For example, a work of art probably was produced several centuries ago. It may contain a plenty of historical information or cultural background. Further, cinematographic works, as one category of "works" protected by copyright law, ordinarily show more or less characters related to culture, like local manners or customs in comedy or a wildly romantic one. "Literature and the fine arts that might make us more conscious of the world as well as delight us".[9] Different culture styles are embedded in diverse types of copyrighted works. In the Enlightenment, terms as "learning" or "science" were commonly perceived to refer to culture.[10]

Moreover, the context in which copyright law making and enforcement relies on certain cultural environment, and also culture factors exert corresponding influence to the copyright law. As culture locates in the realm of superstructure and law is also considered a part of the superstructure. The intersection of culture and copyright law, in this regard, seems inevitable. Besides, it is indeed that culture and copyright law tie a lot to each other.

Culture was represented by concrete forms of "technology". Alternatively, the previous types of culture can be showed by specific technology, as technology has been regarded as a mirror of human beings intelligence that significantly retroacts culture. With the development of technology, the relationship of technology and culture becoming more momentous has been diffusely acknowledged. Technologies interact with social economic and cultural matrix in various aspects, and what matters is cultures have been differentially treated somehow, known as "cultural bias". There hence shaped a culture misunderstanding that advanced technologies were commonly associated with so called "superior" culture. The elements

---

[6]c.19, Anne Act. The original title of this statute, known as "An Act for the Encouragement of Learning, by Vesting the Copies of Printed Books in the Authors or Purchasers of such Copies, during the Times therein mentioned".

[7]Geller [3], p. 256.

[8]Ibid; Also see Justine Pila, "Pluralism, Principles and Proportionality in Intellectual Property", Oxford Journal of Legal Studies, p. 4. http://ojls.oxfordjournals.org/content/early/2013/10/21/ojls.gqt029.full, access date: 31/12/2013. (Original quoted from *Archives Parlementaires de 1787 à 1860,* Receuil complet des débats législatifs et politiques des Chambres françaises (vol xxii, Paris 1887) 210.

[9]Ibid 130, p. 257.

[10]Ibid 130, p. 257.

contained in technologies even interplay each other directly or indirectly.[11] Present technologies had broken through the old socio-cultural ranges through updating knowledge information globally.[12] Since technologies have become competitive instruments of countries' economic progress, the influence on technologies from culture diversity also reduced vastly.[13]

From the machine age in the Industrial Revolution to the current internet times, technologies ranging from hardware to software have turned into the crucial material basis of culture evolution. Even, this type of culture in scholars' mind was termed as "technological culture" or "techculture".[14] Technological culture is a new and popular jargon used for describing social phenomena that technologies and culture act mutually. Similar/same techniques could be embedded in the culture in various ways. It gestates disparate things related to cultural practices under different cultural contexts. Likewise, diverse technologies may be served for the same purpose.[15]

In ancient times, Anglo-Saxon people and tribes in African may use a variety of wooden or metallic tools for hunting animals. In this regard, cultural elements are not determined by the same technology or technique. On the contrary, minor groups of people utilized instead of owning the systematic technologies or "complex" techniques in their societies, which seemed as "minimal" technological culture in other countries. Actually, there is an entity involved in the embedability of technological culture. This ensemble affords both main-stream culture and the alternative one. Therefore, issues about culture exports and culture discrimination thereupon came up. Our civilization has been a kind of culture comprising massive technologies, which is unlike our previous culture in qualitative and quantitative perspectives (Fig. 3.1).

Even in some scholars' opinion, digital rights management system was regarded as an alternative approach for intellectual property protection and implementation of intellectual property law.[16] Digital rights management system allows technology and legislation to supplement mutually, and digital rights management has been the heated and controversial object in technological culture context. Nonetheless, cultural background dissecting behind technologies explores a comprehensive and integrated way for thorough acquaintance of digital rights management.

[11]Vanderburg [6], p. 414.

[12]Ibid 130, p. 412.

[13]Ibid 130, p. 412.

[14]Quintanilla [7], pp. 65–71.

[15]Dusek [8], p. 50.

[16]Bates and Liu [9], pp. 7–26.

Pre-Modern Technological Culture	Modern Technological Culture	Contemporary Technological Culture
Production Development under Primitive Environment	Machinery Lifestyle	Technological Monopoly Existence
Human—Nature Symbiotic Relationship	"Unidirectional" Material Society	Highly Competitive "Deformed" Society
"Nature-Centered" Values	"Technical Products" Focused	"Non-human" Centered Values System

Fig. 3.1 Main paradigms of technological culture (Ibid)

3.1.2 Traditional Value System

There exists a claim from intellectual property system's advocators that its unique character is bound to promote cultural knowledge as well as social innovation indispensably and irreplaceably. They someway are able to automatically treat intellectual property protection system by a logical extension of this point as suitable mechanism for every nations and local citizens since it sufficiently accords with this universal value. China, as one of the most important developing countries in the world, has been struggling with its uncomfortable intellectual property protection system for parallel benefit relationship between international legal obligation and the domestic public.

Previous researches have explored the relationship between developed countries' intellectual property practice and China's intellectual property protection trends as well as its poor environment against intellectual property infringements, but little attention has been paid to the part of local culture or intellectual property acculturation in diverse nations. Chinese traditional civilization, distinct from Westerns' culture system, has wielded an immense influence upon Chinese people over a long time.

While numerous studies of Chinese culture mainly centers around the reason for juristic divergence from others', its historical developments driven by political consideration and legal instrumentalism, very few touches upon what roles Chinese culture plays in intellectual property protection and plunging China into an awkward circumstances where wrongs and contumelies spread.[17] Another sequential tough situation caused by Chinese featured intellectual property culture was found in the aspect of legal execution system deficiency. China's intellectual property regulations, which are more or less incongruous with its national condition, and some provisions, even surpass its endurance capacity.

These findings highlight the potential difficulties encountered by Chinese intellectual property protection and the current recognition of intellectual property system in people's mind affected by deep-rooted Chinese culture. Based upon Chinese culture background introduction as well as comparative analysis of various culture characters and piths between China and the West, in conclusion, the author inclines to explain, not to seek so-called "excuse" for better comprehending to this matter that why China's intellectual property protection got here. Better understanding on cross-culture intellectual property protection system construction will very raise new direction and avenues related to a brilliant intellectual property world.

3.1.2.1 The Concept of Intellectual Property Acculturation

Although it is widely acquired as a proverbial trend that acculturation is a significant part of cross-culture area, consent is hardly reached on defining and measuring it. The concept of acculturation given by some scholars long time ago has been treated as classic, which defined that "acculturation comprehends those phenomena which result when groups of individuals having different cultures come into continuous first-hand contact with subsequent changes in the original culture patterns of either or both groups".[18] This typical definition suggests that acculturation is a mutual and multidimensional synthesis as an outcome of interaction between two different cultural groups, which brings about changes of public beliefs, social values and material traits.[19] The process leading to acculturation was progressive, irreversible and contributed to the ethos of dominant culture group.[20] Nevertheless, acculturation research is more complicated and not only the result of culture groups being interactive with each other.[21]

In current surroundings, there is inevitable for the acculturation of various legal cultures. Increasing trend of globalization makes it impossible that still some communities are absolute seclusion of others in the world.[22] The term intellectual property was introduced in the nineteenth century,[23] but not until the twentieth century, its importance was realized in the United States. In Great Britain, the Statute

[17] Potter [10].

[18] Redfield et al. [11].

[19] Cabassa [12].

[20] Padilla and Perez [13].

[21] Ibid.

[22] Nikolic [14].

[23] Maskus [15].

of Monopolies 1623 and the Statute of Anne 1710 are accredited with the introduction of the patent laws and copyright respectively.[24] As John-Locke's has demonstrated in the well-known statement of property as labor's 'just desert', intellectual property is deemed as "a suitable reward for intellectual labour".[25] Regarding intellectual property acculturation, especially the relationship between the Western culture and Chinese intellectual property culture, it seems convincing that intellectual property acculturation should be more accepted as intellectual property enculturation. According to Padilla (1980, 1987) and Keefe and Padilla's (1987) new perspective on defining acculturation based "cultural awareness" and "ethnic loyalty", the social culture integration inclined to be a supra-constructs synthesis.[26]

3.1.2.2 Chinese Traditional Culture and the West's Ideology

The Western intellectual property culture is based on the individualism, Liberalism and Rationalism, which have been regarded as the humanity basis and the spirit values of the Western modern legal development. The impact on Chinese history inertia and social cognition from its traditional civilization and actual barrier in the process of legal transplantation ultimately posed the influence to intellectual property law localization in China.

Intellectual property culture is a type of culture that multi-dimension, comprehensive and exoteric, which is characteristic of individual unit emphasis, spirit of liberty, and reasonable aspiration embedded in private law culture. Intellectual property culture, specifically divisive from modern legal culture, is the culture more emphasizing consciousness, which differs from legal culture itself that is focusing on social sense and institutional system.

Modern legal culture indicates the attitude, belief and evaluation showed by social citizens towards legal institution and legal mechanism.[27] The emergence of intellectual property law in Western countries has undergone the period of "feudal franchise" from late phase in middle ages to "private property" in initial stage of capitalist times. During the fierce social transformation process, the growth of political, economic, and technological elements afford social condition for the burgeoning legal regime.

3.1.2.3 Values in the West: Individualism, Liberalism and Rationalism

The individualism philosophy has been considered to be the consequence of social revolution of modern law and vicissitudes of social regime. Chinese traditional

---

[24]Proceedings of the annual public conference of the George Washington University, 1958.

[25]Ibid 128.

[26]Ibid 143.

[27]Ibid 162.

cultural psychology and the thinking mode of Chinese people are the obstacles for individualism development. Chinese traditional culture, dominated by Confucius philosophy, asserts "the social ethic based on family unit should be the core of society rather than individual right based on the citizen unit".

The pith of individualism concept is centered on "individual". The philosophy of individualism affords the culture basis in a way for the modern private law construction. Autonomy of private law comes into being through imbibing the essence of individualism. In this regard, intellectual property right as crucial part of private rights stresses specific private right belongs to particular subjects, in other words, intellectual property rights are merely affiliated to particular civil subjects, not the rights enjoyed by the general public.

Individualism leads the progressive trend that public authoritative power has been not allowed normally interfering in affairs relevant private rights, which exists seemingly to arouse the right cognition under private law sphere; whereas liberalism principle has been regarded as the kernel of modern private law.[28] Free thinking and economic liberty, which should be the prerequisites of knowledge innovation and knowledge capitalization,[29] since the Renaissance, have long been the existence from cultural consciousness and cultural policy. The significant contribution of liberalism to modern private legal culture was "discovery of human", which advocated "personality liberty" and "individual capability development".

Statute of Anne in 1709 ("An Act for the Encouragement of Learning, by vesting the Copies of Printed Books in the Authors or Purchasers of such Copies, during the Times therein mentioned") in the UK, which abandoned feudal franchise of publication and feudal publication censorship, to some extent, indicating the liberalism in intellectual property law system, profoundly promoted the dissemination of works.[30] Liberalism, on the one hand, is deemed to provide the ideology foundation for modern law's systematization and codification. On the other hand, the "fair use" doctrine under intellectual property system reflects the "Liberalism Philosophy" full of fairness and justice, which the general public's benefit should be considered. There is little historical connection between the existence of Chinese feudal franchise of publication and the emergence of modern intellectual property law, therefore China had failed to complete the historical change.

Rationalism more reflects the character of human beings in nature that Man is a reasoning creature and all humans have to be restrained by potential rationalism power. In previous theoretical research, a law embodying justice values can be proved once it would accord with nature and reason. Modern Rationalism stressed the unification of laws and attributed rights regarding justice, equality and freedom et cetera as the basis of this unification. In this respect, legal reformers and jurists had been striving to seek for an ideal legal system to incorporate types of principles and

---

[28]Zheng [16].

[29]Zhiping [17].

[30]Spence [18].

rules under natural law as one code. Rationalism was in a way, like Liberalism, deemed to lay foundation for further law systematization. Generally speaking, besides social progresses and developments, harmony between man and nature shall be implication of Rationalism in law.

3.1.2.4 Confucianism as the Dominant Philosophy in Ancient China

When the vantage attitude was rashly disseminated in most Western scholar's comments that the concept of intellectual property indeed did not develop in China at all,[31] even Chinese people themselves, some tenable specific viewpoint towards the critiques neither much felicitous nor ambiguous more than it seems. Late Chinese intellectual property expert Zheng Chengsi ever pointed out straight that a researcher on Chinese intellectual property law might be blind when they have no idea about Chinese history.[32]

The Confucianism has governed the whole Chinese society for thousands of years, which emphasized the "Social Ethic" and "*Lun Chang*" (*Lun Chang* means Feudal Order of Importance or Seniority in Human Relationships). Confucian spirit, which is incompatible with what Western traditional culture advocates.[33] Although the Confucian school was discriminated in *Qin Dynasty* and earlier days in *Han Dynasty*, also was challenged by the Metaphysics the Buddhism around Six Dynasties. Nevertheless, experiencing the unprecedented adversity, the Confucianism has been continuous hereunto, depending on its "self-regulation" for accommodating social changes. Therefore, the Confucianism has rooted deeply in implicit Chinese value system.[34]

Among these values Confucianism admires, "*Li*", as the conduct principle in traditional Chinese society, inherently dominated the spirits embedded in the Confucianism regarding the social relationship between individuals and society. The essence of "*Li*" has been regarded to negate "individuality", which deviates from the innovation spirit, creation capability and speculative ability of human beings. Accordingly, spiritual benefit under Confucianism hierarchy, beyond all doubt, has seldom been considered, and even despised or ignored. It is understandable accepted by the whole Confucian culture that the intellectual creation should be the enlightenment from ancestors or the God without consideration of self-improvement relying on intellectual effort.[35] In traditional Chinese Confucian environment, intellectual creations and noetic outcome are promoted or required to share by each social

---

[31]Marquette University Law School Legal Studies Research Paper Series, Research Paper No.09-03. "What Plagiarism Was Not: Some Preliminary Observations On Classical Chinese Attitudes Toward What The West Calls Intellectual Property", Marquette Law Review. 2009.

[32]Ibid 150.

[33]Li [19].

[34]Handong [20].

[35]Ibid 154.

member unconditionally, which seems more than what creators deserved in Chinese view so far. Consequently, what effect that Chinese traditional culture posed on its social values appears impenetrable to modern intellectual property culture notwithstanding, the significant unshakable influence from Confucianism school to Chinese intellectual property development cannot be underestimated.[36]

- ***Legal Transplantation: The Abortive Intellectual Property Transplantation in China***

Historical experience has expounded that moderate protection on intellectual property right is necessary. In the eighteenth, nineteenth century, Britain, France and Germany were the main technical culture export countries in the world. Concurrently, modern intellectual property laws originated from the three countries and developed significantly subsequently.[37] As a consequence, these countries naturally became the great puissance on intellectual property protection that first appeared in history. However, other European countries, American and Japan, in contrast, belonged to the technical culture importation and legal transplantation countries.[38] However, in the twentieth century, the US, Western Europe and Japan turned into the main forces of intellectual property protection. Technical culture importation countries were replaced by vast majority of nations that included China and other developing regions, in the next round.

Observed by technical culture exportation countries' practices, from coetaneous historical perspective, it was noticeable that intellectual protection levels in those areas were higher than the importation countries.[39] In addition, the former group actively intensified international intellectual property legislation as well. For example, in the nineteenth century, France and Germany jointly push forward the treaty "Paris Convention for the Protection of Industry Property" and "Berne Convention for the Protection of Literary and Artistic Works".[40] Subsequent, TRIPs (Agreement On Trade-Related Aspects of Intellectual Property Rights) was promoted by the US-led developed countries in the twentieth century. As it showed, there has been a "stable" historic association between technical culture exportation entities and its powerful intellectual property protection.

Montesquieu declared his famous opinion in his book, "[Laws] should be in relation to the climate of each country, to the quality of its soil, to its situation and extent, to the principal occupation of the natives, whether husbandmen, huntsmen, or shepherds: they should have relation to the degree of liberty that the constitution will bear; to the religion of the inhabitants, to their inclinations, riches, numbers,

---

[36] Ibid 154.

[37] Handong [21], p. 64.

[38] Ibid.

[39] Ibid.

[40] Paris Convention for the Protection of Industry Property (1883); Berne Convention for the Protection of Literary and Artistic Works (1886).

commerce, manners, and customs".[41] Moreover, as Mr Robert M. Cover stated, "law must be meaningful in the sense that it permits those who live together to express themselves with it and with respect to it…".[42] In this regard, we can conclude that law only can exist in suitable environment. The potential ideological collision between the original transplanted legal system and the receiving system has been regarded seriously with increasing requirement of social recognized acceptance and localization of receiving legal society.

The acceptance of Western civilization, including legal rules for Asian countries, should be regarded as the passive acceptance of legal transplantation. Asian countries had transplanted Western legal system since latter half of the nineteenth century when Western countries pressed onward colonization in Asian area. Chinese scholars in intellectual property area convinced the course of Chinese intellectual property development is more than a process of sinicizing the west.[43] They prefer to believe the whole history of Chinese intellectual property development actually witnesses itself vicissitudes from "forced use" stage to "positive adoption" stage, which was a legal transplantation history as well. Intellectual property law localization through rational selection in China per se reveals how to "root" and "absorb" the essence of Western intellectual property law.[44] China has built its considerable advanced intellectual property system yet since establishment of new China.[45]

Regarding the cultural base of modern private law from the aforesaid, Western individualism claim prepared the ground for subsequent intellectual property culture belonging to part of private legal culture. However, the kernel of old Chinese social tradition had been focused on self-sufficient nature economy culture and patriarchal clan family unit.[46] There was infertile culture soil for intellectual property legal transplantation because of incapable affirmation of human beings as the subjects in the society. Confucianism, uplifting influence on Chinese traditional culture over several thousand years, which was inimical to Western culture, corroborates that it is difficult for China to succeed in transplanting intellectual property culture containing a hefty dose of Western civilization.[47] Hence, it seems predestined for Chinese intellectual property transplantation's failure. Or, rather we might say, China has merely transplanted the outer form of intellectual property legal structure, not entirely the psyche of this culture.[48]

To sum up, there is no consensus on the observation that Confucianism has outright influenced Chinese intellectual property system.[49] Although it is a debated

[41]Montesquieu, The Spirit of the Laws. Cambridge University Press, 1989. Cover [22].

[42]Cover [22]. Also see Zhu [23].

[43]Ibid 182.

[44]Ibid 182.

[45]Ibid 182.

[46]Ibid 173.

[47]Ibid 173.

[48]Ibid 178.

[49]Ibid 178.

proposition that China has attributed massive infringements to Confucianism, we still have to recognize that Confucianism, as the predominant one of three main philosophies (Confucianism, Buddhism and Daoism) in Chinese traditional civilization, affords the most convincing and widespread cultural explanation for Chinese intellectual property current dilemma left much to be desired. Furthermore, the spirit value of Confucianism, clashing with the basic principle and original intention of intellectual property system, has been long regarded as the most irreconcilable feature that militates against Chinese, or even other Asian countries' intellectual property reforms.[50]

Even countries in Europe, had encountered with such intellectual property protection dilemmas between each other under the similar values. Whether domestic copyright matters or transnational copyright distributes, it also appeared to European countries as a challenge that was not smooth to solve. Thriving fiction market in England developed with media industry rising in the nineteenth century,[51] but it got bogged down in piracy trouble in American sales market since there was no global copyright protection system for foreign works protection.[52] Before a uniform code or at least legislation on intellectual property protection establishment, some European countries faced this knotty intellectual property protection problem across borders, like France and Belgium. It did happen a large number of piracies of French publications in Belgium in the nineteenth century.[53] Therefore, the pressing issue that Chinese intellectual property development encounters is time shortage if the whole society cognition would accept intellectual property acculturation as its future destiny.

Summary

Obviously, elements contained in Chinese traditional culture have not simply posed influence, but even osmosis on Chinese intellectual property protection field. Should those people who eagerly criticized Chinese intellectual property protection development or estimated intellectual property's miserable destiny in China withdraw their unsound words after rigorous consideration?

Intellectual property system, as an exotic, is not able to grow up in unaccustomed climate or infertile soil when sown in various countries. In this regard, the foremost challenge for setting up intellectual property protection system and promoting its further development should emphasized how to realize the localization of intellectual property protection system in China. No matter how reasonable the Western statement that China has long been treated as the "exceptionally creative and inventive" country is,[54] or what an obstinate comment is that China has not hitherto

[50]Ibid 125.

[51]Geller [3], p. 233. Original resource see William Briggs, "The Law of international Copyright" 40–41, 1906.

[52]Ibid 128. pp. 58–59.

[53]Ibid 128, p. 233.

[54]Allison and Lin [24].

established an intellectual property protection system yet. The Western tone towards current Chinese intellectual property climate should start from the objective evaluation and clear-cut recognition to China's continuous five thousand years civilization. Otherwise, the conclusions speculated by these scholars in no doubt will be in vain proved nonsensical.

3.2 Social Perspective

If the cultural aspect of the intellectual property protection panorama is regarded as one important part of philosophical analysis, then the social angle discussion would be another essential part in philosophy treatment.

3.2.1 Culture Lag

When the relationship of technology innovation and social change was mentioned, we might work out "Lag Culture" theory. "Lag culture" was expressed by Ogburn, American sociologist, in 1920s: "Where one part of culture changes first, through some discovery or invention, and occasions changes in some part of culture dependent upon it, there frequently is a delay in the changes occasioned in the dependent part of culture".[55] Or "When the material conditions change, changes are occasioned in the adaptive culture. But these changes in the adaptive culture do not synchronize exactly with the change in the material culture. There is a lag which may last for varying lengths of time, sometimes indeed, for many years."[56]

The essence of culture lag mirrors the unsynchronized relationship of the novel technologies adoption and the homologous non-material culture. Material culture transition occurs currently before material technologies change, generally, in culture lag world. Whereas it also did happen that transformations on non-material adaptive culture took place ahead of material culture variation frequently. According to Marxism, material culture was the determinant of non-material culture. Yet, one vital element of non-material culture would be relatively stable and independent once it comes into being.

In the course of social transition, the development of non-material culture has been lagging behind the progress of material culture and technologies advances all times precede the social perception transformation. According to Ogburn's "culture

[55]Woodard [25], p. 388, original resource from William Fielding Ogburn, "*Social Change*", p. 201.1922.
[56]Ibid.

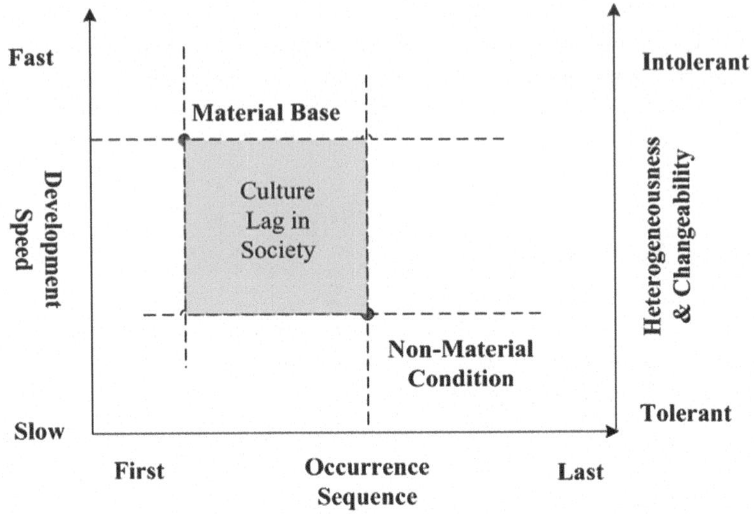

Fig. 3.2 General overview of culture lag in society

lag" theory,[57] regarding the change sequence of objects in non-material culture transition, social regime would first vary, then customs and social morality, and last the social values (Fig. 3.2).

Ogburn used the term of "culture lag" to sum up the time lag of social transition between material culture and non-material culture. Interdependent components under the culture architecture, showed the various development tempos in social progress. Lopsided and incongruous circumstance was triggered by the unsynchronized development of different social culture elements. China has been situating constant and significant social revolutions at this stage, which was the same as what most developing countries had undertaken. In consequence, the condition of culture maladjustment or culture lags in China highlighted thoroughly severe.[58] For instance, a few regions in China, though, brought in advances equipment as its material foundation. However, in contrast, material culture and economy evolution had been restricted by technical information, people qualities and social values.[59]

[57]"The role played by material inventions, that is, by technology, in social change probably received most emphasis in the work of William F. Ogburn. It was Ogburn, also, who was chiefly responsible for the idea that the rate of invention within society is a function of the size of the existing culture base. He saw the rate of material invention as increasing with the passage of time. Ogburn believed that material and non-material cultures change in different ways. Change in material culture is believed to have a marked directional or progressive character......culture lag is defined as the time between the appearance of a new material invention and the making of appropriate adjustments in corresponding area of non-material culture.", http://www.sociologyguide.com/basic-concepts/Cultural-Lag.php, access date: 14/09/2015.

[58]Brinkman and Brinkman [26], pp. 609–627.

[59]Ibid.

The information technology development has provided a stage for culture communication and progress, which nudges human beings down an unforeseen platform. Cyber culture was also occasioned by in information technology growth and its variation. Cyber culture is the outcome of information technology evolution that strikes the traditional culture paradigms. Cyber culture is, as it were, the precondition of culture paradigms conversion. Alike technologies, internet culture has been a double-edged sword so far. Internet culture has crippled tradition culture's predominate position in culture architecture, although it initiated a new culture form.[60]

Information technology enhances the utilization percentage of information resource. However, ironically, cyber culture helped cause new round of "culture invasion". English-dominated Western countries disseminated their ideology, thinking mode and other aspects to non-English speaking regions.[61] Western culture, especially internet culture in the west, in virtue of communication language advantage that it relies on, permeates worldwide.[62] In other words, it failed to spread traditional culture and essence of traditional morality in China through internet. In this regard, it is a great controversial matter that responds to any challenge incurred by cyber culture, which is regarding socio-culture advances.[63]

The heavy burden carried by China historically was expounded above occurred under so-called "Sealed China". In 1978, China's reform and opening-up policy was first contemplated and then launched. It was regarded as the real step that China moved forward to meet the Western world. Massive obstacles in managing mechanism and property rights system previously has been replaced by culture gap although economy disparity reduced (Fig. 3.3).[64]

Intersectional part of two "culture lag" objects reveals the underlying "culture clash", which I mentioned above. Afterwards, a consequential round of culture lags would take place subsequently in the culture conflict course.[65] What discussed under "culture lag" theory corroborated the theme of cultural analysis section. Culture lag, in a way, aggravates rough intellectual property protection situation. Traditional culture value has posed an important influence to people's identical construction on intellectual area. Even in the digital times, this impact would be more significant.

3.2.2 Reciprocal Determinism Theory

Behavior has been deemed as the most essential factors of human beings, handling merely with what might be observed and could be expressed as a function of

[60]Ibid.

[61]Ibid.

[62]Ibid 203.

[63]Ibid 203.

[64]Ibid 203.

[65]Sahay [27].

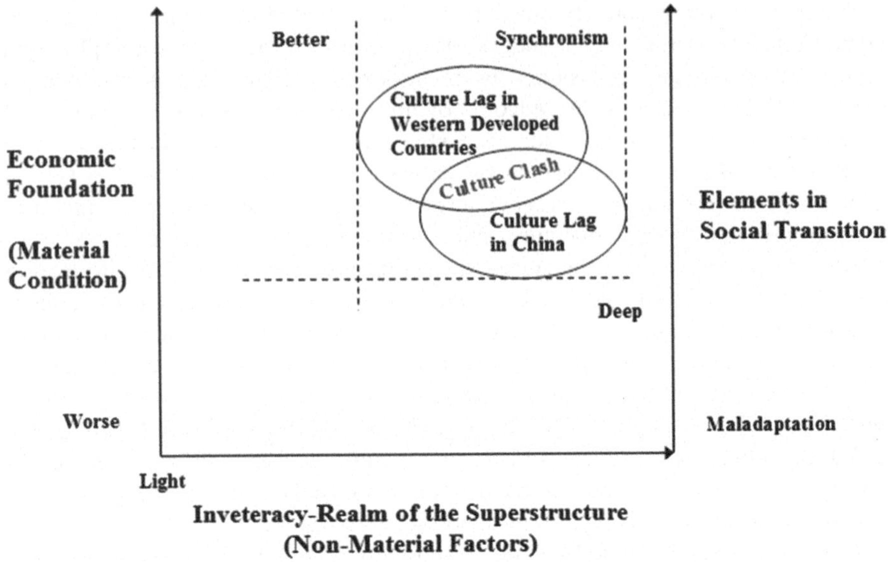

Fig. 3.3 Culture Lag Architecture between China and the Western Countries

individuals and environment.[66] People's behavior has been primarily developed through observation, imitation and modeling,[67] and, is based on constant "interaction between the individual and the environment where they manipulates – a phenomenon described as Social Learning Theory".[68]

In a social circumstance, based on Albert Bandura's concept of reciprocal determinism,[69] the surrounding environment of human beings could be affected by their behavior, which in turn can influence actions (and vice versa), "expectations regarding outcomes within certain situations can influence individuals' decisions and intention to change actions, thus affecting self-efficacy".[70] The theory of Reciprocal Determinism was raised by psychologist Albert Bandura, one of the famous social theoreticians in the twentieth century. Besides social learning theory, Bandura proposed the reciprocal determinism, which involved Environment (E), Persons (P) and Behavior (B). He considers that people's behavior is the result that internal factors of persons (like cognition) interact (select/influence) with environment (like social elements).

---

[66]Sansone et al. [28], p. 119. Lewin's Equation (1939).

[67]Karen L. Williams Middleton, "Developing Entrepreneurial Behavior, Facilitating Nascent Entrepreneurship at the University", p. 23. http://vcplist.com/wp-content/uploads/2013/11/Doctoral-Thesis-Developing-Entrepreneurial-Behavior_Karen-Williams-Middleton.pdf.

[68]Bandura [29].

[69]Bandara [30], pp. 344–358.

[70]Bandara [31], pp. 122–147.

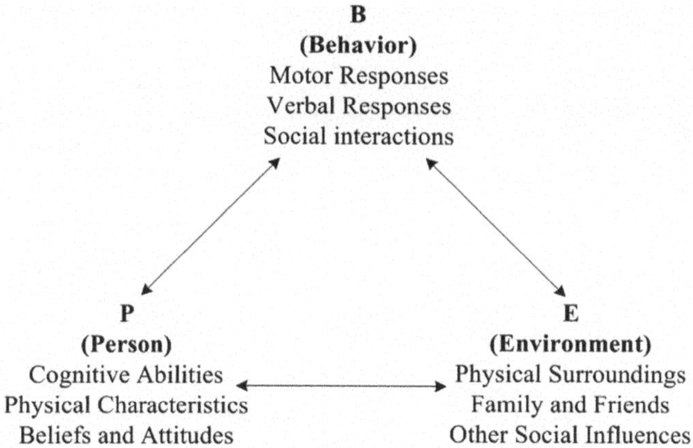

Fig. 3.4 Reciprocal determinism theory architecture (Ibid)

The core principle of Reciprocal Determinism theory illustrates "how what we do and who we spend time with our behavior impacts upon and changes the Life Conditions in the environment we experience and how we respond cognitively and emotionally as a Person to the environmental signal we then receive."[71] The environmental feedback's status will cause different and variable reaction of people's behavior, for instance, beliefs, thoughts and manners. Normally, what people will do are based on what sense they obtain from the feedback (Fig. 3.4).[72]

Therefore, in this regard, an individual cannot be completely free, and get his own way totally. As people's behavior is under the control of environment and society, meanwhile, human beings are not the reactors whom are entirely and passively affected. The interaction between individuals and the society promotes the inner self-regulated system in which cognition is treated as the intermediary agent. They decide mutually and interactively.

For intellectual property architecture in China and Western countries, it is stronger of intellectual property protection awareness in most Western countries than that in China. From Reciprocal Determinism Theory perspective, it would be explained that early capitalism initially burgeoned in certain countries in Europe, where people's thinking was moulded with local condition. Conversely, China's economic system was fully liberated after 1978, "the Reform and Opening-up Policy".

Certainly, the outer context that would pose an influence on individuals' behavior and cognition was poorer that the Western countries.[73] Until now, the economic and civilized development in China has lagged behind those Western nations, although it stepped much faster than those countries. We might observe from the current

[71]"Reciprocal Determinism", available at: http://www.integratedsociopsychology.net/reciprocal_determinism.html.

[72]Ibid.

[73]Ibid.

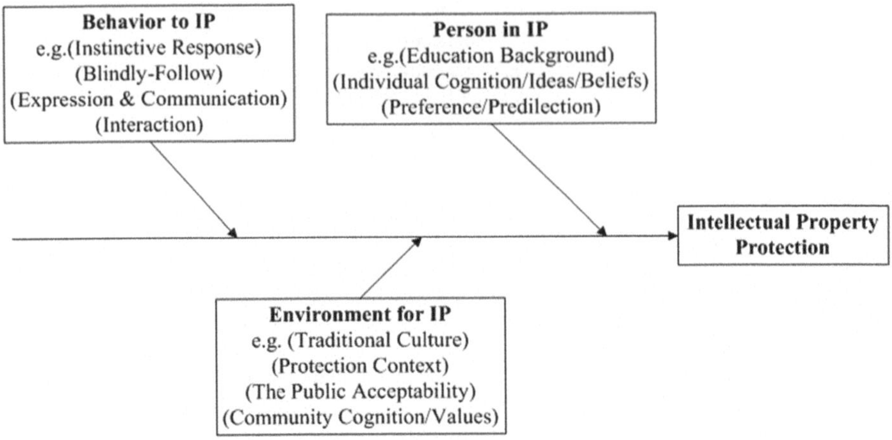

Fig. 3.5 Reciprocal determinism theory-based intellectual property protection system

intellectual property protection situation encountered by China that the external environment at present has not been so helpful in shaping their ideology of intellectual property protection (Fig. 3.5).

3.3 Economic Perspective

Digital rights management regime now has been regarded as the novel method that can do the management of digital copyright, when referred to controversial issue with respect to the conflict between the competition law and intellectual property law.[74] Actually it is visible that the exploitation of digital rights management system is wildly used in the digital environment currently. The impact on the present adoption of digital rights management technology not only benefits the traditional market but also influences the creativity world.

There are a plenty of various definitions with respect to digital rights management meaning from lot of different perspective. In most classical defined concepts, however, it is no doubt that digital right management is more considered as a kind of technical tool that protects and manages intellectual property information and material during the process of creation, communication, distribution and exploitation of the digital content.[75]

Since the birth of digital rights management, its primary target locates within the scope of restricting piracy by technique approaches and also preserve intellectual digital content at the same time to guarantee marketing sales channels about digital

[74] Magnani and Montagnani [32].

[75] Eric Brousseau and Nicolas Curien, 'Internet and Digital Economics: Principles, Methods and Applications', June 2007.

products unblocked. The further goal of digital rights management regime desires to safeguard the lawful right of the authors, publishers and distributors on intellectual property right exploitation and interests.[76] The last but not the least reason of digital rights management technology system existing is prompting the press industry prosperously and finally achieve the interest balance between the private owners and the general public.[77]

Sometimes people prefer to treat the digital rights management system as the extension of intellectual property rights, and they strongly desire that digital rights management can play the same role as intellectual property rights that will affect the competitive market. In relation to the intellectual property rights in light of the principle with respect to digital rights management regime's economic character, which is *per se* not collided with the basic aim of antimonopoly regulations,[78] however, puts its specific and primary function concerning anti-monopoly into the whole intellectual property legislation system.

From active economic perspective of judging the digital rights management technology, it provides a platform for networks users' consuming. Some officers of U.S. Federal Trade Commission insist that it is pretty obvious that digital rights management technology is good for its users in that it offers more choices to purchase or download digital works.[79]

It is understandable that the foremost advantage of digital rights management system is protection of reproducing digital works accords with what the original intention of digital rights management establishment. Although the consensus that copyright works protection could be broken both in physical world and in digital situation. Digital Rights Management is deemed as a groundbreaking and effective attempt towards the copy protection.[80]

According to physical structure of digital rights management technology, it has two functions to protect the digital copyright work against private exploitation without right owners' permission. We have been drawn to the area of digital rights management based on its primary hybrid feature.[81] Whether driven by both the commercial profit and the legal emphasis, digital rights management always shows marvellous opportunities when it is implemented.[82]

First, digital rights management regime existing facilitates the calculation of copyright royalty. Digital rights management automatic calculations system can

---

[76]Ibid 221.

[77]Solove [33].

[78]Weiser [34], p. 534.

[79]*Ibid* 87.

[80]Bill Cope and Robin Freeman, 'Digital Rights Management and Content Development: Technology Drivers across the Book Production Supply Chain, from Creator to Consumer', Oct 2001.

[81]John S. Erickson, Ph.D., Hewlett-Packard Laboratories; D-Lib Magazine February 2002; Volume 8 Number 2 "Digital Rights Management: Business and Technology" http://webdoc.sub.gwdg.de/edoc/aw/d-lib/dlib/february02/02bookreview.html;20/07/2018.

[82]*Ibid.*

precisely tell the result concerning copyright royalty.[83] Second, digital rights management can ensure the transaction security. Digital rights management specifically labels the information in the transmission process to let the transmitters and receiver confirm the order of consumers' identities. Digital rights management could help site administrators observe all the users who would like to download copyright works from website via networks and contribute it to the final admission to digital content according to the existed lawful agreement between users and the websites.[84] For example, if an author merely grants the user to transmit and sale his digital works in domestic market, digital rights management surely is able to restrict and stop any other users' acts of downloading from abroad IP address. It is not doubtful the birth and development of digital rights management have already accommodated the demand of the rapid information and technology renewal in digital world.[85]

Economic exploration on intellectual property hierarchy might apparently arouse two debates that need to be discussed. Copyright holders depend on digital rights management for preventing consumers' unlawful access to copyrighted works. There came an argument that misaligned incentive of digital rights management had been wildly spread nowadays, consequently one assumption would be about whether the abuse of intellectual property more seriously existed in digital times. Intellectual property rights are tied tightly to the markets. Moreover, intellectual property rights are placed at a vital position in information markets construction.[86] The other one might focus on the hypothesis that whether the involvement of digital rights management brought the consumption market unbalanced benefit among copyright holders, content/service providers and the end-users.

The internet has thoroughly changed the business model of the digital content industry.[87] The distribution of digital material has become massively cheap. The piracy of digital works has offered users with low-cost copies in digital world, which made digital rights management existed and developed (Fig. 3.6).

If the relationship among three participants involved in digital economy has to be precisely defined or described, the pellucid term "Money" can fully summarize that. "Money" cannot more vulgarly locate the positions of each party in economic matrix. For copyright holders, they hope reasonable reward will be paid through digital copyrighted works creation and distribution.[88] Content/service providers, as the middleman between copyright holders and end-users, always chase value maximization. Digital content or information is the end product in digital market from consumers' perspective. The factors influencing end-users' consumption activities in

[83]Eckersley [35], p. 85.

[84]John Logie, 'Peers, Pirates, and Persuasion Rhetoric in the Peer-to-Peer Debates', available at: http://ebooksgo.org/engineering-technology/PeersPirates.pdf, Access date: 14th/08/2010, Parlor Press, West Lafayette, Indiana.

[85]*Ibid* 28.

[86]Drahos [36], p. 4.

[87]Melendez-Ortiz and Roffe [37].

[88]Samuelson [38], p. 519.

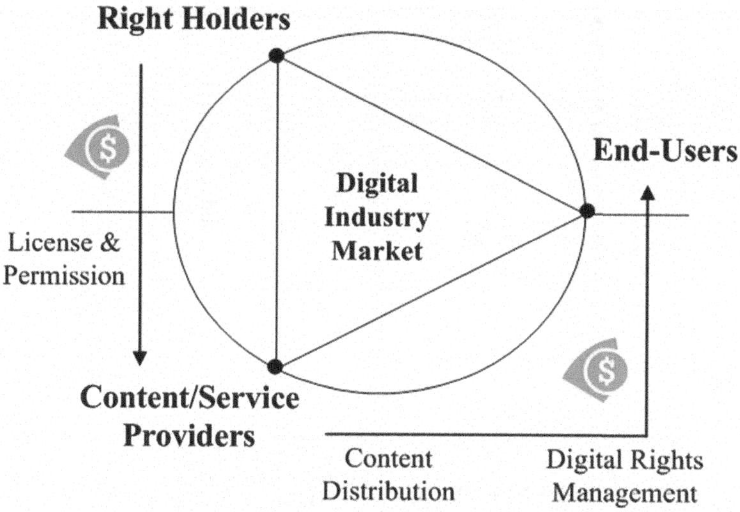

Fig. 3.6 Cross-referencing of three participants in digital rights management system

digital world vary extensively. Competitive pricing would be the one of the top priorities to consumers according to consumer psychology. Alternatively, consumption mentalities of the end-users reflect the important characteristic of cost preference in consumption value analysis.

As illustrated above, content/service providers have to obtain the license or permission from copyright holders and make profit through digital works distribution, then digital rights management systems are the anti-piracy defenses set by content/service providers. The whole system achieves the minimum economic loss of digital copyright and is now adding its appeal for increasing amount of content/service providers.

More than any other business models, rather we might find, programs developed by Apple Company reflected both content owners and end-users, with digital rights management, digital copyrighted works distribution be a win-win result (Fig. 3.7).[89]

Referred to controversial issue with respect to the conflict between the competition law and intellectual property law, we are still able to pay attention to the novel method that can do the management of digital copyright named Digital Copyright Management regime.[90] Actually it is visible that the exploitation of digital rights management system is wildly used in the digital environment in nowadays. The impact on current adoption of digital rights management technology not only benefits the traditional market but also influences the creativity world. Sometimes people prefer to treat digital rights management system as the extension of intellectual property rights, and they strongly desire digital rights management can play the

[89]"Why DRM is Great", http://www.info-mech.com/drm_is_great.html, access date: 26th/01/2014.
[90]Magnani and Montagnani [32], p. 83.

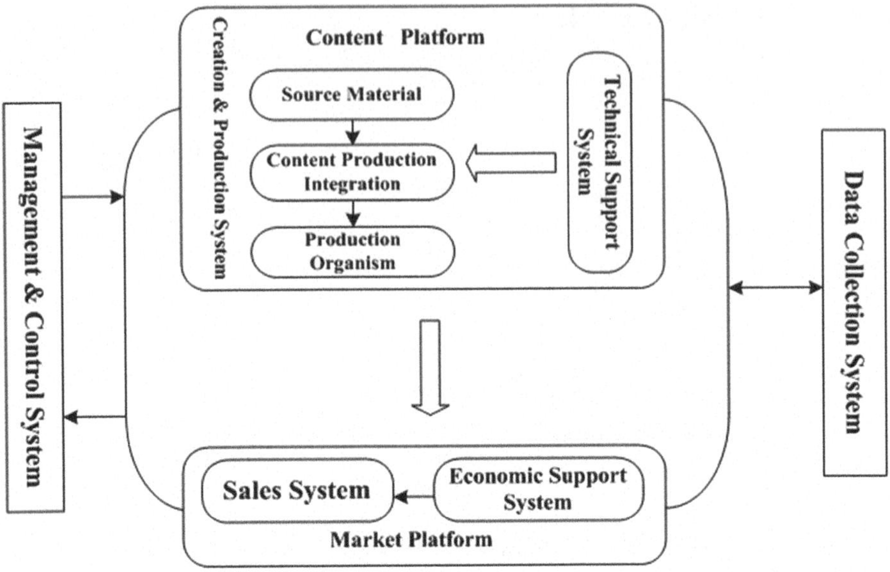

Fig. 3.7 Digital content industry structure

same role as intellectual property rights that will affect the competitive market. In relation to the IPRs,[91] in light of the principle with respect to digital rights management regime's economic character, which is per *se* not collided with the basic aim of antimonopoly regulations, however, puts its specific and primary function concerning anti-monopoly into the whole intellectual property legislation system.

The working principle of digital rights management technology is based on the license center of digital works, which is able to lock encrypted and compressed digital copyright works through the digital private key. It is accessible of private ID and URL of the copyright works license centre. The digital copyright works can be played when the users get the credentials from the license center and unlock the route according to the Key ID and the URL. Otherwise, those users who have not obtained the passport of accessing the encrypted digital works cannot download the works to play the program, which would strictly protect the copyright of digital copyright works.[92]

Designed digital rights management system is consisted of three parts: Content Management, Authority Management and Content Distribution. The following flow-process chart visually reflects their respective function in the whole digital rights management system (Fig. 3.8).[93]

[91] Weiser [34], p. 534.

[92] Ibid 49.

[93] Tang [39].

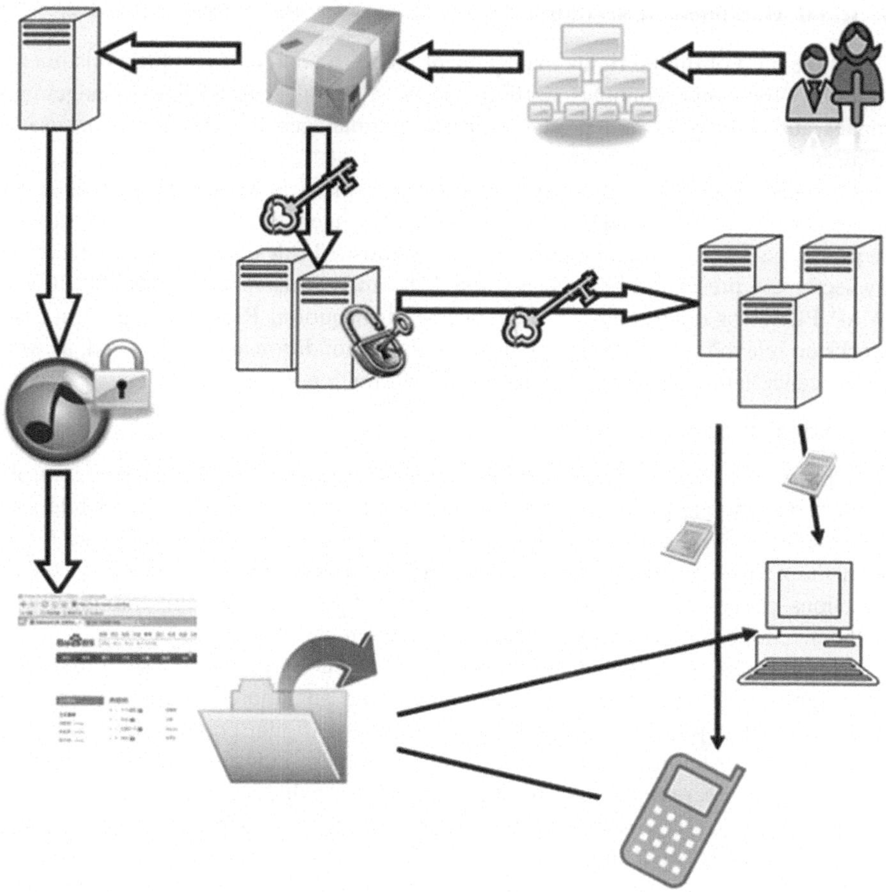

Fig. 3.8 Digital content chain

- **Content Management Section**

The assignment of Content Management focuses on transformation from original media files to encrypted files, which are protected and stored for by digital rights management system. Furthermore, Content Management provides tools for content producing (aims for files forms transformation/information input, etc.) and content encryption/package (aims for files encryption, which have been the final files form protected by digital rights management system). The copyright reserved party (e.g., content/service providers) may apply Content Management function to accomplish the process including content producing, content package, content transformation and content storage management.[94] In this regard, Content Management, as a whole, can be divided into three subsystem in this function: content producing, content package and storage management.

[94]Ibid.

- **Right Management Section**

As the core of digital rights management mode to content users, this constituent, though, which may connotes itself in the most literal sense: Right Management makes authority rules and produces/distributes/manages licenses based on users' request.[95]

Under the specific application circumstance, Authority Management defines the using permission to digital content and issues the licenses according to transaction request type, user's particular demand and established rules. Licenses are encrypted by secret key prescribed beforehand, and distributed to users through HTTP PUSH, WAP PUSH or other ways.[96] After license distribution, Right Management also works on relevant management in line with usage condition and users' need, as well as the cancellation requirement from copyright holders.[97]

- **Content Distribution Section**

It is the very direct connection to the end-users. Content Distribution part controls content distribution/providing/retrieval and interface downloading; meanwhile it is able to obtain users' identification information, accept users' credentials request, and gain the certificates from Authority Management part for users' delivery. Other functions possessed by Content Distribution list as users' administration, users' authentication, transaction reference and fees reference.[98]

Digital rights management is now the most common integrated system in digital copyright world. However, it is often used to be an umbrella term for series of technology that prevents non-permission access to digital content. Digital rights management system basically meets the entertainment industry and media companies' demand: decrease the loss through stopping or reducing piracy; creating profit via establishing a payment platform under instructive conditions or rules, which makes consumers' right clear as well. On the other hand, these users may not be fond of these provisions. Digital rights management is not merely a technology for anti-piracy, but also a platform where content providers are able to work with marketing strategy neatly and consumers may enjoy digital content from any media flexibly.

Digital content produces benefit, while ensuring the content secured should be the premise. Digital rights management excludes security from its systematic function. However, it is admitted that digital rights management system is connected with security since it starts to be implemented. Even to the strictest security system, it also necessarily integrate sort of digital rights management element to be a commercial mode that provides accessible content to network users.

The kernel of digital rights management system is to establish relevant conditions to play or display media content. Digital rights management system identifies digital

---

[95]Ibid.

[96]Ibid.

[97]Ibid.

[98]http://www.masternewmedia.org/online-content-distribution-guide-to-the-best-content-syndication-services/, access date: 14th/08/2015.

content, defines copyright holders'/consumers' right, and further interacts with payment system, which distributes its authorization to users. Digital rights management system in essence builds the commercial rules involved intellectual property.

Digital rights management technologies may be applied to old and new commercial modes, although these modes cannot vanish piracy radically.[99] A deal, should be promoted by not just attractive consumption proposal, along with convenient payment channels. Therefore, a perfect commercial mode shall evaluate what digital rights management can achieve and what digital rights management is not able to do. New business environment affords content proprietors a large number of chances for repeatedly making their existing content and creating pecks of gifts for orientation towards different consumption capacity users.[100] These innovations could produce considerable benefit. It seems a paradox that although piracy in network would create an revolutionary environment for accessing free digital content, other cases from entertainment industry and media industry illustrate the public shall pay for the digital content as long as they believe that is worth paying for it.

3.3.1 Right-Holders

Economic interest is thought of the original impetus for digital right holders' creation. Digital rights management technologies are the protective measures against revenue loss, which sideways reflect right holder's marketing ambition. Technological protection measures have increasingly played another role for helping right-holders make profit.[101]

Right holders deem digital rights management technology as the unique solution for copyright protection in digital world. No matter how great the controversial issues are, technologies is not the answer to the interest balance among right holders, internet content/service providers and end-users because of technologies' neutrality. The balance of interest should be realized by digital copyright regulation.[102] The advent of digital times triggers another debatable matter, which is copyright holders' right abuse.

3.3.2 Internet Content/Service Provider

Those who play intermediate roles include publishers, audio-video products manufacturers, film studios, and broadcasting and television stations. As so-called

[99]Favale [40].
[100]Tran [41].
[101]Ibid.
[102]Ibid.

"gatekeepers" in traditional copyright regime, these mediums, at a time, could not accommodate this particular situation because the social information service providers, represented by internet service/content providers, other than traditional intermediate mediums, has intensified the condition in which traditional copyright communication architecture has been challenged. Traditional communication models has probably collapsed in digital times along with the disruption of gatekeepers rules, which was made by "peer to peer" technologies to be the acme.

Internet content/service providers, unlike right holders, are the clusters those indirectly create digital content, but directly access and distribute digital content in cyber circumstance.[103] The difference between right holders and internet content/service providers, by character, relies on their diverse features. However, when copyrighted works were thrown into the market, especially in digital industry market, multiple objects became copyright holders. The vast distribution of digital works helped digital copyright industry shape various channels for end-users to access works.[104]

Controllability of digital rights management would never have been perfect, especially under the circumstance in which copyrighted works exist without digital mediums. However, this controllability still equips content/service providers considerable economic power. Content/service providers might not merely exert rapid and efficient legal protection on copyrighted works, but also set some other contractual obligations for content/service users.[105]

It is acknowledged that digital rights management, in some scholars' mind, is a tool for fulfilling contracts. Further, digital rights management system facilitates content/service providers to find a more flexible way for making the licenses or agreements with end-users, which are beyond the regulated range of copyright law. To a certain degree, it initiates some novel business models for larger profit in digital content industry.[106] Prices setting or any other benefit gaining channels in articles of contracts or licenses made by content/service providers and end-users would enhance the elasticity of digital content industry marketing.

3.3.3 End-Users

The term of "end-user" is basically used in digital circumstance. It refers those people, who consume the digital copyrighted works on line, or "potential follow-on creators creating based on pre-existing copyrighted works".[107] In other aspect, end-users, as the terminal consumers in digital industry market, are the ultimate

[103]Ibid.

[104]Cahir [42].

[105]Ibid.

[106]Solum [43], p. 1137.

[107]Mazziotti [44], p. 4.

clusters who access and employ copyrighted works. End-user cannot be located as simplification, but diversified pattern. End users might be consisted of individuals, agencies (government department, libraries, universities and so forth), or other business organizations or content operators/carriers.

From the protection aspect, consumers, including the end-users in digital environment, are protected by specific consumer's protection law when they are doing digital content transaction. As the gradual globalization goes into all fields, the internet users have more opportunities to obtain the networks resource from both the local website and other sites abroad.[108] The educated users are more prone to get details about the process of accessing knowledge and information. In other words, the focusing point of new technology for internet users locates at the means how these people get copyright information or material.[109] Those internet users more or less have the common sense about the behavior acted in the digital environment that cannot acquire the copyright works copies without paying any dues.

However, there is one point that we have to raise the attention on that: no matter how advanced digital rights management technology is in under the network context as an effective protection means of copyright in right holder's perspective, the truth is restrictions and limitations of internet users' legal rights under digital rights management regime do not fall into the legal admission scope.[110] It is pretty understandable that the birth of technology somewhat improve the digital copyright protection environment and also pose a challenge to the degree of the public's access or getting of digital copyright works. As the dissemination of lots of information products do not happen merely within national regions, but sometimes transnational.[111] So making the specific regulations clear according to particular situation seems very important.[112]

It is visible that the existing of digital rights management technologies does restrict the private "fair use". If we accept that the system of "fair use" as a kind of restriction to right owners' copyright, then digital rights management scheme would be regarded as another restriction specifically towards "fair use" and "fair dealing".

First, based on the classic authorization—licence model and key element of digital rights management technology, it merely allows internet users to access digital copyright works through successful individual identity certification.[113] Sometimes the certification is far away from accessing or exploring copyright works as digital rights management regime has various levels with authorization. Even the

---

[108]Ibid.

[109]Ibid.

[110]Reducing Digital Copyright Infringement Without Restricting Innovation, Stanford Law Review, Vol. 56, p. 1345, UC Berkeley Public Law Research Paper No. 525662, University of Texas Law, Public Law Research Paper No. 63, University of Texas Law and Economic Research Paper No. 025. (2004).

[111]Ibid.

[112]Ibid.

[113]Liu et al. [45], pp. 49–58.

internet users have already got the "passport" to access to the intellectual works, they still wait for permission of the real access right.

Moreover, fair use regime helps the general public to achieve the aim of exploring the copyright works freely within certain scope. However, there is no any specific scope with respect to "fair use" of copyright works in digital world. The absolute fact aroused by digital rights management technologies is that this technology controls the channels that connected with exploitation of digital copyright works and consumers buy the digital works, still in vain. For example, if an internet user get the permission of downloading a single song from one music website, under the digital rights management technologies principle, he/she will be limited by digital rights management and could play this piece of music merely on his own PC while not others. This kind of "repression" concerning exploitation from digital rights management technologies themselves of digital intellectual works is deemed as the chief reason that digital rights management regime is not as popular as expectation among the massive internet users.[114]

The exploitation of digital right management regime causes privacy problems, as well which appears a little knotty to handle within domestic scope. This digital rights management system that can facilitates the process with respect to collecting of users' private data are hard to supervise and administer beyond national jurisdiction. In a certain number of countries, users are allowed to adopt some measures to circumvent technical protection to restrict gathering or diffusing of private information.[115]

The copyright owners are able to escape from developing nations' copyright system limitations and usually sign a contract to transfer their copyright to obtain the considerable profit. The principle of digital rights management technology is allowing its users to access the digital copyright works or encrypted material is based on the terms with respect to "automatically-enforced license"[116] in contracts between foreign copyright owners and digital rights management companies. It is understandable that copyright legal protection system in developing nations, what seems effective legal approach, actually have non-sense to restrict the giant developed regions' trick of circumvent the local copyright regulations.

It is no doubt for the general public that they do not need to explore the information and resource in public domain with the permission of the authors. However, the digital rights management technologies are not as familiar as the knowledge in public domain. Therefore, no wonder some jurisdictions demonstrate the users were sued by copyright owners since they have no clear recognition on the

---

[114]Ibid.

[115]Manon Ress, 'DRM and developing countries', CPTech, Washington DC, USA on: 29/04/05 available at: http://www.indicare.org/tiki-read_article.php?articleId=97, access date: 15/08/2016.

[116]Gordon, Wendy J.; Bahls, Daniel, 'Public's Right to Fair Use: Amending Section 107 to Avoid the Fared Use Fallacy', 2007 Utah Law Review 619, 2007, available at: http://heinonline.org/HOL/LandingPage?collection=journals&handle=hein.journals/utahlr2007&div=26&id=&page=, access date: 14/08/2014.

legal status of digital rights management technologies.[117] In other words, the digital rights management technology causes the uncertainty of commerce when the laws allow some measures to circumvent digital rights management, which intends to preserve copyright content and right holders' interest.

It is much more risky for developing countries if they use digital rights management technology like the developed nations' exploitation and place digital rights management at a crucial position, whereas, the reason that can explain the knotty situation to developing nations is pretty visible to understand for us users.[118]

Digital rights management was deemed as a monopoly tool of right owners that restricts users from developing regions to get or access to the digital copyright material in any types through encrypting digital content by domestic digital rights management technology.[119] Sometimes even worse, the restriction of external accessing or exploring digital content narrowed its scope and also prevents the legal exploitation regulated by copyright laws. That digital rights management system might restrict the resale concerning the digital copyright products with regional licence code via different areas is considered as another negative aspect on developing nations.[120]

Last but not the least, regulations concerning digital rights management or anti-circumvention may cause a mega passive influence to the developing countries' innovation development.[121] According to American experience of exploitation of it has proved that if the copyright owners inappropriately explore the rules with respect to digital rights management mechanism and anti-circumvention technology to limit the competitive rival ship in market, it would indirectly lead monopolies. In other word, small companies are confronted by the hazardous situation brought by the inappropriate exploitation of digital rights management technology and survival of the fittest market choices.

Both the copyright owners and digital rights management technology distributors take the point that the authorities should exclude the main bodies that have the right to set the unified interoperability criteria. However, they are so avaricious that the administrations could do them a favor on harmonization of the various solutions because sometimes private means conflicted with official's approach and local regulations may collide with international treaties with respect to the protection of technological protection measures and the knowledge sharing with the general public. Many opponents disagree with the exploitation of digital rights management

---

[117]Ibid.

[118]François Bar, Hernan Galperin, 'Geeks, Cowboys, and Bureaucrats: Deploying Broadband, the Wireless Way'. The Southern African Journal of Information and Communication, Issue No. 6. available at: http://www.sajic.org.za/index.php/SAJIC/article/viewArticle/155, access date: 08th/08/2013.

[119]Vathitphund [46], pp. 9–10.

[120]Ibid 16.

[121]Paul Ganley, 'Access to the Individual: Digital Rights Management Systems and the Intersection of Informational and Decisional Privacy Interests', available at: http://ijlit.oxfordjournals.org/cgi/content/abstract/10/3/241, access date: 15/08/2010.

technology and technical protection measures that have already raised a lot of controversial discussions because they pose an adverse influence on many aspects. Just as I mentioned above that digital rights management technology and other digital copyright protection means affect the development of innovation and the technology research. The existing and development of digital rights management system more gradually prove that its prospect of market will be challenged by the increasing cost and narrow consumption market.[122]

Summary

In nowadays, as the much concern of digital rights management technology from the general public, the authoritative international and domestic bodies are testing digital rights management regime's economic potential and other aspects feedback.[123] As the under-developed level of education and culture in developing regions asks for a large amount on information products import, the increasing cost on digital copyright protection measures like digital rights management technologies makes these countries sacrifice their price that has gone beyond their ability. Even worse, the developed nations fancy reaping the profits by suppressing sale and re-sale of products protected by copyright law in developing countries through unfair contract terms against developing nations' local copyright law.[124]

3.4 Socio-Cultural and Economic Matrix for Copyright and Digital Rights Management

The rationality of copyright protection on Technological Measures can be proved by economic analysis.[125] Knowledge possesses the characters of public products, and delineation of rights can be adopted to correct external economy, make knowledge products become efficient, and provide authors with monopoly rights. Traditional copyright system cannot meet the demand of copyright holders and it is difficult to correct external economy. Therefore, new systems arise at the historic moment. External economy refers to the situation that activities carried out by individuals or manufacturer (homo economics) directly affect others without compensations or payment, which is not reflected in the monetary or market transaction.[126]

---

[122]Melendez-Ortiz and Roffe [37].

[123]Ibid.

[124]Franklin and Morris [47], p. 1213.

[125]O'Connor [48], pp. 973–1000, George Mason Center for the Protection of Intellectual Property's Conference, Common Ground: How Intellectual Property Unites Creators and Innovators, October 2014., University of Washington School of Law Research Paper No. 2015-28.

[126]Ibid.

3.4.1 *The Rationality of the Technological Protection Measures of Copyright*

Copyright holders can get profits while providing products, and are able to benefit others (homo economics). However, they can only get part of profits of whole social revenue based on approval price. Even though the creators are responsible for the cost of creation, the whole society obtains profits.[127] If there should be externality in the market, the allocation of market conducted on products is inefficient. In terms of knowledge products, such as copyright, policies that can be used to correct it and make it internalized should encourage external economy, namely to prevent free-loaders without payment.[128] Because of new technology, digital technology makes copying with tiny payments but accuracy possible, which adds accesses for people to get works. What's more, these accesses are convenient even without payment. Besides, the risk of using, adapting and copying without authorization significantly increases; in addition, the copyright holders, users and publisher are highly fragmented. Each consumer shall become potential infringer and disseminator, who then will become potential competitors against copyright holders. Traditional copyright law based on limiting the copying technology is no longer able to prevent the strengthening external economy, and copyright works ask new system. In the case of Technological Measures' nature, it aims to control illegal access and copying: the legal sense of Technological Measures is to punish others from copyright infringement, and those equipment and services makers who deliberately provide techniques to carry out infringement activities, which indicate the strengthening of power to control external economy.

The clear connotation of negotiation steps defined by Navarro is: 'Both parties or more entities involved try mutual efforts to reach a consensus through discussion on the disputes and solutions based on equal dialogue'.[129] Chong believes that contract refers to the agreement that every participants should take on duties and responsibilities.[130] The negotiation mechanism is composed of a series of trigger conditions and dialog steps, which are important compositions and links to reach a contract. In the second chapter of this paper, it makes a clear declaration that the digital rights management should be correctly regarded as the implementation and execution on electronic contract. Therefore, correspondent negotiation mechanism should be necessarily come up with. Lee puts forward that agreement strategies based on computer processing mode include two significant elements[131]: the first is to carry out completely formal specification of the contract; and the second is to set up or authorize reliable agencies with availability to assist in the processing of each key

[127] Ibid 151.

[128] Ibid 173.

[129] Guillermo et al. [49].

[130] CheunNgen et al. [50].

[131] Wei et al. [51].

steps. Besides, Bonatti[132] raises another two added demands on the mechanism of automated Negotiation. First, there should be a proper language to define the rules used to handle matters, which should also be adopted to comment and judge the items involved in the negotiation process. Second, there are important elements that should be ignored: the language has to correctly demonstrate the appealing and decision-making behaviors of participants. In this chapter, there are two protocol modes put forward, which are deepened and detailed. Moreover, after comparison of current protocol evaluation modes, petri net is finally selected to act as the analysis and simulation tool of formalized description and construction because it is convenient to describe the relationship between process sequence supervene, conflict and synchronization. Comparing to other system network model, it has unique advantages of clear description. As a system model, petri net cannot only describe the structure but also the dynamic behavior (such as the state changes). It adopts petri net to analyze the nonexistence of deadlock and reachability analysis of various expected conditions so as to fully elaborate the established protocol to have integrity and robustness.

In terms of social field, it discusses the possible behavior models of various participants as well as the influence the processes make on the final result; in terms of industrial field, it takes Multi-Agent System as the research hotspot in the Distributed Artificial Intelligence field.[133] Agent originates from a conceptual model of DAI with objects, behaviors and knowledge, which is able to independently complete specific tasks and to reach a certain goal based on ability, conditions, resources, relevant knowledge and external information with plans and activities. The Agent put forward by Amamiya is a physical or abstract object, which can complete system object with concerted action between agents in the premise of satisfying constraints.[134] It focuses on system construction principle as well as the coordination mechanism of several entities. Traditional DAI mainly studies on the DPS (Distributed Problem Solving), which breaks problems into subtasks and solves them with different processors, and then collects each result.[135] It is a top-down system. To some extent, DPS aims to solve the problem of computational efficiency. However, it is difficult to deal with conflicts among different entities. Aimed at this situation, people put forward the idea of Multi-Agent System. Multi-Agent System is a down-top system, which defines the independent agent and then it researches how to complete multi-solutions.[136] The starting point is that the behaviors of the system are based on the partial information and objectives of every agent, which can complete the overall object with interaction and coordination of multi-agents

[132]Piero and Daniel [52].

[133]Guo and Zhang [53], pp. 3029–3090.

[134]Xu and Brussel [54], p. 115.

[135]Daniel Freund, Andreas F Raab, Tobias Küster, Sahin Albayrak, and Kai Strunz, 'Agent-based Integration of an Electric Car Sharing Fleet into a Smart Distribution Feeder',3rd IEEE PES Innovative Smart Grid Technologies Europe (ISGT Europe), Jan, 2012.

[136]Tanenbaum [55].

based on limited knowledge and resources. Therefore, MAS can better reflect the intelligence of human beings than DPS, which can be better adapted to the e-commerce environment. In this digital rights management application environment, the DPS mainly shows in the following situations: the interaction between end users and copyright holders, interaction between end user and copyright agents. Li[137] makes a discussion on various influencing factors of negotiation strategy and protocol development process, which include the number of participants, interest groups, reproducibility of communication process, the number of consultation provisions, and the third party intervention.

3.4.2 *Types of Consultation Mechanism*

The using permission of digital rights management should be the contract achieved between copyright holders and consumers.[138] However, the current using permission is only customized by copyright holders. It can be indicated that the following mechanism of digital rights management is not available: it allows end users to raise objections and make modifications of relevant items and conditions issued in the using permission. Zhang suggests that the current rights expression language has limitations that cannot allow consumers to demonstrate their appealing.[139] At the same time, when the current RMS sets using permissions for users, it does not make it clear that which segment can be used for users to show their appealing.[140] Consequently, it is necessary to take mutual negotiation mechanisms into consideration while designing and constructing protocols and rights expression language to promote the communication between consumers and copyright holders. Its aim is to enable consumers to communicate with copyright holders about relevant items of using permission to further meet the fair and reasonable principle and demand of copyright law.

Usually, there are two participants in using permission mechanism: copyright holders and end users. This paper adopts the popular 'request-respond' model, which can be divided into the following steps: first, end users make a request to use their copyright and make modifications; second, copyright holders will comment on the above requests, and carry out check and validation of the applicants; besides, copyright holders provide users with one or more service life; finally, users can choose one privilege set or make a request that the provided permission package should be perfected.[141] This processing mode provides a new business model, namely, users with different using permission rights should pay different cost,

[137]Bin et al. [56].

[138]Ibid.

[139]Jiang et al. [57].

[140]Ibid.

[141]Ibid.

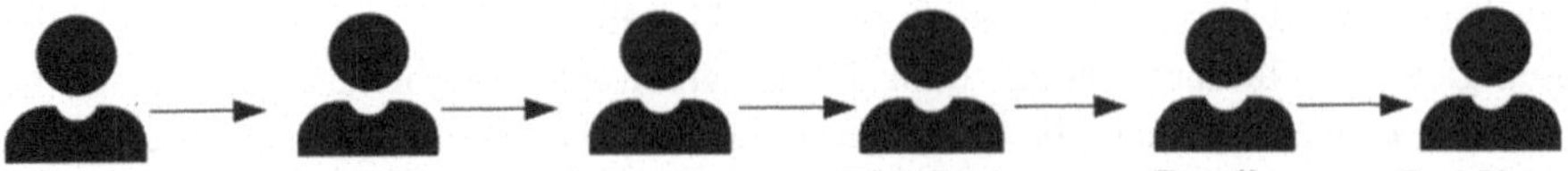

Fig. 3.9 Value chain of digital content (Creator (create/rewrite work; Publisher (provider of digital content); Integrator (Service Provider); Distributor(Content Service Provider); Retailer(Content Service Provide); End Users (purchasing/limited media))

which has flexibility. Garcia[142] puts forward the demand analysis of consultation mechanism systems, namely there should be a certain language to describe the rules during the communication process. Meanwhile, the language can also be adopted to correctly show the negotiate willingness. However, Garcia does not come up with concrete implementation plans and strategies.[143]

Negotiation steps refer to the process to reach a certain contract. Negotiation mechanism can be divided into the following types according to the actual operation and possible business models of digital rights management:

1. Tendering manner: it can also be distinguished as the offer price, which is a way of purchasing. Bidder is the buyer (end users), who releases announcement or sends invitation for specific suppliers or contractor with the bid nature, quantity, quality, technical requirements, time of delivery, and the procurement qualifications of other suppliers and contractors; tenders are sellers (copyright holders) who can provide products, engineering, and services with refunds and reward. Through this mode, users search for services or products they are interested in online and put forward inquiries on suppliers' product pricing.[144] Users can choose one or more suppliers based on comparison. At present, current DRM cannot support this model.
2. Auction: it is a reverse process of the first type with sellers acting as bidders (copyright holders) submit the products and conditions and buyers (end users) acting as tenders to compete in buying. Subsequently, sellers will select the buyers based on the consideration of credit and their own demands. Afterwards, they will sign a contract. Selling at marked price is similar to auctions, both activities are competitive transactions launched by a certain party. However, there are obvious differences between them. At present, most of the digital rights management systems are able to control the dealing course with prices as the leading factors.[145]
3. Bargaining: It is the most flexible and comprehensive mode among all negotiation mechanism, which allows all of the participants to conduct dynamic amendment and fairly satisfy their own demands and appealing (Fig. 3.9).

[142]Roberte and Rosa [58].

[143]Ibid.

[144]Stamp [59].

[145]Ibid.

Creators and publishers always have the copyright of digital content, who are owners and providers of digital content. Integrators act as the role of service providers during the content spreading process, who are responsible for collecting digital contents of content providers and then select and arrange the contents so as to provide support and services for digital products. Publishers and retailers belong to content service providers. Publishers are responsible for the publishing of digital products while retailers are responsible for the marketing. It should be noted that in real content spreading, there may not be all of the roles. In different spreading models, roles involved are different and many roles can be assumed by a same entity.

References

1. Williams R (1985) Keywords: a vocabulary of culture and society. Oxford University Press
2. Yu PK (2012) The Confucian challenge to intellectual property reforms. WIPO J. Drake University Law School Research Paper No. 12-37
3. Geller PE (2000) Copyright history and the future: what's culture got to do with it? J Copyr Soc USA 47:211
4. Havelock EA (1963) Preface to plato. Blackwell, pp 93–94
5. Hearn G, Mandeville T, Joseph R (2003) Public policy in knowledge-based economies: foundations and frameworks - new horizons in public policy series. New horizons in public policy Series. Elgar, Cheltenham
6. Vanderburg WH (1985) Technology, society, and culture, a framework for understanding. Technol Soc 7:414
7. Quintanilla MA (2000) Tolerance and technological culture. Philosophica 66(2):65–71
8. Dusek V (1993) Philosophy of technology: an introduction. Paragon House, New York, p 50
9. Bates BJ, Liu T (2010) A cultural approach to DRM implementation in China. Westminst Pap Commun Cult 7(1):7–26
10. Potter PB (2005) The Chinese legal system globalization and local legal culture. Taylor and Francis e-Library
11. Redfield R, Linton R, Herskovits MJ (1936) Memorandum for the study of acculturation, American anthropology, 1921–1945: Papers from the American Anthropologist. University of Wisconsin Press
12. Cabassa LJ (2003) Measuring acculturation: where we are and where we need to go. Hispanic J Behav Sci 25(2):127–146
13. Padilla AM, Perez W (2003) Acculturation, social identity, and social cognition: a new perspective. Hispanic J Behav Sci 25(1):35–55
14. Nikolic D (2011) Legal culture and legal transplant, Serbian Report. Isaidat Law Rev 1(1)
15. Maskus KE (2000) Intellectual property rights in the global economy. The Peterson Institute for International Economics
16. Zheng C (2004) Intellectual property law: a number of research focal points at the beginning of the new century. China Law Press, Beijing
17. Zhiping L (1999) The past, current and future of Chinese law. China University of Political Science and Law Press, Beijing
18. Spence M (2007) Intellectual property. Clarendon Law Series, Oxford University Press
19. Li L (2010) How has Chinese traditional culture an impact on China's intellectual property legal system? Would this influence be a problem in the protection of folklore by the intellectual property legal system?. Int J Interdiscip Soc Sci 5:15
20. Handong W (2007) A cultural explanation of composition and transfer of IP law. China Legal Sci, 6

21. Handong W (2005) Essential issues research on intellectual property. Renmin University Press, p 64
22. Cover RM (1993) Narrative, violence, and the law: the essays of Robert cover. University of Michigan Press
23. Zhu N (2005) A case of legal transplant: the possibility of efficient breach in China. Georgetown J Int Law 36:1145
24. Allison JR, Lin L (1999) The evolution of Chinese attitudes toward property rights invention and discovery. Univ Pa J Int Econ Law 20
25. Woodard JW (1934) Critical notes on the culture lag concept. Soc Force 12(3):388
26. Brinkman RL, Brinkman JE (1997) Cultural lag: conception and theory. Int J Soc Econ 24 (6):609–627
27. Sahay (1997, Summer) Cybermaterialism' and the invention of the cyber-cultural everyday. New Literary Hist 28(3)
28. Sansone C, Morf CC, Panter AT (2004) The Sage handbook of methods in social psychology. Sage Publications Inc, p 119
29. Bandura A (1977) Social learning theory. General Learning Press, New York
30. Bandara A (1978) The self-system in reciprocal determinism. Am Psychol 33:344–358
31. Bandara A (1982) Self-efficacy mechanism in human agency. Am Psychol 37:122–147
32. Magnani P, Montagnani ML (2008) Digital rights management systems and competition: what developments within the much debated interface between intellectual property and competition law? Int Rev Intell Prop Compet Law 39:83
33. Solove DJ (2004) Digital person: technology and privacy in the information age. Law, Technology and Society, Ex Machina
34. Weiser PJ (2003) Internet, innovation, and intellectual property policy. Column Law Rev 103:534. Available at: http://heinonline.org/HOL/LandingPage?collection=journals&handle=hein.journals/clr103&div=25&id=&page=. Accessed 14 Aug 2012
35. Eckersley P (2004) Virtual markets for virtual goods: the mirror image of digital copyright? Harv J Law Tech 18:85
36. Drahos P (1996) A philosophy of intellectual property. Dartmouth Publishing Company, p 4
37. Melendez-Ortiz R, Roffe P (2009) Intellectual property and sustainable development: development Agendas in a changing world (Elgar Intellectual Property and Global Development). In: Edward Elgar Publishing Ltd
38. Samuelson P (1999) Intellectual property and the digital economy: why the anti-circumvention regulations need to be revised. Berkeley Technol Law J 14:519
39. Tang M (2008) Application of digital right management in music area. University of Electronic Science and Technology of China. http://www.cnki.net/
40. Favale M (2014) Death and resurrection of copyright between law and technology. Inf Commun Technol Law 23(2):32
41. Tran JL (2016) A primer on digital rights management technologies. In: Chapter 3 in digital rights managements: a librarian's guide, August 17, 2015. Scarecrow Press
42. Cahir J (2007) The structure of control communication system and copyright law. In: Westkamp G (ed) Emerging issues in intellectual property trade, technology, and market freedom: essays in honor of Herchel Smith. Queen Mary Intellectual Property Research Institute, Centre for Commercial Law Studies, University of London
43. Solum LB (2005) The future of copyright. Tex Law Rev 83:1137
44. Mazziotti G (2008) EU digital copyright law and the end-user. Springer, Berlin, p 4
45. Liu Q, Safavi-Naini R, Sheppard NP (2003) Digital rights management for content distribution. In: Conferences in Research and Practice in Information Technology Series; Vol. 34, Adelaide, Australia, pp 49–58
46. Vathitphund T (2010) Access to knowledge difficulties in developing countries: a balanced access to copyrighted works in the digital environment. Int Rev Law Comput Technol 24 (1):9–10

47. Franklin JA, Morris RJ (2002) Symposium on constructing international intellectual property law: the role of national courts: international jurisdiction and enforcement of judgments in the era of global networks: irrelevance of, goals for, and comments on the current proposals. Chicago-Kent Law Rev, 1213
48. O'Connor SM (2015) Creators, innovators, and appropriation mechanisms. George Mason Law Rev 22(4):973–1000
49. Guillermo N, Babak F, Rissanen S (2003) Constrained delegation in XML-based access control and digital rights management standards. In: Proceedings of the IASTED International Conference on Communication, Network, and Information Security, New York, NY, United States. International Association of Science and Technology for Development
50. CheunNgen C, Ricardo C, Jeroen D (2006) LicenseScript: a logical language for digital rights management. Annales des Telecommun 61(3):284–331
51. Wei X, Jinpeng H, Yunhao L (2005) Access control policy negotiation for remote hot-deployed grid services. In: The First International Conference on e-Science and Grid Computing, Melbourne, Australia. Institute of Electrical and Electronics Engineers Computer Society
52. Piero B, Daniel O (2007) Rule-based policy representation and reasoning for the semantic web. In: Lecture notes in computer science. Springer, Dresden, Germany
53. Guo Q, Zhang M (2009) A novel approach for multi-agent-based intelligent manufacturing system. Inf Sci 179:3029–3090
54. Xu H, Brussel HV (1997) A behaviour-based blackboard architecture for reactive and efficient task execution of an autonomous robot. Robot Autonom Syst 22(2):115
55. Tanenbaum AS (1996) Computer networks, 3nd edn. Prentice-Hall
56. Bin Z, Min F, Shipeng L (2005) Secure key management for flexible digital rights management of scalable codestreams. In: IEEE 7th Workshop on Multimedia Signal Processing. Institute of Electrical and Electronics Engineers Computer Society, Shanghai, China
57. Jiang Z, Bin L, ShiQiang Y (2005) FLMP: a flexible license management protocol for digital rights management. In: Proceedings of SPIE - The International Society for Optical Engineering. International Society for Optical Engineering, Beijing, China
58. Roberte G, Rosa G (2006) An OWL copyright ontology for semantic digital rights management. In: Lecture notes in bioinformatics. Springer, Montpellier, France
59. Stamp M (2003) Digital rights management: the technology behind the hype. J Electronic Commerce Res 4(3). http://www.csulb.edu/web/journals/jecr/issues/20033/paper3.pdf. Accessed 14 Aug 2015

Part II
Comprehensive Analysis of Digital Rights Management

Chapter 4
Legislations

4.1 Correct Positioning and Proper Application of Copyright Technological Protection Measures

The application condition of technological protection measures is not ideal because of the passive influences put forward above. These measures deviate from the track of technology neutrality, which will become tools for copyright holders to gain profits. Then, should we totally abandon technological protection measures? In this paper, technology acts as a psychical means that objectively exists with neutrality.[1] Thus, how do these measures play its role can be determined by the attitude and approaches made by us, and the key point is to correctly recognize and properly use these measures.

4.1.1 Correct Positioning of Technological Protection Measures in Digital Era

Although technological protection measures have passive influences on copyright, they also play significant roles in the future construction of copyright, which do not only play an important role in the current copyright system but also in various exploration protection models. To begin with, judging from legislation, technological protection measures have become important components in modern copyright system. Since 1996, technological protection measures have been introduced into copyright law when the *Internet Convention*[2] is recognized. Digital Millennium

[1]Burk [1], p. 537.

[2]Article 11 of WPT.

C. Xu, *Regulatory Model for Digital Rights Management*,
https://doi.org/10.1007/978-981-15-1995-6_4

Copyright Act (DMCA)[3] of America, the EU Copyright Directive[4] and Copyright Law of China[5] have all stipulated the perfect technological protection measures and anti-circumvention. In addition, although the result of technological protection measures being introduced into copyright law may be because of lobbying of copyright industry, which have deviated from technology neutrality. It is undeniable that technological protection measures have become basic technological measures to protect copyright in the digital era.

Moreover, technological protection measures have become important means for copyright holders to face difficulties in the digital era. IFPI believes that digital rights management provides flexibility and protection for consumers, and most digital music is obtained from digital carriers.[6] Charlie McCreevy, Chairman of International Market and Service Committee of European Commission, believes that 'Digital rights management is a direct means of payment to provide contents to consumers'.[7] From the perspective of the European Commission, a digital rights management infrastructure, which is global and compatible based on consensus of various parties, is an important guarantee of current legal system, and is also the premise to effectively provide and get secured contents. Technological protection measures have become important means to protect copyright in the network environment. Third, technological protection measures are the bases for theoretical models of copyright protection.[8] While facing the challenge of digital technology, a glittering array of scholars has put forward new theoretical assumptions. For example, the Creative Commons issued by a famous American network law expert-professor Lessig, and copyright compensation system come up with by American copyright law scholar William. W. Fisher, etc. This system is based on the technological protection measures.[9] The network environment is an interactively virtual environment with a dazzling array of works. Moreover, the protection models adopted are all based on technology, which require technological protection measures to play the role of clearing the copyright ownership and benefit distribution. To conclude, technological measures are products resulted from digital technology attacking copyright system. They have shortages, but play important roles in the future pattern construction of copyright system.

[3]1201 (a) (1) of DMCA.

[4]Article 6 (1). 6(3) of Directive 2001/29/EC of the European parliament and the Council of 22 May 2001 on the Harmonization of certain aspects of Copyright and Related Rights in the Information Society.

[5]Article 47 of Copyright Law of People's Republic of China.

[6]http://www.ifpi.org/content/library/chinesedmr08.pdf.

[7]McCreevy [2].

[8]Ibid.

[9]Ibid 23.

4.1.2 The Proper Application of Technological Protection Laws in Digital Era

Technological protection measures have inherent defects. Only with proper applications, can these measures try ultimate to design the future protection pattern. At first, stick to the technology neutrality. The reason why current technological protection measures have above negative influences is that these measures are unilaterally driven by copyright holders without paying attention to social benefits and violating the principle of technology neutrality. In future copyright system, we have to change the role copyright holders played as usual, and head to the way of technology neutrality.[10] As technological tools, technological protection tools cannot be taken as tools for copyright holders to achieve benefits, which should be technological means to safeguard interests between copyright holders and the public as well as ensure the proper function of new mechanisms of copyright law. In addition, fully play the value of technological protection measures. On the one hand, fully play the role of technological protection measures in protecting works to avoid the situation that works may be totally free of charge in the network environment to help copyright owners obtain expected business benefits[11]; on the other hand, change the situation that technology tightly controls consumers to give them more freedom and space. Besides, be on guard against the control of technological protection measures on end consumers. The fundamental reason of technological protection measures having so many negative influences is the end-control characteristic, which is fully controlled by copyright holders.[12] To avoid this, the following two points have to be paid attention to: first, distinguish work access and other productive use. Technological protection measures cannot distinguish whether users reasonably or unreasonably use the work, and the controlling of access means that the way to get to the copyright works is inefficient. Therefore, in digital era, we have to pay attention that the access to works cannot be controlled. In fact, if the copying and spreading right is in the control of copyright holders, the access to the copyright works will not create threats to the economic interest of them.[13] Hence, the public should be allowed to read books, listen to music and watch movies online. Then, the public is granted with access to the copyright works and rules set will also play the function. Second, change the control objects of technological protection measures. In the network environment, copyright compensation system can be conducted and technological protection measures should not control the behaviors of being exposed to works, using works and spreading works with only payment of certain behaviors.[14] Based on this, control objects of technological protection

[10]Lessig [3].

[11]'The Infringement Age: How Much Do You Infringe On A Daily Basis?', https://www.techdirt.com/articles/20071119/015956.shtml, access date: 14th/08/2015.

[12]Gasser [4].

[13]Armstrong [5], p. 49.

[14]Gasser [6].

measures change from being exposed to, using works to paying. Some scholars believe that 'The support of consumer is the key factor for the survival of copyright holders'. Judging from this point of view, the demand to protect copyright should not cause burden on the digital content receivers. Thus, the digital rights management with limitations as basis can be abandoned to turn to the models with supervision that has access to get the secured contents at any time. The potential demand of this change and payment has significant meanings for the successful market of digital rights management. The change of control objects markedly decreases the level of control on end consumers, which enables the public to use works freely and at the same time guarantees the economic interest of copyright holders.[15]

4.1.3 Fully Introduce New Technology

Digital and network technologies have provided tremendous convenience for human beings to acquire knowledge and information, which set a convenient path for us to build up a fairly new society. Nowadays, the technological protection measures have big flaws because measures excessively control the adoption of new technology by end consumers. In the future, the design of copyright protection model cannot follow the tracks of an overthrown chariot—recommit the same error. 'Since the emergence of copyright law, it has experienced countless challenges.[16] The strong adaption and flexibility to new technologies reflect while facing with techniques for photography, recording technology and satellite technology, which are also sources of vitality for copyright law's ever-lasting existence.' Moreover, copyright law should take the initiative to adapt to the development of new technologies, which will not only help to the survival of copyright law but also introduce new power to better benefit human kind.

Technology occupies an important position in the future pattern of copyright law in the digital environment. However, excessive emphasis on technological protection measures is harmful especially when they are adopted as tools for copyright holders to achieve benefits, which will lead to the destruction of the original balance and the information flow retardation, and even affect basic human rights such as privacy and freedom to further damage the basic social values. In the digital environment, if there is no participation of technology, any copyright protection modes will no longer exist.[17] The current exploration of copyright protection models has cleared the practical advantages. However, the key problem is to recognize both the demerits and merits of these measures to fully play their roles in the future pattern construction and meanwhile avoid their demerits being over-exposed.

---

[15]Petrick [7].

[16]Reidenberg [8], pp. 1074–1095.

[17]Ginsburg [9].

The legal legitimacy of "contact control technological measures": To carry out the stipulations of technological measures protection in the WCT, copyright laws of our country and many other countries protect "contact control measures", which aim to prevent unauthorized enjoyment of literary works and application of computer software as well as copyright infringement like copying and propagating works without authority. However, there has a big debate about the legal legitimacy of copyright laws protecting "contact control measures".[18]

Of the two kinds of technological measures, the legitimacy of copyright laws protecting "copyright protective measures" has never aroused big disputes, because objects protected by "copyright protective measures" have the exclusive rights given by copyright laws clearly. "Copyright protective measures" are effective means of right holders to protect their exclusive rights, and the protection of copyright laws to "copyright protective measures" is an approval to the self-reliance protective method in effect. The drafter of Regulations for the Protection of Information Network Distribution Right pointed out when explaining the terms of technological measures protection: under the network environment, as measures to prevent infringement, technological measures could safeguard economic rights of right holders effectively. Since "copyright protective measures" are proper means of copyright owners to protect their exclusive rights, the protection of copyright laws to "copyright protective measures" is also legitimate.[19]

However, the protection of copyright laws to "contact control measures" gave rise to great theoretical confusions and debates—the paralleling of "contact control measures" and "copyright protective measures" demonstrated that "contact control measures" were not used to protect copyright directly.[20] Of acts of contacting works without authority, reading, enjoying and pirating literary and artistic works are not copyright infringement in any country, and application of pirated software belongs to copyright infringement only under certain circumstances. The current debates about the legal legitimacy mainly include the following three categories:

(1) "reproduction protective right";
(2) "contact protective right";
(3) "protective copyright indirectly".

But the writer believed that "contact control measures" are means of copyright owners to protect their legitimate interests in copyright laws besides exclusive rights to copyright, and the protection of copyright laws to the legal legitimacy of "contact control measures" is sourced from the legitimacy of interests protected by "contact control measures".[21] The one goal of copyright laws is to stimulate and encourage more people devoting themselves to creating activities by allowing copyright owners

[18]Ibid.

[19]Dimitriou [10].

[20]Cohen [11], pp. 575–617.

[21]Day [12].

benefit from application of the works.[22] The benefits are legitimate interests of copyright owners from copyright laws. The traditional means of copyright laws used to realize the legislative goal is to endow copyright owners with exclusive rights to prevent others using the works in certain ways. If others want to take actions under the protection of exclusive rights, they must obtain permission from and pay to copyright owners, through which copyright owners can benefit from the works.

Under the situation that copyright owners enjoy a certain exclusive right and can control some action, they could surely take technological measures to prevent others carrying out the action without authorization to protect their legitimate interests according to copyright laws.[23] If some software is recorded in a light disk through special technological means and thus others cannot copy the software with conventional methods, others would be prevented from duplicating the software without authorization directly. However, although copyright laws do not endow copyright owners with exclusive rights to make others use a work with a certain method, it just indicates that the unauthorized action is not a direct infringement but that others have rights to carry out the action and that copyright owners cannot prevent such an action through self-reliance methods.[24]

It is a major approach of right holders to obtain interests from application of works and realize their legitimate interests according to copyright laws by exercising exclusive rights endowed by the laws, but not the only one. Although right holders do not have the so called access right and cannot file a suit of copyright infringement against people contacting the works without authority, it does not mean that customers have the positive right of contacting the works and that copyright holders cannot adopt self-reliance means to safeguard their legitimate interests. Besides exclusive rights, copyright owners can adopt other methods only if they do not conflict with copyright laws and other laws to make sure only paying users can appreciate literary and artistic works or use computer software and thus they can benefit from their works, and "contact control measures" belong to this kind.[25] For example, in China, it is not an infringement act for users using pirated software non-commercially and software copyright holders cannot insist accountability for people's non-commercial application with no authorization, but it does not mean that copyright owners can't apply the "contact control measure" of setting "serial numbers" to guarantee that only paying users can apply the software.[26] Since "contact control measures" protect legitimate interests of right holders according to copyright laws, it is also legitimate for copyright laws protecting them. The action of cracking "serial numbers" and selling them will give rise to that copyright owners cannot make users pay for software through "serial numbers" thus to realize the goal of obtaining reasonable earnings. The protection of copyright laws to the "contact

[22]Slater et al. [13].

[23]Kerr and Bailey [14].

[24]Favale [15], pp. 1–25.

[25]Favale and Derclaye [16].

[26]Gunn [17].

control measure"—"serial numbers" can make sure that copyright owners can realize their legitimate interests according to copyright laws.

In the case between MDY and Blizzard at the end of 2010, when refuting the opinion that the protection to "contact control measures" was to prevent copyright infringement, the 9th U.S. Circuit Court of Appeals pointed out that if the prevention from copyright infringement was regarded as a premise to the protection of "contact control measures", we would deprive an important tool of copyright owners endowed by the parliament which can make sure that copyright holders can gain compensation from non-infringing contact to works.[27] For example, copyright owners can apply "contact control measures" when providing movies or music through network to obtain direct and indirect reward from users enjoying the movies and music. In fact, it was admitted that the goal of the protection of copyright laws to "contact control protection"[28] was to guarantee that copyright owners can obtain benefits from the public enjoying works, which was the base of the legal legitimacy of copyright laws protecting "contact control measures". The explanation to the legal legitimacy cannot only provide evidence to the legitimacy of the protection; what is more important is that it can offer legal basis for copyright owners abusing "contact control measures".

In this part, the author tries to discuss what the appropriate legal protection of digital rights management technologies is.[29] The objective of the paper is to highlight the deficiencies of the present legal practices in US and the EU. Compared with private remedy, such as making license and using technological protection measures, anti-circumvention rules will bring more widespread influence and probably rebuild the new benefit rules in copyright system.[30] The theory of anti-circumvention legislation has been far away from the principle of traditional copyright since its emergence, which means there is not much experience that merits attention by current copyright system, even anti-circumvention rules in various countries no doubt provides legal support and so-called "lawful basis" for creators' rights expanding.[31] The methodology adopted in this paper is mainly based on comparative legal research.

It is time to adjust copyright system appropriately with the aim of answering how to keep new balance of interest in digital era. This adjustment can be adapted to digital rights management prototype, which must be deemed as the fundamental approach of copyright's future development. All diverse practices collected so far have pointed out imperfect digital rights management rules as the motivation of a new digital rights management scheme. The combination of their distinct advantages of the practices should be the priority.[32] Part I introduces digital rights management

[27]Balboni and Partesotti [18], pp. 345–358.

[28]Ibid.

[29]Ibid.

[30]Quintais [19].

[31]Ibid.

[32]Ibid.

concepts and its development panorama. Part II summarizes the core technical problem of digital rights management: Technological Protections Measures (TPM) and Part III compares different regulations on TPM in various countries. Part IV analyzes the impact of anti-circumvention legislations before their evaluations in Part V. The article appraises different restriction practices of digital rights management technology and presents advise on interest balance to analyze the dilemma encountered by digital rights management system.

Digital rights management is a tool that the creators defend for the utmost interest based on their own benefit in modern copyright system. Digital rights management scheme strictly controls the public's access and further use of digital content as a result that right holders are able to overstep the boundary of their specific right, which is protected by copyright. In digital environment, and probably in right holders' opinion, the creation of new right on "access to works" ("access right"), is evitable and this right to a certain degree has already become the core of digital copyright system instead of "reproduction right". Lacking of standardization is acknowledged by scholars and professional insiders as the crucial problems nowadays nagged by digital rights management technologies and the matter to be solved promptly by digital rights management software designers and legislators. The digital rights management is short for digital rights management and its appearance decided by the special feature of digital information times.[33] Digital environment is glutted with plenty of digital works, which means that it cannot deal with these controversial digital issues without specific regulations or approaches.[34] The working principle of digital rights management technology is based on the license center of digital works, which is able to lock encrypted and compressed digital copyright works through digital private key. The digital copyright works can be played when the users get the verification from the licence center and unlock the access according to the Key ID and the Universal Resource Locator (URL). Otherwise, those users who have not obtained the authorization of accessing the encrypted information cannot download the works.[35]

Summary There are a plenty of definitions with respect to digital rights management from a lot of different perspectives. In most classical defined concepts, however, it is known that digital rights management is more considered as a kind of technical tool that protects and manages intellectual property information and material during the process of creation, communication, distribution and exploitation of the digital content.[36] Digital rights management's primary target locates within the scope of restricting piracy by technical approaches and also preserving intellectual digital content to guarantee marketing sales of unblocked digital products unobstructed. The second goal of digital rights management regime is to safeguard

[33]Rothman [20], p. 1595.

[34]Nicita and Rossi [21], pp. 17–40.

[35]Maurushat et al. [22], p. 7.

[36]Brousseau and Curien [23].

the lawful right of the authors, publishers and distributors on intellectual property right exploitation and interests. The last but not the least, the reason why digital rights management technology system exists is prompting the press industry prosperously and finally achieving the interest balance between the private owners and the general public.[37]

4.2 The Background of Anti-Circumvention Rules Emergence

The comprehensive digital rights management system includes multiple elements such as licence, technology and law. Prof. Stefan Bechtold deemed that "Digital rights management systems are not only technological phenomena: they pose complex legal, business, organizational and economic problems".[38] Although digital rights management system is able to provide high-level technology security protection, there is no absolutely and totally very good system for all.[39] The case of SDMI (Secure Digital Music Initiative) also indicated there is no so-called "Fully Secure" system to count on, although these technological factors and design structures contained are more innovative and thorough. Technology system would be cracked by much more advanced technology, if specific research time provided based on the complexity. More significantly, digital content and authorised works secured by technology scheme would be spreading once the technology shield had been destroyed or wrecked. This situation also brought about irreversible impact and losses to copyright owners. Considering the inherently risky result, scholars in copyright law area insist that protecting digital copyrighted works through technological approach proves entirely futile.[40] Therefore, the right holders had started their journey to search for a new tool for intensive copyright protection in digital era besides combined protection of licences and technology, which presented us the arrival of anti-circumvention rules thereupon.

The term "anti-circumvention rules" adopted in this article aims to clarify general expression in a whirl in present research upon digital rights management system. The concept of "anti-circumvention rules" discussed in the paper embraces "anti-circumvention legislations" and "rights management information". The figure[41] with branches below shows what the relationship is among anti-circumvention rule, technological measures legislation, rights management information legislation, anti-circumvention legislation and anti-device legislation (Fig. 4.1).

---

[37]Solove [24].

[38]Ibid 68.

[39]Sander [25].

[40]Doctorow [26].

[41]Dongjun [27], p. 22.

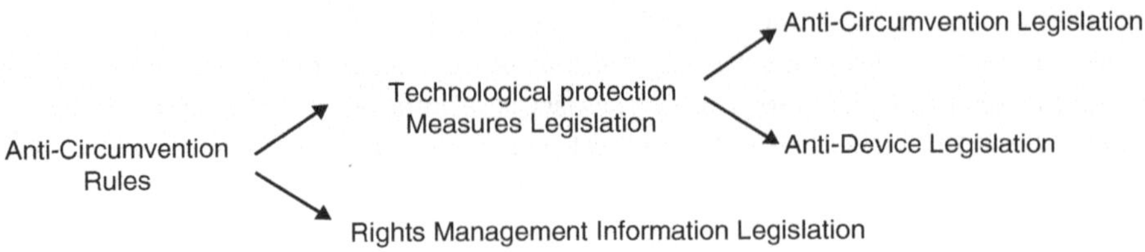

Fig. 4.1 Architecture of anti-circumvention rules

4.2.1 Technological Measures Legislations

To enhance the safety of digital rights management system integrally, the new technological measures legislations motivated by copyright industry development has been passed. These acts (so-called "preparatory activities"[42]), which circumvent technological protection measures and produce or sell the devices that can be used as circumvention means of technological protection measures are illegal. A retrospective of the idea that forbids a special technology via domestic legal provisions has traced back to Audio Home Recording Act of 1992 [17 U.S.C.§1002 (c)]. Article 1002 (c) of prohibition on the circumvention act of Serial Copy Management System (SCMS) is about "prohibition on circumvention of the system".

No person shall import, manufacture, or distribute any device, or offer or perform any service, the primary purpose or effect of which is to avoid, bypass, remove, deactivate, or otherwise circumvent any program or circuit which implements, in whole or in part...[43]

On the international horizon, the World Copyright Treaty (WCT) and World Performance and Phonogram Treaty (WPPT) under World Intellectual Property Organization (WIPO) structure both contain the similar provisions to ban circumvention behavior of technology protection measures.[44] The Article 11 of WCT stated that:

Contracting Parties shall provide adequate legal protection and effective legal remedies against the circumvention of effective technological measures that are used by authors in connection with the exercise of their rights under this Treaty or the Berne Convention and that restrict acts, in respect of their works, which are not authorized by the authors concerned or permitted by law, and Article 18 of WPPT states like that:

Contracting Parties shall provide adequate legal protection and effective legal remedies against the circumvention of effective technological measures that are used by performers or producers of phonograms in connection with the exercise of their rights under this Treaty and that restrict acts, in respect of their performances or phonograms, which are not authorized by.

---

[42]Ibid.

[43]Hovenkamp [28].

[44]Ibid.

In 1998, the American Congress passed the Digital Millennium Copyright Act (DMCA), which includes relevant technology protection measures provisions. Regarding DMCA, we could first find it designed the technology protection measures from two different but parallel points. One of them is "access control" rule, which controls the general public's access to the copyrighted works and the other one is "use control" regulation, which aims to "secure the right owners' copyright". Another important aspect in DMCA is about the partition from "direct circumvention acts" to "preparatory activities",[45] and the "use control" technology merely applies to the "preparatory activities".

In the EU, technological protection measures legislations were established through passing multi-directives related to copyright law. The Article 7(1)(c) of "Software Directive" in 1991[46] pointed out that:

> any act of putting into circulation, or the possession for commercial purposes of, any means the sole intended purpose of which is to facilitate the unauthorized removal or circumvention of any technical device which may have been applied to protect a computer program.

The Article 4 of "Conditional Access Directive"[47] also has the similar provisions:

> [T]he manufacture, import, distribution, sale, rental or possession for commercial purposes of illicit devices; the installation, maintenance or replacement for commercial purposes of an illicit device; the use of commercial communications to promote illicit devices.

The most important technological protection measures legislation is the Copyright Directive in 2001.[48] Article 6 (1) of this Directive forbids acts against the circumvention of any effective technological measures. Further, Article 6 (2) prohibits "import, distribution, sale, rental, advertisement for sale or rental, or possession for commercial purposes of devices, products or components or the provision of services" or devices "have only a limited commercially significant purpose or use other than to circumvent" or "are primarily designed, produced, adapted or performed for the purpose of enabling or facilitating the circumvention". Generally speaking, Article 6 (1) and Article 6 (2) provided digital rights management system the comprehensive protection.

4.2.2 Rights Management Information Legislation

Unlike the anti-circumvention legislations, rights management information legislations have not been reproached by universal odium, which probably summed up on

---

[45]Ibid.

[46]Council Directive of May 14, 1991 on the legal protection of computer programs (91/250/EEC).

[47]Directive 98/84/EC of the European Parliament and of the Council of November 20, 1998 on the legal protection of services based on, or consisting of, conditional access.

[48]Directive 2001/29/EC of the European Parliament and of the Council of May 22, 2001 on the harmonization of certain aspects of copyright and related rights in the information society.

account of its non-restriction on people's use of digital content. In other words, rights management information legislations do not directly limit the Internet users to get digital copyrighted works. Provisions related to rights management information in WCT and WPPT are explicit and specific. Article 12 (1) of WCT involving "obligations concerning rights management information" expresses:

> (1) Contracting Parties shall provide adequate and effective legal remedies against any person knowingly performing any of the following acts knowing, or with respect to civil remedies having reasonable grounds to know that it will induce, enable, facilitate or conceal an infringement of any right covered by this Treaty or the Berne Convention:
>
> (i) to remove or alter any electronic rights management information without authority[49];
> (ii) to distribute, import for distribution, broadcast or communicate to the public, without authority, works or copies of works knowing that electronic rights management information has been removed or altered without authority.[50]

Which are similar to Article 19 of WPPT.

4.3 Legal Protection of Technological Protection Measures in Different Regions

To a certain degree, the anti-circumvention rules in various countries from the perspective of the global legal measures' implementation, are deemed to be the outcome under American's pressure in the structure of WIPO.[51] WCT and WPPT granted the implementation right of specific means against circumvention acts to their signatories.[52] Also, they merely provide general principle of legal solutions concerning these acts, like "enough protection" and "effective legal remedy" on this issue. In this respect, besides inherently similar with each other, every single member of WCT and WPPT builds their own legal system for circumvention behavior out of respective legal value orientations.

4.3.1 US Level: Digital Millennium Copyright Act in 1998

Digital Millennium Copyright Act (DMCA) is regarded as one of the most authoritative statute in recent years. Section 1201 in DMCA states three types of anti-circumvention of both copyrighted works protection and copyright protection

[49] Article 12 (1) of WCT.

[50] Ibid.

[51] Ibid 335.

[52] Ibid 335.

behavior. The anti-circumvention categories include direct circumvention, providing means for circumvention and indirect circumvention.[53] Although these practices were welcomed by Internet content providers and accepted by digital copyright regulations, the general public still has a strong aversion to the digital rights management system.[54]

Most contribution of DMCA is to divide two kinds of technological protection measures: "access control" and "use control", which is a highly contentious issue as well. In the practice, there is no unambiguous distinction on the two measures, or even confusedly mixed up sometimes. DMCA created a new doctrine of liability fixation that is completely separated from the traditional doctrine under the digital copyright system through those articles. The right holders claimed specific lawsuit about ones' circumvention acts, and there is no need for them to provide any evidence of the existing infringement acts or even the proof of substantial circumvention occurrence. The only thing is sustained by judges once plaintiffs show "technologies", "devices" or "services" accused the very eligible objectives under the definition of "circumvention devices" in anti-device legislations.[55] The anti-circumvention legislation in DMCA, especially the anti-device legislation has been negative influenced in digital copyright system. "Technology" itself, not the making use of technology, is treated as "illegal" in DMCA, which may be widely accepted as the absurd problem in DMCA.[56]

4.3.2 *The EU Directives*

The EU has provided legal protection to technological measures for a very long time, and it has formed a systematic system of management rules constituted by Orders of the EU on Computer Software, Green Book of Copyright and Neighbouring Rights in Information Society of the EU, Suggestions and Orders on Copyright and Orders on access to Appendix.

The earliest clause about technological protective measures of the EU can be seen in the orders on legal protection to computer procedures (which was called "Software Directive") issued in 1991.[57] Article 7 (1) Special Protective Measures of the Directive listed the actions that Member States should sanction according to their domestic laws and the third clause stipulated to prohibit investing in, circulating or possessing any equipment for commercial purpose (if the only goal of the equipment

[53]Travis [29].

[54]Ibid.

[55]Ibid.

[56]Yen [30], pp. 649–698.

[57]Directive 91/250/EEC, on the legal protection of computer programs, entered into force on May 14, 1991, http://europa.eu.int/eur-lex/lex/LexUriServ/LexUriServ.do?uri=CELEX:31991L0250:EN:HTML, access date: 26/09/2015.

was for the convenience of unauthorized deletion and circumvention of any technological equipment aiming to protect computer procedures).[58] Since the Directive was only limited to the protection to technological protective measures of computer procedures, its scope of protection was relatively narrow and the Directive just prohibited two kinds of actions: the one was anti-circumvention of circulation of equipment, and the other was possession of anti-circumvention of equipment.[59]

Moreover, the definition of anti-circumvention was also clear, and the judging standard was whether it had the only purpose, that is to say, whether equipment specialized in providing convenience for unauthorized deletion and circumvention of technological devices used to protect computer programs, but the definition also imposed restrictions on affirmation of anti-circumvention equipment. Because of the above-mentioned restrictions, the implementation of the Software Orders had shortcomings in practice, for example, the requirement of only-purpose was too strict. If several other functions were added on purpose when designing anti-circumvention equipment, it would be very easy to evade this regulation.

In July 1995, the EU issued Green Book on Copyright and Relevant Rights in Information Societies[60] (which was referred as Green Paper below). Mainly starting from the aspect of right holders, the report stated issues about copyright protection to new products and services in information societies in detail. In the section of Technical Systems of Protection and Identification, it had a specific discussion on technological measures of copyright protection. Its essential point was that if a proper protective system was installed, digital technologies could make works and other protected objects identified, tattooed, protected and automatically managed and that if information societies wanted to operate successfully without damaging interests of right holders, these protective systems must be introduced and accepted internationally. In general, the Green Paper stressed the importance of copyright protection in information societies from the standpoint of copyright and right holders of relevant rights, required coordination of various countries and provided protection to technological measures as a part of the EC.[61] However, the technological measures involved in the Green Paper were still limited to identification, and the suggested protective scope of technological measures was also limited.

In November 1996, based on wide consultation, the Commission of the EU issued the subsequent green book on copyright and relevant rights in information societies

---

[58]'The WIPO Treaties: Technological Measures', March 2003, http://www.ifpi.org/content/library/wipo-treaties-technical-measures.pdf, access date: 26/09/2015.

[59]Ibid.

[60]European Commission Green Paper of 27 July 1995 on Copyright and Related Rights in the Information Society COM(95) 382 final, http://europa.eu/scadplus/leg/en/lvb/l24152.htm, access date: 20/09/2015.

[61]'The content of Commissions Green Paper on Copyright and Related Rights in the Information Society26 considered how the information society ought to function, showing the importance of the information society for the European Community and which current issues relating to copyright and related rights should be looked at… The "voluntary measures" established by Article 6, paragraph 4 represent measures taken by the right holders to protect their rights', da Motta Perin [31].

(referred as "Subsequent Green Paper"[62] below), which investigated copyright in single market from economic, social and cultural aspects and believed a legal framework of information societies should be constructed based on the community. Compared with the Green Book, the Committee had a statement on active and positive effects of technological measures of legislation priority based on the community in the second chapter of the Subsequent Green Paper.[63]

The Committee held that the digital management and protection system of copyright was beneficial for right holders identify and monitor piracy, but it also pointed out that it would have a positive effect on privacy of users. In addition, different from that the Green Paper only concerned about technological measures of identification, the Subsequent Green Paper observed that application of new technological measures such as access control, anti-copying and personal use would have a great impact on copyright protection. Members of the Committee considered the large-scale introduction of electronic management and protection system of copyright depended on whether a set of standardized projects could be developed to solve interoperability of these systems. Therefore, the Committee encouraged all parts to keep trying in standardization, appealed to take actions based on the community, and coordinated legal protection to technological identification and protection systems.

After the two treaties WTC and WPTP were passed in the diplomatic conference of the WIPO, the Committee of the EU quickened its legislative process of legal protection to technological measures as well. In December 1997, the Committee submitted the suggestions on coordination of several orders of copyright and relevant rights in information societies[64] (referred as Suggestions on Directive of Copyright below) with the purpose of adjusting and improving the current legal framework, especially copyright issues of new products and services with intellectual property, including on-line products and services, physical loaded DC, CD—ORM and digital light disks to protect the single market of copyright and relevant rights as well as to stimulate creation and investment of the EU.[65] The Suggestions on orders of copyright included that the EU asked Member States provide full legal protection to effective technological measures used to protect copyright and relevant rights, sanction actions of breaking above-mentioned technological measures as well as actions of manufacturing and issuing breaking equipment, products and components and providing breaking services. The suggestion further made clear of the definition of breaking equipment or services, that was, actions of propagating, popularizing and marketing equipment or services for breaking, or equipment and services taking breaking technological measures as its only goal or major commercial purpose, or equipment or services designed, manufactured, adopted or

[62]Commission Green Papers on encrypted services, Commercial Communications and the protection of minors in audio visual services, and the proposed Directive on a transparency mechanism.

[63]Guibault et al. [32].

[64]Little [33].

[65]See Burk [34], p. 35.

performed to break technological measures protection to copyright and relevant rights.

In November 1998, the EU passed Legal Protection to Conditional Access (Conditional Access Directive)[66] with the purpose of protecting broadcasting services of radio and TV stations that charged or had conditions for access as well as other services in information societies, including audio-visual services, on-line information services and electronic publishing provided as required. In February 1999, the law was submitted to the European Parliament for a first reading vote, and the parliament put forward 58 amending suggestions. In September 2000, the Council of ministers of the EU finally came to a political agreement on an integrated copyright law,[67] that was, common position of copyright law of the EU and thus entering into a second reading procedure. In February 2001,[68] after another discussion, Law on coordination of copyright and relevant rights in information societies (Copyright law in information societies), which had been under discussion for 6 years, was finally born and was officially carried out on December 22, 2002. The law stipulated protection to technological measures in the third chapter and definition of technological measures in Article 6.

From law-making stipulations of criminal protection to technological measures of copyright at broad, we can know that most countries punish both perpetrating and preparatory acts of circumventing technological measures, such as America and Germany. Only very few countries just punish preparatory but perpetrating acts, like Britain. For acts of providing services for technological measures circumvention, some countries like Japan do not punish, but most countries do. Thus, "proper and full protection" required in Article 11 of the WIPO Copyright Treaty[69] is a provision with broad meaning. As for what protection is proper and full, it is decided by conditions of a country.

Comparing with the provisions related technological protection measures in DMCA, the EU directive shows the similar articles on this part, which is specific characteristic as follows:

First, in the anti-circumvention provisions, it stated that the person who has to be liable for "circumvention of technological protection measures" only under the case "if such person knows, or has reasonable grounds to know", while DMCA has no same provision. It seemingly that the restriction scope of circumvention acts of the EU directive is much narrower than that in DMCA, which in fact is not true. Since the direct circumvention acts seldom happened in the case that the one did not know his behavior belonging to "circumvention of technological protection measures".

[66]Directive 98/84/EC of the European Parliament and of the Council of 20 November 1998 on the legal protection of services based on, or consisting of.

[67]Ibid 356.

[68]Directive 2001/29/EC, on the harmonisation of certain aspects of copyright and related rights in the information society, entered into force on June 22, 2001. http://eurlex.europa.eu/pri/en/oj/dat/2001/l_167/l_16720010622en00100019.pdf. Access date: 26/09/2015.

[69]Article 11 of the WCT.

Owing to the high requirement of technological skills on "circumvention of technological protection measures", it is unbelievable that in the situations that no one knows what they did for technological measures is the act of "circumvention of technological protection measures", even if it did exist. What the most focusing point in copyright holders' mind is that anti-device legislation contained anti-circumvention rules. Once the possibility that the public can obtain the circumvention tool was excluded, the importance of anti-circumvention legislation would not be that prominent. Therefore, this condition in the EU Directive did not distinguish its legal effect in practice from DMCA. The positive affirmation of the EU Directive is that it still kept the prudent attitude towards defining the scope of the liabilities of infringement, unlike DMCA's rash decision. Although the EU Directive has not listed the denumerable provisions with regard to the acts of circumvention of "access control" and "use control" technology, however, the EU Directive essentially differentiate these two acts through the definition of what the "effective" technological protection measures are. It is worthwhile to note that the circumvention act of "use control" is not forbidden under the DMCA, but is banned by the EU Directive. This means that the scope of application of "anti-circumvention legislation" in the Directive [Article 6 (1) and 6 (2) provide stronger protection] is wider than that in DMCA.

Although most countries added technological measures of copyright into copyright laws, no countries regarded copyright technology as contents of copyright law. Even in Japan, technological measures of copyright are considered as a part of anti-unfair competition law, therefore, crime of technological measures circumvention do not belong to infringement of copyright but an independent crime. Moreover, it has independent criminal law articles to perpetrating and preparatory acts of circumventing technological measures of copyright and the acts have their own constitutive elements of crime as well.

4.3.3 The Path of Digital Rights Management Regulatory Model in China

The earliest anti-circumvention technological measures in laws and regulations of our country can be seen in the Interim Measures on Software Products Management issued by the Ministry of Electronics Industry in March 1998, Article 18 of which stipulated that actions like producing pirated software and decoding software as well as software whose main function was to decoding technological protective measures were forbidden. With the limitation of domestic economic and technological development then, there were no protective clauses about technological measures in the Copyright Law issued in 1991. On October 27, 2001, the new Copyright Law was put into effect, which stipulated in Article 47 (1) item 6 that it was an infringing act for person avoiding or destroying technological measures which were adopted by right holders to protect their copyrights or relevant rights on their works, videos and audio records without permission of copyright owners or right holders related to copyright except there had clear laws and administrative regulations.

In addition, the Regulations for the Protection of Computer Software carried out on January 1, 2002 stated the protection to computer software in Article 24 (3) which went like acts that avoid and destroy technological measures adopted by right owners to protect their software copyright with no permission were infringement, except there had specific stipulations in the Copyright Law of the PRC and other laws and administrative regulations, and people committed the infringement must assume civil, administrative and criminal liability according to the situation. Meanwhile, for restrictions and exceptions of technological measures protection, some other new exceptions were specified through administrative laws and regulations besides stipulations in the new copyright law.

Compared with the DMCA, the laws and regulations in our country have the following characteristics: 1. the fault principle was adopted for affirmation of infringement against technological measures while the DMCA adopted the non-fault principle; 2. the laws and regulations in our country put emphasis on actions of avoiding technological measures while the DMCA on the prohibition of technological measures circumvention; and 3. technological measures stipulated in the laws and regulations of China only referred to measures preventing application of copyright but measures for access control while the DMAC included the two of them. Furthermore, the prohibition in relevant laws of our country to technological measures and equipments circumvention is not as wide as that of the DMCA, which is more beneficial to the development of the information industry; meanwhile, relevant laws in our country well handle the balance between public interests and rights of copyright owners, which safeguards the rights of the public obtaining information to some extent. However, the protection of our current legal system to technological measures protection has some problems, including weak operability, narrow protection objects, and shortage of corresponding terms of sanction to manufacturing and selling equipment cracking technological measures or providing decoding services, which are places needing improvement.

In February, 2010, China revised the Copyright Law for the second time and it realized its protection to technological measures of digital rights management by endowing copyright holders an exclusive right, which was declared in Article 48 (6) and (7) in the Copyright Law. General protective clauses to technological measures just allow right holders adopt technological measures protection to protect their copyright and relevant rights and make violators accept punishment, but their practical application are difficult and uncertain to a certain degree. The over-general stipulations about legal protection to technological measures of digital rights management in our country was caused by the passivity of relevant legislation of China's digital rights management to some extent, and compared with the Copyright of Information Societies Directive 2001/29/EC of the EU and the DMCA, the Copyright Law of China do not have a detailed and specific illustration to technological measures, rights management information[70] and relevant prohibiting and circumventing actions.[71] Although Article 36 of Enforcement Regulations of the Copyright Law further stated punishment to infringing acts including circumventing and destroying technological measures as well as deleting and changing rights management information, there still have no specific application rules to protection of technological measures.

With the improvement of the system of socialist laws of China and the laws and regulations of copyright, China issued and implemented a series of laws and regulations successively including Regulations for Protection of Computer Software, Implementation Measures for Administrative Punishment of Copyright, Collective Management of Copyright, and Explanation of the Supreme People's Court on Several Issues of Law Application in Computer-Network Related Copyright Cases. In July 2006, China started to carry out Regulations for the Protection of Information Network Distribution Right that involved technological clauses of digital rights management, and it became a contracting party of the two Internet treaties, namely, WCT and WPPT, which further strengthened protection to the anti-circumvention of digital rights management technological measures.

Regulations for the Protection of Information Network Distribution Right had a specific statement to the definition of "technological measures" and "electronic information of rights management" in Article 2 (2) (3). The Regulations laid a solid foundation to anti-circumvention legal protection of digital rights management of China starting from definition, and from the aspect of definition of technological measures, although China did not divide technological measures into control type and rights protection type clearly, we can knew that the laws of China provided protection to the two types from expressions like "avoiding browsing works with no authority" and "preventing providing works to the public without permission". The Regulations stipulated corresponding protective legal provisions to technological measures and electronic information of rights management of digital works respectively. For legal protection to technological measures, the Regulations had an all-sided prohibition that covered from direct infringement acts like circumvention and destruction to indirect ones like manufacturing, importing and providing equipment, components and services with the major purpose of avoiding and destroying technological measures. For electronic information of rights management, the Regulations also had specific regulations to direct deletion or change of rights management measures and illegal supply of works that can delete and change electronic information of rights management. Thus, we can see that compared with the legal protection of the Copyright Law to digital rights technological measures that only

[70]Article 7(2), Directive 2001/29/EC.

[71]The following acts are target by Article 7(1): (a) the removal or alteration of any electronic RMI; (b) the distribution, importation for distribution, broadcasting, communication or making available to the public of works or other subject-matter protected under this Directive and Directive 96/9/EC from which electronic RMI has been removed or altered without authority.

had over-general rules to infringing acts and accountability, the Regulations is more objective, specific and operable.

For accountability and punishment of avoiding technological measures of digital works or deleting electronic information of rights management, the Regulations also had specific application rules. For direct infringing acts like avoiding or destroying technological measures, deleting or changing electronic information of rights management, and providing works whose electronic information are deleted or changed, infringers must assume not only civil liabilities, but also administrative responsibilities such as confiscation of illegal gains and a huge sum of penalty according to illegal business transactions if they harm interests of the public. In addition, if circumstances are serious, criminal liability is possible. For indirect infringing acts to technological measures, the Regulations had detailed and specific protective rules which stipulated that people who manufactured, imported or provided equipment or components which were mainly used to avoid and destroy technological measures or provide technological services to others to avoid or destroy technological measures must assume corresponding legal liability.

Compared with Article 48 of the Copyright Law that stipulates direct infringing acts only from the level of accountability, the Regulations is more specific, standard, applicable and practical on provisions for legal protection to technological measures of digital works. In addition, The Article 24 of Regulations for the Protection of Computer Software and the Article 6 of Explanation of the Supreme People's Court on Several Issues of Law Application in Computer-Network Related Copyright Cases had specific regulations as well for legal protection to technological measures of computer software and digital works. Since computer software is a kind of special digital works, and it has characteristics like universality, the tendency to be infringed and wide users, the Regulations had clear legal protection to the technological measures and electronic information of rights management of computer software. Furthermore, it had a higher upper limit to penalty for infringing compared with other infringing acts, which further illustrated the importance of technological measures protection. With the flourishing of digital network and the increasing of infringement of network service providers, the Explanation had stipulations on direct infringing acts of network service providers, which further expanded the coverage of legal protection to technological measures.

The revised draft of the Copyright Law issued at the end of 2013 had many modifications and adjustment to the current Copyright Law of China. The revised draft for Approval of the Copyright Law would be an independent chapter from clauses related to technological measures and rights management information that protected digital rights management and have detailed and specific stipulations. The revised draft for approval made more specific stipulations for legal protection to technological measures from the four aspects, namely, definition, rights of right holders, limitation of rights and liability for tort based on absorbing and learning from Regulations for the Protection of Information Network Distribution Right. In definition, application objects of technological measures in the revised draft for approval added in broadcasting and TV programs and application goals added in duplication, operation and adaptation. In addition, application objects of electronic information of rights management added in broadcasting and TV programs and broadcasting and TV stations as well as right holders of broadcasting and TV programs. The law further made clear that the legal protection to technological measures covered the two types, namely, contact control and rights protection. In scope of rights protection of right holders, the revised draft for approval still followed the detailed and specific rights contents, being highly consistent to the Regulations. In liability of tort, the revised draft for approval stated liabilities for tort specifically, such as avoiding and destroying technological protective measures and deleting and modifying rights management information. Compared with the Regulations, it did not only integrate liability terms of direct and indirect infringement, but also expanded indirect infringing ways of electronic information of rights management with actions including duplicating, issuing, renting, performing, playing and transmitting works to the public through network although knowing or supposed to know rights management information was deleted or changed. Although the revised draft for approval was not legally valid, as the first revised draft of the Copyright Law, it could be official copyright law. We can know that the legal protection to technological measures of the digital rights management is getting complete from actions like it takes legal protection to technological measures as an independent chapter, make the definition of technological measures specific, make rights of right holders clear, and take liability of tort harsher. On January 16, 2013, the executive meeting of the State Council's modification on fine of the four administrative laws and regulations including Enforcement Regulations of the Copyright Law, Regulations for the Protection of Information Network Distribution Right and Regulations for the Protection of Computer Software further strengthened the force against circumvention and damage of technological measures of digital rights management and deepened the protection to digital copyright.

Furthermore, in 2013 before the two national sessions, the center of the China Association for Promoting Democracy organized some members of the national committee of CPPCC to have a deep investigation to digital piracy and submitted the proposal on Strengthening Digital Rights Management and Constructing a Unified State-Level Public Service Platform for Digital Copyright. The center of the China Association for Promoting Democracy proposed to perfect legislation of laws and regulations on digital publishing, perfect system of informing and deleting, relieve rights safeguarding loan on copyright holders, further protect rights and interests of right holders, make clear indemnification standards for infringement against copyright laws, strengthen enforcement of administrative laws and pay attention to popularizing and educating work of digital copyright. Thus, protection of digital copyright has attracted great attention, and before long, China will establish a more perfect and sound system for digital rights management.

Summary Similar legal status of technological protection measures in different countries signifies digital rights management architecture has located its protection onto the whole framework of digital copyright protection. As an aside, various protection standards and thresholds for technological protection measures of digital rights management pyramid in Western countries and China can even be treated as portrayals responding to the societal and cultural issues mentioned above.

For the specific articles, digital rights management regulatory model in China more or less was branded with Western logo. To a certain degree, it has invoked subsequently a series of problems in legal practices. It is, perhaps said that China has the greatest motivation for adjusting the whole digital rights management regulatory model.

4.4 The Impact of Anti-Circumvention Legislations

Although the wording is sort of accepted that anti-circumvention legislations in various countries has been passed basically for implementing their own obligation under WCT and WPPT. However, the irony worth cogitating is that, these new laws on anti-circumvention, merely made for world treaties' duty implementation, to a large degree, are not necessary at all. In fact, the core of anti-circumvention legislation is anti-device rules, which substantially weights the liabilities of devices providers. It is precisely based on this character of anti-circumvention legislations that the right holders may not only strengthen their protection through the combined approach of private remedy and new legal provisions, even also potentially put a premium on another capability for their exclusive rights extending to the related technology and products market. The possibility of anti-circumvention legislations abuse restrains the new disseminating technology at its embryonic stage, and moreover increases the general public's cost. As some scholars put like that, "A government copy protection mandate passes the cost of intellectual property protection to all taxpayers, in the form of enforcement costs for new criminal and civil laws accompanying the mandate".[72]

According to the legislation background of famous DMCA, we could probe into it as the outcome of American copyright industry that politically influenced almost the world copyright regime. The right holders would prefer to choose anti-circumvention legislations for protecting their technological protection measures. Numerous attentions of copyright owners simply put on their own benefits in digital copyright environment (ab ovo usque ad mala), rather than these harmful impact on public users.

Technological protection measure is regarded as a kind of "private remedy" tool, which emerged for the sake of stopping massive Internet piracy to maintain their interest since the advent of new technology times. In addition, the existing of anti-circumvention legislations confirms the lawful position of this so-called "private remedy" from copyright owners. In this regard, anti-circumvention legislations normally are seemed as part of copyright law system nowadays, which sounds ridiculous to the majority. As the essence of protection provided by

[72]Plummer [35], p. 12.

anti-circumvention legislations for technological measures or digital rights management entirely alien from the exclusive rights protection under copyright law system. It is blind of anti-circumvention legislations to provide protection of technological protection measures as the private remedy, which has aggravated interest unbalanced.

Summary Provisions under anti-circumvention legislations in different countries almost throughout the full text centered around detailed technological measures protection instead of any likelihood about right holders' abuse or possible threat posed on the general public, which had triggered legal loophole in lack of related restrictions on digital rights management.

As a matter of fact, any private right would be possible abused in perspective of theoretical analysis, while a sequence of corresponding limitations in legal right regime should be inseparable element. Anti-circumvention legislations undoubtedly enhance copyright owners' controlling force on both their copyrighted works and the development of digital technology, which initiate another dramatic evolution of copyright law nature from "concept of law" to "concept of technology".[73]

4.5 Anti-Circumvention Legislations Analysis and Evaluation

Anti-circumvention legislations reflected the contradiction between the copyright owners and the general public. Take the US as an example: Internet piracy had hit the Hollywood market in the whole world. The producers and investors have already become the advocators and supporters to legalize circumvention measures, while the information industry has been one of the high-speed growth entities in American economic development, which has been conflicted with the requirement of anti-circumvention legislations. For anti-circumvention legislations forbid producing the devices used for circumvent technological protection measures. No wonder the elites who paddled at the incoming tide from Silicon Valley boosted the morale of anti-circumvention legislations as part of DMCA. Another saying of legalization process of anti-circumvention measures is mocked kind of "war between Hollywood and Silicon Valley".

Notwithstanding the American's DMCA or the EU Directives, the regulations related to anti-circumvention are out of crucial economic influence consideration. Uncle Sam expected reduced adverse balance of trade under the aid of its domain position in copyright industry to convert the current economic development's main direction from manufacturing industry to information industry. The EU would like to decrease the trade barrier inside of the whole union so that it can build European United Market through legislation integration with regard to technology measures

[73]Jackson [36], p. 608.

protection. The common intention of the US and the EU both took attempted to pass their own anti-circumvention legislations first, and then to enforce the legislation model as soon as possible or at least pressed other countries to keep unanimous with its legislation logic. This act probably would be encouraged to leave enough space to updated technology after copyright amendment, to expand copyright owners' specific right and to control each act type of copyrighted works access caused by innovative and valuable technology in digital copyright system. However, the fundamental aim of copyright protection is to ensure and promote intellectual works created and disseminated positively to benefit the general public from intellectual creation of authors. As John Locke's has demonstrated in the well-known statement of property as labor's "just desert", intellectual property is deemed as "a suitable reward for intellectual labor".[74] The purpose of copyright law should behave as it was whether at national level or international range. The developed countries and the developing countries are closely related and mutually dependent, and in particular, economic benefit is bound up with each other. "Technological protection measures" is developed countries' gunboat diplomacy for increasing their gross national product (GNP), which not only induced unprofitable creation and also was harmful to the development of the world harmonization.

Nevertheless, balance of interest is the indispensable constraint in the protection of private right, which defines that copyright owners are not able to achieve the goal beyond the balance of interest purpose in physical or digital copyright world. The preface parts of copyright treaties or related conventions under WIPO structure made clearly that one of their objectives is maintaining the balance of interest between "authors' right" (including performers' and phonogram producers' right) and "the general public interest", especially the interest balance among "education", "research" and "access information". What the principle discussed above same applies to the "technological protection measures". In other words, protection of "technological protection measures" cannot collide with this significant rule of copyright system. Provided that we say yes to right holders' monopoly acts and prohibition of authorized works appropriately got or used by eligible ones via technological measures, there will be another intensively severe situation encountered with copyright law system. A new private area hereupon will come out and therewith trigger numerous infringements in public area. Regulations concerning digital rights management or anti-circumvention may cause a mega passive influence on the developing countries' innovation development.[75] According to the American experience of digital rights management exploitation, it has proved that if the copyright owners inappropriately explore the rules with respect to digital rights management mechanism and anti-circumvention technology to limit the competitive rival ship in market and indirectly lead monopolies. Simply, small companies are confronted by the hazardous situation brought by inappropriate exploitation of digital rights management technology and survival of the fittest market choices.

[74]Christopher [37], p. 7.

[75]Ganley [38], pp. 241–293.

In fact, technology in digital rights management system does not inevitably at all shape obstacles for balance of interest in copyright regime. Technology's neutrality character indicates various adoption ways of technology are the reflections of social value. Therefore, it is possible for digital rights management system to find an updated friendly form that is more beneficial for end-users.

This paper aims to clarify erroneous remarks about digital rights management scheme in the context of digital world based on literature analysis. Technological protection measure is the kernel of digital rights management system and copyright holders' technological means to protect their copyrighted works and to evaluate legal approach for protecting these technological protection measures (Anti-Circumvention Rules). Anti-circumvention rules, as the new content in copyright system, have been legislated worldwide despite of their unreasonable feature.

Summary As the influence from digital technology on copyright system has not been completely revealed, copyright system has not yet fully responded to these effects, either. The existing situation of unbalanced interest under copyright system and chaotic applicability of copyright law provisions is treated as the requisite stage towards a perfect copyright world.

The explanation to the legal legitimacy cannot only provide evidence to the legitimacy of the protection, what is more important is that it can offer legal basis for copyright owners abusing "contact control measures".

References

1. Burk DL (2005–2006) Legal and technical standards in digital rights management technology. Fordham Law Rev 74:537. http://heinonline.org/HOL/LandingPage?collection=journals&handle=hein.journals/flr74&div=27&id=&page=. Accessed 15 Aug 2015
2. McCreevy C (2018) Address to the EABC/BSA (European American Business Council/Business Software Alliance) Conference on Digital Rights' Management. http://ec.europa.eu/commissionbarroso/mccreevy/docs/speeches/2005-10-12/euamen.pdf
3. Lessig L (2005) Free culture: the nature and future of creativity. Penguin Books
4. Gasser U (2004) iTunes: how copyright, contract, and technology shape the business of digital media-a case study. Berkman Center for Internet & Society at Harvard Law School Research Publication No. 2004-07
5. Armstrong TK (2006) Digital rights management and the process of fair use. Harv J Law Technol 20:49. University of Cincinnati Public Law Research Paper No. 07-10
6. Gasser U (2006) Legal frameworks and technological protection of digital content: moving forward towards a best practice model. Berkman Center Research Publication No. 2006-04
7. Petrick P (2004) Why DRM should be cause for concern: an economic and legal analysis of the effect of digital technology on the music industry. Berkman Center for Internet & Society at Harvard Law School Research Publication No. 2004-09
8. Reidenberg JR (2007) The rule of intellectual property law in the internet economy. Houston Law Rev 44(4):1074–1095. Fordham Law Legal Studies Research Paper No. 1012504
9. Ginsburg JC (2007) The Pros and Cons of strengthening intellectual property protection: technological protection measures and Section 1201 of the US Copyright Act. Columbia Public Law Research Paper No. 07-137

10. Dimitriou C (2015) Digital rights management systems and data privacy. March 1, 2015. https://doi.org/10.2139/ssrn.2571859. Accessed 26 Sep 2015
11. Cohen JE (2003) DRM and privacy. Berkeley Technol Law J 18:575–617. Georgetown Public Law Research Paper No. 372741
12. Day BR (2011) In defense of copyright: creativity, record labels, and the future of music. Seton Hall J Sports Entertain Law 21(1)
13. Slater D, Gasser U, Smith M, Bambauer DE, Palfrey JG Jr (2005) Content and control: assessing the impact of policy choices on potential online business models in the music and film industries. Berkman Publication Series Paper No. 2005-01
14. Kerr IR, Bailey J (2004) The implications of digital rights management for privacy and freedom of expression. J Inf Commun Ethics Soc 2. Troubador Publishing Ltd
15. Favale M (2012) The right of access in digital copyright: right of the owner or right of the user? J World Intellect Prop 15(1):1–25
16. Favale M, Derclaye E (2010) 'User contracts' (demand side). J Intellect Prop Law 18(1)
17. Gunn MA (2015) Peer-to-peer file sharing as user rights activism. West J Leg Stud 5(3)
18. Balboni P, Partesotti C (2014) Digital right management in the cloud. In: Li KC, Li Q, Shih TK (eds) Cloud computing and digital media: fundamentals, techniques, and applications. Chapman and Hall/CRC, London, pp 345–358
19. Quintais JP (2012) On peers and copyright: why the EU should consider collective management of P2P. Munich Intellectual Property Law Center-MIPLC, Bd. 14, Nomos
20. Rothman JE (2014) Copyright's private ordering and the 'Next Great Copyright Act'. Berkeley Technol Law J 29:1595. Loyola-LA Legal Studies Paper No. 2015-10
21. Nicita A, Rossi MA (2013) Spectrum crunch vs. spectrum sharing: exploring the 'Authorised Shared Access' model. Communications & Strategies, No. 90, 2nd Quarter, pp 17–40
22. Maurushat A, Tacit CS, Kerr IR (2002–2003) Technical protection measures: tilting at copyright's windmill. Ottawa Law Rev 34:7. Available at: http://heinonline.org/HOL/LandingPage?collection=journals&handle=hein.journals/ottlr34&div=8&id=&page
23. Brousseau E, Curien N (2007) Internet and digital economics: principles, methods and applications. Cambridge University Press, June
24. Solove DJ (2004) Digital person: technology and privacy in the information age. Law, Technology and Society, December
25. Sander T (2002) Golden times for digital rights management? Financial Cryptography, Springer
26. Doctorow C (2004) Microsoft Research DRM Talk. June 17, 2004. Available at http://www.authorama.com/microsoft-research-drm-talk-1.html
27. Dongjun W (2011) Studies on problems of legal restrictions on digital rights management. China National Knowledge Infrastructure (CNKI) as Internet resource for database, p 22
28. Hovenkamp HJ (2013) Innovation and competition policy, Chapter 1: competition policy and the scope of intellectual property protection, 2nd edn. January 11, 2013. https://doi.org/10.2139/ssrn.1937207. Accessed 26 Sep 2015
29. Travis H (2008) Opting out of the internet in the United States and the European Union: copyright, safe harbors, and international law. Notre Dame Law Rev 83(4). Florida International University Legal Studies Research Paper No. 08-03
30. Yen AC (2003) What federal gun control can teach us about the DMCA's anti-trafficking provisions. Wisconsin Law Rev:649–698
31. da Motta Perin AC (2007) Technological measures for protection of copyright in the European Union, United States of America and Japan. Munich Intellectual Property Law Center
32. Guibault L et al (2007) Study on the implementation and effect in Member States' Laws of Directive 2001/29/EC, on the Harmonisation of Certain Aspects of Copyright and Related Rights in the Information Society. http://www.ivir.nl/publications/guibault/Infosoc_report_2007.pdf. Accessed 20 Sep 2015
33. Little V (2008) Audiovisual Media Services Directive: Europe's modernization of broadcast services regulations. J Law Technol Policy 2008(1). http://www.jltp.uiuc.edu/recdevs/little.pdf. Accessed 26 Sep 2015

34. Burk DL (2004) Legal and technical standards in digital rights management technology, p 35
35. Plummer J (2005) Expanding the market's role in advancing intellectual property, March 29, 2005, p 12. Available at http://www.cei.org/pdf/4452.pdf
36. Jackson M (2001) Using technology to circumvent the law: the DMCA's push to privatize copyright. Hastings Commerce Entertain Law J 23:608
37. Christopher (2000) A global political economy of intellectual property rights: the new enclosures? Routledge Taylor & Francis Group, May 2000, p 7
38. Ganley P (2002) Access to the individual: digital rights management systems and the intersection of informational and decisional privacy interests, pp 241–293. Available at http://ijlit.oxfordjournals.org/cgi/content/abstract/10/3/241

Chapter 5
Case Law Analysis

5.1 Cases in the US

5.1.1 Felten v. Recording Industry Assoc. of America

Felten was a council member of EFF, and he was also a professor of computer science and public affairs of Princeton University. In addition, he was one founder of the information and technology policy center of Princeton University. Felten once took part in many lawsuits against RIAA and Microsoft. In the case of "America charging Microsoft", Felten played the role of the chief expert witness of computer science of the Ministry of Justice of America.[1] In this case, Microsoft was accused of abusing its monopoly position in fields of operating system and browser. Felten and his group once cracked the SDMI (Secure Digital Music Initiative) music encryption technology, but he suffered legal threat when he prepared to publish an essay on cracking technologies. In 2001, People including Felten accused RIAA and SDMI with the help of EFF, requesting the court affirm that the publishing of an essay on cracking technology was not illegal. He even doubted that the Digital Millennium Copyright Act went against the constitutional spirits.

Through investigation, the court thought there were no disputes in this case. Felten regarded himself as a Galileo who fought against tyranny, but in fact, he was just a Don Quixote who was irritated by a pinwheel. Therefore, his lawsuit was rejected. Meanwhile, considering the Ministry of Justice indicated there were no actual disputes in this case in Motion to Dismiss because organizations like RIAA accusing Felten with DMCA lacked legal basis, people including Felten decided not to appeal and the essay was published successfully later.

[1]Nate Mook, "Scientists Take Recording Industry to Court", http://betanews.com/2001/06/06/scientists-take-recording-industry-to-court/.

C. Xu, *Regulatory Model for Digital Rights Management*,
https://doi.org/10.1007/978-981-15-1995-6_5

The case of Felten v. RIAA[2] enlightened us, after introducing the copyright system in the information era represented by DMCA, how we should balance protection to rights and others' freedom of action. As Mr. Wang Zejian said, the goal of tort laws was to give consideration to the two instead of being partial to rights of right holders. However, no matter what, one's own opinions should not be approved by misinterpreting facts.

5.2 Cases in Europe

5.2.1 Finnish CSS Cases in 2007

On May 25, 2007, the local court of Helsinki, Finland made an extraordinary judgment to the case about DVD-CSS technological measures. The judgment pointed out that since methods used to circumvent the CSS encryption technology were widely used in Internet, the CSS technology did not belong to effective technological measures stated in the copyright law, and thus the action that the defendant cracking the CSS technology was not an act of "circumventing technological measures". The reason was that the accusation of "cracking technological measures" suggested by procurators must be specific to effective technological measures. Since hackers from Norway cracked the CSS technological measures in 1999, some cracking software of this kind diffusion in internet were free, and some computers even preset cracking software. For common users, it became very easy to circumvent CSS technological measures, thus CSS technology could not realize the original goal of protecting DVD products. Since expert witnesses of the both parties approved this, CSS technological measures were no longer effective. Therefore, the accusation to the defendant should be rejected.

However, in 2004, in the case of "321 Studios v. Metro Goldwyn Mayer Studios"[3] with the same background, the local court of California, America made a totally opposite judgment with the idea that CSS technology was an effective technological measure. The CSS case in Finland was identical to that hackers from Norway released DeCSS procedures to crack CSS technology. In January 2006, the two defendants of the case also released the software used to crack CSS technological measures in Internet and provided services specializing in cracking and circumventing technological measures.[4] The local prosecutors appealed to the local court with the opinion of "cracking technological measures" and asked for corresponding penalty. But the local court of Helsinki refused the accusation of procurators.

---

[2]Felten v. RIAA Case No. 01-CV-2669, (filed D.N.J. 2001).

[3]307 F. Supp. 2d 1085 (N.D. Cal. 2004).

[4]http://www.pigdog.org/decss/, access date: 14/09/2015.

In the case of "321 Studios v. MGM", the defendant, a film company, accused a website that reprinted CSS decoding of violating laws about protection to technological measures. When deciding the efficiency of CSS technology, the local court of California, pointed out that we could not consider that it was no longer an effective technological measure because methods of circumventing CSS were widely spread in Internet. "Protecting rights of copyright holders effectively" stated in laws and regulations referred to prevent, restrict or limit others exercising rights of copyright holders in process of usual operations. In this case, CSS could undoubtedly control users accessing to DVD films effectively and protect rights of copyright holders.[5] And the court did not consider if the decoding to CSS technology could be realized through common sense and legal common tools or it must be with the help of specific cracking tools or services provided by hackers. On the contrary, the court believed the only legal ground to judge "efficiency" was whether CSS technology could prevent duplication in process of normal operations. According to the logic of unlimited popularization of the local court of California, any technological measures were effective.

The method of the Finland court that judged the "efficiency" of technological measures according to prevalence of cracking methods was hard to have fair and reasonable results. As we all know, most technological measures could be decoded and the convenience of internet could make a cracking method spread over to every common user rapidly. Therefore, under the condition of high technology, very few technological measures could be free from cracking. If most technological measures were considered non-effective according to this, chances of copyright holders using technological measures to protect their own interests were deprived.

It was noteworthy that the judgment made by the local court of Helsinki was based on the copyright amendment passed by Finland in 2005, and the amendment was formulated for implementation of the Orders.[6] The related clauses about technological measures were almost adopted by the copyright amendment of Finland as they were. Therefore, the judgment of the local court of Helsinki was the first specific explanation and application to relevant clauses of the Orders. Whether the explanation was completely right, it was worthy to be highly concerned. Judgment standards to "efficiency" of technological measures could decide whether a balance between protecting copyright and safeguarding public interests can be realized, which was a very complicated issue and could not be understood as a whole.

[5]Perry and Chisick [1], p. 261.

[6]http://www.engadget.com/2007/05/26/finnish-court-rules-css-dvd-protection-ineffective/, access date: 14/09/2015.

5.2.2 *Nintendo v. PC Box*

With regard to the legality of digital rights management measures, the Court of Justice of the European Union (CJEU) ruled on this issue for video games on January 23, 2014,[7] which made consistent trend of "positive decisions against the sellers of circumvention devices".[8] The Interactive Software Federation of Europe even held the opinion that, "CJEU has now confirmed a robust level of protection for technological protection measures in line with existing legal norms".[9]

The plaintiff Nintendo was a video game giant, who sued PC Box for infringement. Nintendo adopted technological measures to prevent illegal copies of its games being played on Nintendo DS and Nintendo Wii. PC Box is an Italian company that sells users mod chips and game copiers for playing unauthorized games on Nintendo systems by circumvention. In this case, PC Box argued that Nintendo's main purpose was not to protect copyright, but to prevent third party independent multimedia content being played on Nintendo's consoles and systems, which is not "proportionate" under the EU law.

Digital rights management again became "the target for attack". In other words, bargain on technological measures in Europe has incurred a constant chatter. In the EU, Article 6 (chapter III) of the Copyright Directive (Directive 2001/29/EC of the European Parliament and of the Council of 22 May 2001 on the harmonisation of certain aspects of copyright and related rights in the information society) provides protection of technological measures against circumvention actions.

The CJEU ruled that, although Article 6 of the Copyright Directive defines technological measures widely, the legal protection applies to digital rights management that are "proportionate" under the EU law.[10] In this case, relevant factors considered by the court for judging the proportionality of digital rights management:

- Whether the DRM prohibits devices or activities which have a "commercially significant purpose or use other than to circumvent the technical protection (emphasis added)"[11];
- A comparison of the cost and effectiveness of the DRM versus available alternatives;
- A survey of evidence on the purpose and actual use of a circumventing device: namely how often the device was used for copyright-infringing purposes and other purposes;

---

[7]Case C-355/12 Nintendo v. PC Box. (January 23, 2014).

[8]"CJEU Ruling in Nintendo v PC Box case CJEU Ruling in Nintendo v PC Box case". http://www.isfe.eu/about-isfe/news/cjeu-ruling-nintendo-v-pc-box-case.

[9]Ibid.

[10]Case C-355/12 Nintendo v. PC Box. (January 23, 2014).

[11]Recital 48 of the Directive 2001/29/EC of the European Parliament and of the Council of 22 May 2001 on the harmonisation of certain aspects of copyright and related rights in the information society.

- The current state of technology[12];
- (The copyright holder's particular intention of use is not relevant to the analysis.)[13]

Obviously, a copyright holder with 'proportionate' technological measures could be able to rely on the legal protection of digital rights management as a basis to challenge providers of technical devices. According to the CJEU, legal protection is "granted only with regard to [DRMs] preventing or eliminating, as regards works, acts not unauthorized by the right holder of copyright [. . .]" and "[t]hose measures must be suitable for achieving that objective and must not go beyond what is necessary for this purpose." Thus, "if such measures prevent also acts which do not require authorization then, if they could have been designed so as to prevent only acts which require authorization, they are disproportionate and do not qualify for protection."[14] In the circumstances, the right holders cannot rely on the digital rights management shield.[15]

5.3 Cases in China

5.3.1 *Jiangmin Company "Logic Lock" Case in 1997*

The case of "Jiangmin Company" in our country in 1997[16] can illustrate the problem. Jiangmin Company was a domestic enterprise that specialized in software development and its "KV300" antivirus software was welcomed by markets. However, the encryption measures of the software were cracked by a website named "China virus-island forum" and it provided users with "MK300V4" software which was exclusive to cracking encryption measures of "KV300". Losses of Jiangmin Company were conceivable. To copy with the cracking software, Jiangmin Company had to set a "logical key" in the newly developed software. Thus, once someone applied the "decoding key" provided by "China virus-island forum" to duplicate pirated software and ran it in computers, the "logical key" would be automatically started immediately and crashed computers of users. However, the action of Jiangmin Company was charged of endangering computer system by the Public Security Bureau of Beijing and was imposed with administrative penalty.

Another case is the China Academy of Building Research accusing a Mr. Zhang from Sichuan and "computer news" of Chongqing. The China Academy of Building Research developed the integrated CAD system software PKPM that held 20% of

[12]AG Opinion, Case C-355/12 Nintendo v. PC Box (September 19, 2013), para. 52.

[13]AG Opinion, Case C-355/12 Nintendo v. PC Box (September 19, 2013), para. 67.

[14]AG Opinion, Case C-355/12 Nintendo v. PC Box (September 19, 2013), para. 52.

[15]Strowel et al. [2].

[16]http://www.66law.cn/lawarticle/4397.aspx, access date: 14/09/2015.

market shares in the architectural design industry. Moreover, the system was sold abroad with over 6000 users and the annual output value of 20 million Yuan. However, the encrypting key disk of the software was cracked by Mr. Zhang from Sichuan and he developed the backup production software of the key disk for the unique use of manufacturing key disks that could start various modules of PKPM system software. Although knowing the action of Mr. Zhang was not authorized, "Computer news" of Chongqing still advertised his pirated key disks and marketed unencrypted key disks of 21 modules of PKPM software through the software department and various exclusive shops. Each time when the defendant sold an unencrypted key disk, the plaintiff would loss a market share, let alone potential shares.[17] In 2008, Microsoft started a new round of legitimate value-added plans independently: if users of WindowsXP did not pass the genuine advantage, their computers would be blackened once an hour and there would be a permanent noticing and reminding dialog box in bottom right of screens; and if Office users did not pass the genuine advantage, a "non-original" mark would be added in 30 days later. Microsoft claimed the only purpose of the actions was to help users identify whether the software in their computers was original and they were reminders in good faith.[18]

Even for a technological measure legally proved by law, its implementation would be limited to a degree. Implementation of legitimate technological measures must not endanger the safety of computer information system and legitimate users' right, damage legal interests of customers, infringe commercial secrets as well as privacy right and reputation right of the public, and use technological measures for industry monopoly and unfair competition.[19] In addition, technological measures should also spare a room for intelligent use of the public. The action of "blackening screens" of Microsoft brought panic and inconvenience to users, and even affected normal use of other legitimate software in computers of users, being suspected of infringing users' right to use other legal properties. The genuine advantage process of Microsoft collected, monitored, and tracked data of users and even conducted some operations, putting individual privacy and commercial secrets of users in an unsafe state, being suspected of infringing privacy right and trade secret right of users.[20]

Without permission from administrative enforcement authorities and judicial departments, Microsoft blackened and imposed pirated mark to computers of users was an act of enforcing laws by itself with no judgment but depended on its genuine advantage alone, thus it was suspected of abusing rights and infringing reputation right of users.[21] Technological measures of copyright could not go beyond necessary

[17]http://www.66law.cn/lawarticle/4397.aspx, access date: 14/09/2015.

[18]Ibid.

[19]http://www1.any2000.com/Articles/show/1563_1.htm, access date: 14/09/2015.

[20]Ibid 384.

[21]http://searchsecurity.techtarget.com/feature/Spotlight-article-Domain-8-Laws-Investigations-and-Ethics, access date: 14/09/2015.

limits of copyright protection and could not be evolved into revenge and punishment to final users of software and go against the legal idea of “anyone cannot consider himself as the judge”.[22] Software copyright should be and must be protected in practice, which is not only the interest appeal of Microsoft but also the guarantee to development of the software industry in China. However, rights should be exercised through legitimate approaches and methods. If surpassing necessary limits allowed by laws, actions like Microsoft blackening screens could evolve into “copyright violence” and fall into the dilemma of “answering violence with violence”.[23]

5.3.2 Beijing Jingdiao Technology Ltd. v. Shanghai Naikai Electronic Technology Ltd.[24]

In the case, the plaintiff claimed that he developed the CNC engraving system which mainly consisted of three parts, namely, CAD/CAM software or JDPaint software, engraving CNC system and basic machine. The application of the system relies on two computers, one is used to processing and programming computer and the other is a numerical control computer. The two computers that run two different procedures need to exchange data, or to say, data file. To be more specific, JDPaint software generates Eng data files by processing and programming computers, and then the data files are received by the control software run in numerical control computers and turned into processing commands. The plaintiff has copyright to the above-mentioned JDPaint, which is not sold to the public but equipped in digital engraving machines produced by the plaintiff. In early days of 2006, the plaintiff found that the defendant advertising that the NC—100 CNC engraving and milling machine can fully support all engraving Eng files in his website.

The above-mentioned Ncstudio software in the CNC can read Eng data files output from JDPaint, but the plaintiff had encrypted the Eng format.[25] Therefore, the defendant did circumvent or destroy technological measures adopted by the plaintiff to protect his software copyright by illegally decoding the encryption of Eng format, thus the defendant did infringe the copyright of the plaintiff. The action of the defendant allowed other NC engraving machines can receive Eng files illegally, reducing sales volume of engraving machines of the plaintiff and causing economic loss. Thus, the plaintiff requested the court have the following judgment[26]: 1. the defendant must stop the development and marketing of CNC system that supported various Eng formats of JDPaint; 2. the defendant must extend an apology in

[22]Meadows [3].

[23]Ibid 386.

[24]上海市第一中级人民法院 民事判决书 2006年沪一中民五(知)初第134号, http://china.findlaw.cn/chanquan/zhuzuoquanfa/zzqal/20316.html, access date: 14/09/2015.

[25]Ibid.

[26]Ibid.

non-advertising space except the center part of Xinmin Evening News and Strait News; and 3. the defendant must pay for economic loss of 485,000 Yuan.

The defendant argued that[27]: 1. the Ncstudio software developed by the defendant was control software of the engineering industry that applied for copyright protection on December 6, 2001,[28] while the JDPaint software whose copyright was possessed by the plaintiff was graphic software of the industry of arts and crafts manufacturing, and the two were different in interface, function and application environment; and 2. Ncstudio software can read Eng data files output by DJPaint software because Eng data file and Eng format used by the file did not under protection of computer software, thus the action of the defendant was not an infringing act and did not need to assume compensation liability appealed by the plaintiff. The plaintiff made clear that JDPaint software and Ncstudio software were not identical since Eng files output by JDPaint software was data files of Eng format.[29]

In April 2006, the entrusted agent of the plaintiff applied for evidence perpetuation of relevant information in Internet to the Notary Office of Mentougou District of Beijing. The agent used the computer and other Internet facilities in the Notary Office to search and log in www.weihong.com.cn, open columns including company news, product introduction, activities and news, and hot news in the home page of the company and printed related reports as well under supervision of notaries.[30] The Notary Office of Mentougou District of Beijing proved it with a notarization.[31] The reports in the columns mentioned above included: in December 2005, Naiky released the NC-1000 engraving and milling machine that fully supported various Eng files and was developed because of users' appreciation to the software JDPaintV5.19.[32]

Moreover, it was found out that Ncstudio software can read Eng files output by JDPaint software of the plaintiff, that is to say, Ncstudio software was compatible with Eng files output by JDPaint software. The court thought the dispute focus of this case was whether that the Ncstudio software of the defendant was compatible with Eng files of JDPaint software of the plaintiff infringed software copyright of the plaintiff; in other words, whether Eng files under encryption protection which were output from JDPaint software of the plaintiff was within the protection scope of computer software.[33]

---

[27]Ibid.

[28]Ibid.

[29]http://www.lsbar.com/caseContent/5141, access date: 14/09/2015.

[30]Ibid.

[31](2006)沪高民三(知)终字第110号, http://china.findlaw.cn/info/wenshu/fayuan/minpan/208471.html, access date: 14/09/2015.

[32]Ibid.

[33]Ibid; and also, http://www.pkulaw.cn/fulltext_form.aspx?Db=pfnl&Gid=117529046&EncodingName=, access date: 14/09/2015.

The plaintiff believed that since JDPaint software whose copyright was possessed by the plaintiff was mated with his engraving machines and it was not offered to the public, moreover, the plaintiff adopted three-level encryption to Eng file output from JDPaint software that it cannot be directly read through other control systems except engraving control system, that Ncstudio software of the defendant read Eng files was an act of circumventing or destroying technological measures adopted by the plaintiff to protect his software copyright, thus infringing the software copyright of the plaintiff. While the defendant argued that Eng format was a method to record geometric data imported by users after procedures of JDPaint software were performed by computer, it was not a software program but a treating process of JDPaint software to data and its thought of describing mathematical concepts. Furthermore, Eng data file was not a software program and cannot be operated and executed by computers. The data file was not included in mediums released by JDPaint software or in installation directory of the software after software was installed.[34] Therefore, both Eng files and Eng format were not under protection of computer software.

According to relevant stipulations in Copyright Law of the People's Republic of China, the court believed that computer software was under the protection of the Copyright Law. Article 2 of the Regulations for the Protection of Computer Software[35] stipulated that computer software referred to computer programs and related documents. Further, Article 3 said: 1. computer program was a coding instruction sequence that can be executed by devices which had information processing capability like computer with the purpose of realizing certain results, or a signifying instruction sequence or signifying statement sequence that could be converted into coding instruction sequence automatically. The source program and target program of a same computer are the one thing; and 2. files were literal data and charts used to describe contents, constitutions, design, functional specification, development, test results and application methods, such as design instruction of programs, flow chart and user's manual. Therefore, we can know that the current laws just protect programs and files of computer software. In this case, the copyright registration certification of computer software provided by the plaintiff proved that he possessed the copyright of JDPaint software whose programs and related files should be protected by laws. Thereafter, the plaintiff claimed that Ncstudio software of the defendant reading Eng files output from JDPaint software had infringed the software copyright, thus whether Eng file was a part of JDPaint software which was under legal protection was the focus of this case.

After investigation, Eng files output from JDPaint software were data files, and their output format Eng format was the result of target program of JDPaint software executed by computers; while the data files of this format were not a coding instruction sequence or signifying instruction sequence or coding statement sequence and could not be run or operated by computers. In addition, according to

[34] Ibid.

[35] Ibid; 《计算机软件保护条例》.

the statement of the plaintiff, Eng files were data files generated from JDPaint software run in processing and programming computers. It can be known that data recorded by the files were not exclusive to JDPaint software of the plaintiff but were generated from engraving processing information input by software users. Therefore, data and document formats included in data files of Eng format were not programs of JDPaint software, thus they were not under protection of computer software and should not be protected by laws.[36] Accordingly, the plaintiff argued that Ncstudio software's capability of reading Eng files was compatibility of software and data files in fact. It lacked legal basis that the plaintiff accused the defendant of software copyright infringement since his software received Eng files when the plaintiff did not market JDPaint software to the public and encrypted data files of Eng format, the court did not give its support.

References

1. Perry M, Chisick CM (2000) Copyright and anti-circumvention: growing pains in a digital millennium. N Z Intellect Prop J: 261
2. Strowel A, Clancy M, Kim H-E (2014) The CJEU's Nintendo v. PC Box: 'Proportionate' DRMs? http://www.insidetechmedia.com/2014/02/20/the-cjeus-nintendo-v-pc-box-proportionate-drms/. February 20th, 2014
3. Meadows C. Where digital rights meet fair use rights: the Unlocking Technology Act of 2013. http://pc.answers.com/file-sharing/where-digital-rights-meet-fair-use-rights-the-unlocking-technology-act-of-2013. Accessed 14 Sep 2015

[36] http://www.lawxp.com/case/c11963.html, access date: 14/09/2015.

Chapter 6
Digital Rights Management Practices

6.1 iTunes Model

Computers, internet and digital communication technologies have surrounded our daily life globally. The development of digital technologies, especially networks, facilitates knowledge spreading. The communication of information has broken through the national boundary, which seems a limitation in physical circumstance. On the contrary, excessively restriction may result in the public's privacy or other issues. Digital technologies improved people's life greatly, which initiates an innovated business model for copyright protection. iTunes Music Store model has been deemed as one of the classic case on digital rights management in digital copyright times.[1]

6.1.1 The Emergence of iTunes: Substitute for Illegal File-Sharing Platform

P2P technologies, as a "Peer to Peer" file-sharing communication approach, have broken the monotonous way for exchanging information in digital circumstance.[2] Unlike other downloading means, which are based on "server-terminal", when the global three major record companies brought Napster into the lawsuit eddy for its liability of downloading music, the centralized model of file-sharing communication had seemed to foresee its misfortune. Later, the record companies also sued the representatives of decentralized communication model, like Grosker and KazaA. During that period, these servers made profit by advertisement input, as digital information spreading to the public had been free of charge online.

[1] Farrand [1], pp. 508–513.

[2] Yang [2].

C. Xu, *Regulatory Model for Digital Rights Management*,
https://doi.org/10.1007/978-981-15-1995-6_6

Most traditional communication platforms were operated by the same business strategies. Even Napster intended to negotiate with record companies for a "value-added" service as a profit allocation method, which was eventually dismissed. The combination of contracts law, copyright law and communication technologies has been comprehended in iTunes architecture, which integrates various copyright systems from transnational perspective.[3]

The internationalized process of iTunes also presents the course that how the policies of Apple Company are employed. It is fruitful and effective of iTunes way in different copyright holders' eyes for digital rights management implementation in copyright protection field. iTunes music stores, in this regard, has obtained more record authorization or licenses, and multiple digital works in diverse countries or regions.[4]

6.1.2 *iTunes Online Music Store (iTunes Store): Prospective on Digital Rights Management Model*

Nowadays, intellectual assets have been the most essential property type compared with other property varieties. The success operation, at least at current stage, of iTunes platform shows that digital technologies has been "a nuisance, not a mortal threat" to the copyright system. The establishment of relevant copyright law environment is in favor of novel copyrighted works transaction models.[5]

Prof. Jane. C. Ginsberg has pointed out that iTunes would be an authorized highly valued—and marketable platform where digital rights management technologies embedded in copyrighted works can be downloaded. Ginsberg believed that iTunes has commendably combined digital technologies, copyright protection and controlled-access of copyrighted works from the public. In other words, iTunes, in essence, has achieved the goal that the benefit of the copyright holders and the general public would be balanced.[6]

6.1.2.1 Merits of iTunes Online Music Stores

In America, iTunes works well based on its favorable copyright law, pragmatism of commercial incentives mechanism, as well as obvious local protectionism. Constant

---

[3]Gasser [3].

[4]Sharpe and Arewa [4], p. 331.

[5]Rayna [5].

[6]Klebanow and Wu [6].

infringement lawsuits initiated by copyright holders and the vast compensation claims have been regarded as a strong deterrent so that a large number of internet users dare not to download unauthorized music or other copyrighted works online.[7]

Vocational pirates has been struck severely, on the one hand, at the joint function of copyright regulations and digital anti-piracy technologies. On the other hand, the general public inclines to adapt high quality service and stable technical support from authorized internet service providers or legal platforms. From the angle of iTunes' strategy effect, the vivo sphere of piracy has been shrunk, since the arisen time of digital rights management technologies uniting with legal foundation extends longer, and the digital rights management scheme in digital copyright market perfects degree of gradual adequacy of comprehensive system for sure.[8]

Apple, Inc., as the distinguished brand in digital technology field, has taken upon the whole industrial chain from hardware (iPod), software (Media Player Software) to internet service (iTunes Online Music Stores). All related marketing and economic actors included in this chain were organized and processed by Apple as its business model. "Hardware + Content" pattern turns iTunes into the sole official synchronous software with iPod. iTunes——iPod, succeeded reciprocally whereupon as the synonyms that were tightly associated, while the fashionable designed appearance of iPod and its remarkable performance promoted these fans of Apple products to grow steadily.[9]

This so called "Seamless" business model, thus far, has sought out a fresh channel for earning profit for musicians, copyright holders and Apple, Inc. Foremost, the consumption market position orientated by Apple, Inc. was highly targeted, as it signed a series of agreements or licenses with the Five Record Companies (EMI, Universal, Warner Bros., Sony Music Entertainment and BMG (Sony Music Entertainment and BMG merged as Sony BMG). It built a copyrighted works database which appealed to the consumers irresistibly and accumulated enough financing of marketing.[10] Further, iTunes itself offers numerous customized superior service to the users. For instance, the retrieval mode of five-star evaluation system would provide the perfect reference datum or information of price discrimination in future practices.[11]

---

[7]Ibid.

[8]Solo [7], p. 169.

[9]Ibid 407.

[10]Heald [8].

[11]Ibid 407.

6.1.2.2 Disadvantages of iTunes Online Music Store

Technology swings between two worlds, which are unrestricted world (free world) and property world.[12] From the perspective of technological protection measures, iTunes is not compatibility with other media players except iPod. In other words, if the consumers would like to be served with high quality and optimal compatibility, they have to choose iTunes. FairPlay, created and used by Apple, Inc., is a digital rights management technology, which largely locked its users on iPods. However, if users have chosen the iPod, it does not mean they have selected iTunes.[13]

The absolute protection from technological protection measures, which are usually aiming at users' access, seems impossible, although diverse companies have been sparing no effort on technologies development. Technological protection measures are increasingly employed in digital copyright area, which customers were compelled to pay out more, but consumers would hardly recognize their existence. As far as we know, technologies are vulnerable, vast amount of technology adopted would result in potentially privacy and security issues.[14]

Alternatively, if the iTunes users are purely treated as "consumers", one fact definitely will be overlooked: it might be derived when most works are employed by the users. Derived exploitation of original works may create new works, which turns simple consumption into the creation. At one time, if the internet service providers or copyright holders overstressed the digital rights management, it would pose a threat to the basic "peer to peer" structure on internet. This deterrent has been attracted our keen vigilance since technological protection measures has until now been undoubtedly a decent option, not an ultimate solution though in the future. The combination of technological protection measures and legal contracts in iTunes model has intensified exclusiveness, which aggravated the non-equivalence position of the negotiation between the licensors and licensees.[15]

iTunes business model implies that digital copyright legal control has been replaced by technological control. It also potentially shows a serious case that information or message could be controlled or manipulated by private person when the obligees design a series of programming codes for a new "copyright law" that is in favor of themselves. Licenses for end-users became the public rules, while internet content providers turned themselves to the rules-makers. These articles in the licenses often challenged the boundaries of the current copyright law system. The previous balance between copyrighted works protection and

---

[12]Rowe [9].

[13]Ibid.

[14]The Recorded Music Industry and the Emergence of Online Music Distribution: Innovation in the Absence of Copyright (Reform) George Washington Law Review, Max Planck Institute for Intellectual Property & Competition Law Research Paper No.11-09.Vol.79, Issue 6, pp. 1783–1813 (2011).

[15]Ibid.

information freedom has been destroyed, which even jeopardized the exception system of copyright law as well.[16]

Currently, many countries or companies has requested Apple, Inc. to remove FairPlay protection as they believed that limitation from iTunes business model has violated interoperability or consumers' rights and benefit. It is considered by the French parliament that no interoperability of Apple products would be a monopoly of digital market. Thus, the French parliament once was supposed to establish a specific law to push Apple, Inc. to a compromise on the interoperability with other digital players of its music in 2006.[17]

6.1.2.3 Copyright Mode in the Future

In 1990s, copyright substitution issue has been emphasized by the Western scholars along with the rapid development of digital technologies. The proposal on substitutive copyright means put forward involved creative commons, copyleft models and so forth. Nowadays, creative commons is not only used, but also widely spread in digital circumstance and educational institutions.[18] It is admitted that creative commons has been accepted to take the fancy of aim of copyright legislation that intends to at least protect the interest of the public. However, it is impossible for creative commons to be expected as popular as iTunes Online Music Stores.[19]

Many records producers are unwilling to throw their works into the public domain at once or in a relatively short period. In a way, it would be impractical to promote this strategy in a large-scale. The licensing mechanism of creative commons, notwithstanding has portrayed a distinct and latent feasible plan under international framework; it would be abortively operated in case there is no any good toll system for profit collection and property right.

It is distinguished between digital environment and analogue surroundings where copyrighted works are created and communicated. As this difference would not fade away shortly, it is impossible to implement the same copyright regulations in these two disparate worlds. It is insisted that traditional copyright law should protect works fixed on physical medium, and the protection issue of digital works might be dealt with a new approach which is improved from traditional solution accordingly.[20]

iTunes affords a particular business model of "Online collective licensing fees on price"(网上集体许可对价征收使用费),which benefits all participants at each link. This business model, has simplified copyright law, at the same time, has internally

---

[16]Ibid.

[17]Laurence Frost [10].

[18]Fisher [11].

[19]http://freemusicarchive.org/member/chriszabriskie/blog/Why_I_Went_CC_BY, Access date: 14/09/2015.

[20]Ze Mer [12].

adapted a dual-track approach within copyright architecture. It is deemed as a supplement with high feasibility of current copyright scheme.

Some thought iTunes is a monopolistic entity essentially in digital products market; some disliked the bigger expense charged from iTunes business model; some advocated that there should be a substitutive flexible system for Apple, Inc. At the present phase, whatever arguments on iTunes or Apple, Inc. are dejected, as iTunes model has been proved the effective idea among few choices.

iTunes has applied comprehensively contract law, copyright law and technological means to create an international legal system for downloading music globally, which has been proved feasible. The triumph of iTunes operation has largely restrained the furious piracy or infringements online; likewise, copyright protection consciousness has embedded in the mind of the public.[21] iTunes freely spread or provided millions of digital works to the public when it helped copyright holders' to defend their interest, which coincides with copyright law's goal. In this regard, Apple, Inc. or at least iTunes has succeeded partly.

6.2 Amazon Kindle

E-book readers and tablet PCs are hardware products for reading e-books. When allowing readers read, they have many other merits such as portability, high capacity and environmental protection.[22] Among them, e-book readers are devices specializing in reading of e-books. Compared with printed books, it is just a kind of change of medium. While tablet PCs integrate multi functions like reading e-books, watching movies and listening music, reading is just a segmenting function of it. To guide revolution of e-books, Bezos started to organize a group to develop Kindle readers as early as 2004.[23] After three years of experiment, the first generation of Kindle came out in 2007. Later on, he upgraded and updated Kindle readers several times. Furthermore, he has issued the series of Kindle Fire tablet PCs since 2011. To sum up, Amazon e-book reading devices have the following characteristics:

6.2.1 High Updating Speed of Devices

In November 2007, Amazon released its first Kindle readers, and they were recognized and welcomed by markets and customers quickly after marketed, causing the

[21]Ibid 407.

[22]Larkey [13].

[23]Campbell [14], p. 1.

situation that was out of stock.[24] Very soon, Amazon updated products quickly and released a new generation of Kindle products. In February 2009, Kindle 2 was released; in May of the same year, Kindle DX was born; in August 2010, Kindle 3 was released; Kindle Touch and Kindle 4 came into being in September 2011; and in Sep. 2012, Kindle Paperwhite was released. Meanwhile, to meet challenge of iPad, Amazon released its first tablet PC Kindle FirCc in September of 2011 as well as Kindle Fire 2 and Kindle Fire HD in September of the next year. During the short five years, Kindle products were upgraded and updated several times, manifesting the power of Amazon, a scientific and technical corporation driven by technology and innovation, and its concerns to Kindle products. Moreover, Amazon brought readers with better reading experience.[25]

6.2.2 Abundant Supported Formats

Although Kindle e-books enjoy the unique AZW format, document formats supported by Kindle readers are increasing, from indirect support of PDF format to direct support, from AZW to AZW3, from simple MP3 audio format to Audible (Audible Enhanced(AA、 AAX))、 AAC、 MPS and WAV, and so on. The enrichment of supported formats of Kindle readers expanded documents accessible to readers and reduced fussy conversion between formats and devices.[26]

6.3 Adobe Content Server

Digital rights management products of Adobe support cutting-edge digital rights management framework, mainly including Adobe Content Servers and Adobe eBook Readers. Adobe Content Server mainly takes the responsibility of establishing, encrypting, packaging and releasing contents. Adobe has the leading encryption technology authorized by the RSA lab. At present, it adopts 64 and 128 level encryption. Coordinating with Adobe Content Server, Adobe eBook Reader will lock downloaded e-books into personal book stack of Adobe Reader

---

[24]Ibid.

[25]Lehdonvirta [15].

[26]Hovenkamp [16].

automatically so that they could not be sent to other users unless lending or presenting permission is given.[27]

Based on Adobe PDF, Adobe Content Server can guarantee the highest security standards and access control while sending hi-fi e-books and other digital contents to users all over the world. Its major advantage lies in that PDF format is widely used and can be easily integrated with currently published and distributed software.[28]

6.4 Foxit Digital Rights Management

The Foxit Software Company put forward the solution of Foxit digital rights management which had its own characteristics, for example, operating authorization of supporting sending same digital contents to several devices or users, realization of encryption requirement which has nothing to do with format, separation treatment of certification of users and data encryption, which has realized double insurance, adoption of mixed encryption with multiple keys, which has improved safety strength effectively, support of recognition related to hardware and system environment, and permission of customizing digital rights management encryption scheme according to requirements of publishers and content providers.[29] The Foxit digital publishing platform based on the scheme is also online officially, but the platform does not support off-line reading so far.

6.5 Ubisoft and Blizzard

Blizzard officially confirmed that it would give up digital rights management on-line certification system on Assassin's Creed: Brotherhood. Digital rights management was a specialized anti-piracy system developed by Blizzard. In its contest with hackers, it allowed Assassin's Creed to keep a well record of not being decoded for a long time, but it did not survive from decoding of hackers, instead, it brought much inconvenience to users of original copies.[30] Did the Assassin's Creed: Brotherhood's abandonment of the digital rights management system indicate that Blizzard gave in to crackers?

Recently, press spokesperson of Blizzard announced that the Assassin's Creed: Brotherhood would give up the digital rights management system, which was acclaimed by many players. As early as last week, when the steam platform did

[27]Desai [17].

[28]Ibid.

[29]http://blog.foxitsoftware.com/the-basics-of-pdf-security/, access date: 14/09/2015.

[30]Andrei Dumitrescu, 'Nintendo, Blizzard and Ubisoft Are the Best Videogame Developers', https://twitter.com/intent/follow?screen_name=softpediagames, access date: 14/09/2015.

not list digital rights management information of the work, some people had this thought. Since the existence of the digital rights management on-line anti-piracy certificate system, disputes kept going; moreover, it brought inconvenience to many original players.[31] However, Blizzard claimed that the Assassin's Creed giving up the digital rights management did not mean other new works would either. The company had not given up the anti-piracy mechanism so far.[32]

6.5.1 Blizzard was Proud of the Digital Rights Management System

The system of Blizzard was opened with the release of The Settlers. After Assassin's Creed 2, which took a long time for hackers to crack, Blizzard was very proud, and the high-level managers once said: if we did not have confidence to the anti-piracy technology, we would never release the PC edition. We cannot say that the new Digital Rights Management system must be created by God and it was perfect or could not be cracked, but we had confidence in it. After the release of Assassin's Creed 2 in March 2010, the digital rights management system did help the game against cracking of hackers, allowing the game free from cracking of any organizations for over one month. It was luckier than other PC games in the recent years which suffered cracking very soon. However, in April, the famous decoding organization "Skid Row" announced it had cracked the digital rights management system of Blizzard, and Skid Row wrote in "Readme" that it was grateful to Blizzard for bringing a so interesting challenge, but the small problem was not enough to let us shrink back.[33] Next, you should pay more attention to production of games instead of the digital rights management with so many manpower and material resources. What else, it brought a disaster to your loyal legal users. We cracked it just because we wanted to make life simpler.[34]

When developing the system, Blizzard did spend a huge number of manpower and material resources and had high expectations to it, hoping it could get rid of the situation of being cracked, but the results were disappointing. What is worse, the digital rights management brought inconvenience to original game players. The system required original users maintain the on-line state all the time. For users who could not connect Internet, they cannot go along even for single player games; moreover, if servers or network which were used by Blizzard or places where players were broke down, the game would not run and many players would curse Blizzard for destroying game progress; besides, if Blizzard planned to stop maintaining the digital rights management server in a old game, player could not

[31]Ibid.

[32]Ibid.

[33]http://www.wired.co.uk/news/archive/2011-08/01/ubisoft, access date: 14/09/2015.

[34]Ibid.

continue to play it as well. Many original users were dissatisfied with the system of Blizzard.[35]

Players were pleased that Blizzard would not use the digital rights management system in Assassin's Creed: Brotherhood. Surely, original users were delighted because they could not put up with the stupid setting of going online from time to time anymore. While users of pirated apps would be more pleased, there would have no mysteries about decoding the game. Did Blizzard give in to crackers? Certainly, the thought was over conceit. It was believed that Blizzard giving up the digital rights management out of more considerations to experience of original users.[36]

At present, among popular games in PC platform, although single plot is still a key point concerned by players, it is online multiplayer mode that players spend most time on, and the focus of games is partial to producing more wonderful multiplayer modes. It just needs several or dozens of hours for players to experience single plot, while online multiplayer games can make players have passion for the game for months. Among most foreign games, users can enjoy online services freely for life only if their purchase legitimate games. Although users of pirated apps can play parts of games, they could not enjoy online services like players of legitimate copies. Not a few players would buy the legitimate one if they think the game is cool after having an experience of single plot and use CDKEY to join in online fighting.[37]

In Assassin's Creed: Brotherhood, the hero did not fight alone anymore, instead, he built his own assassin organization. The news before claimed the online multiplayer part would be more wonderful. I believed it was this that attracted more people to purchase legitimate copies. Blizzard giving up using the digital rights management did not mean it gave in to piracy but just its strategic shift.[38]

Cracking has been a headache to game developers who have spent a lot in fighting against crackers with no desirable results. Actions like Blizzard using the DRM system to prevent piracy but affecting original players are not advisable. However, with the improvement of online modes, more and more players purchase legitimate copies, which could be an effective way to compete with pirates.

---

[35]"Dear Ubisoft and Blizzard: Please stop this madness", http://www.wired.co.uk/news/archive/2011-08/01/ubisoft, access date: 14/09/2015.

[36]Ibid.

[37]"Blizzard 'Surprised' By Fans Outrage Over Diablo 3 Online Requirement", http://megagames.com/news/blizzard-%E2%80%98surprised%E2%80%99-fans-outrage-over-diablo-3-online-requirement. August 7, 2011.

[38]Hilbert Hagedoorn, "Blizzard: DRM a 'losing battle'", http://www.guru3d.com/news-story/blizzard-drm-a-losing-battle.html. 05/28/2010.

6.6 National Digital Library Project in China[39]

In 1995, the national library started to track the research and development of the international digital library and had accumulated a large number of technologies and experience. In 1996, the national 8630 key project, which was based on research and development of the multimedia information retrieval system, was under the control of the computer technology research institution of the Chinese Academy of Sciences and the national library to track and study the research and development of retrieval systems of international digital libraries.[40] In 1997, the project of SGML library of the Ministry of Culture was developed by the national library and the computer research institution of the Peking University. In the same year, the national key scientific and technological project—China pilot digital library approved by the State Development Planning Commission was finished by the six libraries at provincial or municipal level under the guidance of the national library. In 1998, the 863/306 project—digital library system of the Ministry of Science and Technology was controlled by the national library and the computer technology research institution of the Chinese Academy of Sciences.[41]

In 2000, the 863/300 project—China digital library application system with the China hi-speed information pilot network as operating environment was assumed by the national library and the hi-speed pilot network group of the Ministry of Science and Technology.[42] In the same year, the national library was on the control of the study of Chinese metadata standards made by the Ministry of Culture. In 2002, the Ministry of Science and Technology approved the project of study on digital library standards of China and the national library took part in the project. Earlier studies on Chinese digital libraries mainly focused on technologies of processing, releasing and multimedia, but now it expands to legal status, scientific management system and long-term storage of digital resources gradually. Moreover, some problems of earlier studies on digital libraries have been cleared gradually.

6.6.1 Copyright Protection and Construction of Digital Library

Because of the effect of carriers and recording methods adopted by traditional literature, some of them were damaged. To preserve the literature and support long-term use of them, digital libraries applied digital technologies to convert traditional literature into digital ones to pass on the knowledge of the literature.

[39]"国家数字图书馆计划".

[40]http://www.nlc.gov.cn/dsb_footer/gygt/ghgy/. Access date: 14/09/2015.

[41]Ibid.

[42]http://news.xinhuanet.com/it/2002-05/27/content_411044.htm.

Studies of later generations on the literature can be done through digitalized methods, achieving the goal of studying and reserving the literature. However, when protecting and serving to the literature with digitalized methods, we must protect the copyright so that we can on the one hand meet needs of readers to digitalized literature and on the other hand prevent interests of copyright holders from being infringed.

Therefore, copyright is one issue that digital libraries encounter with and should be solved gradually. At present, system designs of digital libraries mainly adopt the two methods: the one is centralized system design and the other is distributed system design. DILAS designed by Shenzhen library is a centralized system design that redesigns and re-implements the automatic system of the library and the digital library system. For units which have realized library automation, the design makes it easy to construct a digital library system according to catalogue, because traditional library is mature for management of physical resources and added functions, like collecting and manufacturing, publishing and serving, and management of digital resources.

Considering that the digital library system of the national library is confront with complex data, a large number of digital resources and diversified services, we adopt the distributed system design identical to CALIS and CSDL. However, it is different to them in design philosophy because it stresses on the integration of automation of traditional libraries and digital libraries.[43]

Moreover, the library system and the digital library system is integrated through standard interface, and the whole system adopts external standards which allow libraries, resource service structures, and even network search engine companies all over the world can have interoperation and communication with the national library easily and conveniently.[44] The Z39.88 protocol of the national library and the search engine of Google have been linked and have passed system tests of domestic products of Open URL protocol. The OAI protocol has passed the tests of the international OAI protocol; the Z39.50 system has been linked with libraries at home and abroad; and the agent servers of the national library can connect with the authorized resources at home or abroad.

The national library has conducted the exchange between MARC and XML through OAI protocol and has related studies on exchange between MARC and XML. ILL is mature inter-lending among libraries. URI is resource scheduling protocol of digital libraries which has integrated several objects scheduling modes like URL, URN, ISBN, ISSN and DOI.[45] Only resources requiring certification need the resource scheduling protocol, while resources requiring no certification are processed through open linking protocol. Z39.90 protocol is the network reference consultation protocol, through which the national library can coordinate with

---

[43]http://www.nlc.gov.cn/index_old.htm, access date: 14/09/2015.

[44]http://www.cdlc.cn/, access date: 14/09/2015.

[45]http://www.yuan0.cn/Article/462698.html, access date: 14/09/2015.

reference consultation network of all national libraries and can combine with the reference consultation network of CALIS and CSDL by adding a conversion layer.[46]

(1) Metadata processing system. The resource producing systems of libraries are richer. The traditional library automatic system is transformed to national union catalog system after being improved, catalog records of which are not only data resources but also data used for resource management. Users of the system include both cataloguing institutions of the national library and that of all libraries in the country. The public can use the OPAC system to retrieve catalog records, to locate corresponding libraries, and to locate various digital resource supply system, virtual reference resources and interlibrary loan by opening the linking protocol.
(2) Literature digitalized system would assume the job of converting traditional literature in libraries into digital ones, allowing information in traditional literature spread through digital resources, making it possible to print unique copies for preservation, and keeping and publishing digital contents.
(3) Knowledge processing system mainly takes the job of constructing single-point knowledge and systematic knowledge, which is the core of knowledge processing of digital libraries. Processed knowledge can be preserved and published.[47] Website obtaining system mainly gains corresponding websites and webpage from obtaining strategies and themes and conducts metadata processing for storage or publishing. Resource presentation system is a specialized system for publishing agencies submitting online resources and college essays which are preserved or published according to agreements. Purchased resources can be published or preserved.[48]
(4) Literature delivery system is a service system that delivers copies of corresponding physical resources to service systems of users through various methods according to requirements of users, which is one of extended networked and digitalized businesses of traditional libraries. Rapid printing system would reprint resources lacked in the national library for long-term storage, and copy unique copies of the national library and generate microfilms as well.[49]
(5) Resources publishing and service system mainly includes metadata retrieval system, old full-text retrieval system, full-text retrieval system, and online reading system (reading books, listening music and watching video) based on digital resources. Portal system and universal retrieval system are convenient for users to access to look for resources they need.

[46]http://lib.jlau.edu.cn/wxcd.htm, access date: 14/09/2015.

[47]Ibid.

[48]Ibid.

[49]http://www.huawei.com/cn/, access date: 14/09/2015.

6.7 China Unicom/China Telecom Platform

The ever-increasing value-added services of Internet and mobile network increases demand of digital contents to digital rights management. Mobile digital rights management has brought new energy to wireless service. High technologies such as smart phones, broadband, 3G and 4G enrich people's mobile life.[50] Reading books, listening music, playing games and watching movies with phones can be seen everywhere. Phone has become a new platform for value-add of contents. How to obtain interests of copyright? It is necessary to bring mobile value-added services to digital rights management.

Mobile digital rights management products include server and client. As a new link of the digital industry chain, manufacturers must cooperate with CP/SP, operators, third-party platforms and manufacturers of terminal equipment during the development process. In corporation with CP/SP, cooperation involving wireless business is not much, wireless businesses can be often seen in cooperation with operators, third-party platforms and manufacturers of terminal equipment. Operators need manufacturers of digital rights management to build a mobile digital rights management platform to maintain servers and provide testing services to 3G.[51] Third-party platforms must develop service ports to access to Digital Rights Management servers, and manufacturers of terminal equipment should cooperate with manufacturers of digital rights management according to digital rights management client.[52]

OMA (Open Mobile Alliance) is an organization initiated by leaders of the mobile industry. Founded in June 2002, the organization consists of nearly 300 world leading mobile manufacturers, manufacturers of mobile terminal equipment, providers of mobile network equipment, providers of information technology, and providers of contents and services, for example, Nokia, IBM, Motorola, Alcatel-Lucent, China Mobile and China Unicom. OMA created the famous digital rights management standards. In November 2002, it issued the first international mobile digital rights management standard—OMA digital rights management 1.0 Enabler Release which provided guidance to establish a digital rights management system in mobile network. After OMA digital rights management 1.0 was released, giants of the industry including Nokia and Motorola did develop and found many problems, thus they had several discussions and modifications on OMA digital rights management 1.0. On June 14, 2005, OMA issued OMA digital rights management V2.0, formulated a security and trust mode based on PKI, released the function system and language standards of rights description of mobile digital rights management, digital content format (DCF) of digital rights management and the rights object acquisition protocol (ROAP).

[50]http://www.yhwit.com/list.asp?ProdId=0171, access date: 14/09/2015.

[51]http://www.enet.com.cn/article/2010/1105/A20101105771379_2.shtml, access date: 14/09/2015.

[52]Ibid.

OMA digital rights management standard is an open one, which has been supported and applied by many operators and equipment suppliers. At present, digital rights management systems of most European and American operators have basically adopted OMA digital rights management. However, mainstream mobile phone manufacturers like Nokia, Motorola, Samsung, LG and Sony Ericsson preset OMA digital rights management Agent in their phones to support the application of OMA digital rights management 1.0; meanwhile, companies like Nokia and LG have started to preset the Agent which is based on OMA digital rights management 2.0 to realize the evolution from OMA digital rights management 1.0 to 2.0. Therefore, as for OMA digital rights management, the biggest advantage is the standardization and openness of platform ports.[53]

OMA digital rights management 1.0 has realized the four modes, namely, controlled transmission, combined delivery, separate delivery and super distribution, and it has the following merits[54]:

- content is sent to mobile phones through GPRS after AES encryption;
- authority limits and keys are sent to mobile phones through WAP push;
- keys are preserved in safe areas of mobile phone operating systems;
- media contents are convenient for transmission;
- flexible control over business strategies;
- media contents are possible for renewal;
- renewal just requires files of authority limits, saving bandwidth.

OMA digital rights management was applied at home long ago, and the four biggest operators took OMA digital rights management 1.0 as standards.[55] China Telecom and China Network have applied OMA digital rights management 1.0 in OTA download at present and started to apply them to music and streaming media.[56] As a member of OMA, China Mobile also considered to apply OMA digital rights management to various fields as technologies for copyright protection, especially whole-song download which was under test of China Mobile was the cutting-edge and core business in developing its digital music. China Mobile is considering whether to adopt private standards of manufacturers or OMA digital rights management basing on open interface. It is said that China Mobile has decided to apply more open and standard OMA digital rights management, and this has been affirmed by China Mobile.[57] Considering whether shortcomings of OMA digital rights management 1.0 would affect record companies providing copyright of whole-song

[53]'Digital Rights Management Approved Version 1.0–15, Open Mobile Alliance OMA-Download-DRM-V1_0-20040615-A', http://technical.openmobilealliance.org/Technical/release_program/docs/DRM/V1_0-20040625-A/OMA-Download-DRM-V1_0-20040615-A.pdf, June 2004.

[54]Deng et al. [18].

[55]http://3gca.org/newsletter-june-2013/, access date: 14/09/2015.

[56]http://www.well.com/user/lonewolf/main/vera.html, access date: 14/09/2015.

[57]Russell Shaw, 'Will OMA DRM 2.0 be the solution?', OMA digital rights management, http://www.zdnet.com/article/will-oma-drm-2-0-be-the-solution/, IP Telephony, February 16, 2007access date: 14/09/2015.

download, China Mobile had consulted the four record companies and had been supported by them to use OMA digital rights management 1.0 as copyright protection technology for whole-song download. In addition, after applying OMA digital rights management 1.0 in the Java platform, China Unicom also considered to apply OMA digital rights management to its new music business.[58]

In addition, with the wide use of OMA digital rights management in the industry, private digital rights management protection technologies have some development and a group of companies adopting private standards spring up. Private standards keep some small apps under protection of digital copyright; however, with the increasing of apps, some problems exposed themselves.[59] First, the limitation of private standards made digital rights management apps rely on providers of private standards. Thus, both expansibility and substitutability were poor. Second, with the increasing demand to copyright protection, many companies embezzled current standards and developed their own private digital rights management, which put many apps in risk of lawsuit. Therefore, relevant specialists suggested that for large digital rights management apps, digital rights management with open standards was recommended to avoid above-mentioned risks.[60] Considering the hidden danger of private standards, Telefonica changed private standards into OMA digital rights management standards after it developed its whole-song download business. With the development of mobile network, new apps emerge in endlessly and more and more contents require copyright protection. Thus, as for OMA standards organization, it has more chances to develop OMA digital rights management in China. Because of this, more and more digital rights management manufacturers considered to cooperate with Chinese enterprises, such as CoreMedia, BeepSience and SafeNet,[61] they wanted to establish partnerships with domestic manufacturers.

6.8 Founder Information Industry Group: Apabi Technology

On digital rights management technology for e-books, the representative technology would be the DAS from the Microsoft, Adobe Content Server, etc., while in China's e-book industry market, Apabi digital rights management technology has been regarded as the most advanced architecture for digital copyright protection.

[58]'The Future Of Music Copyright In A Digital World', http://www.soundonsound.com/sos/mar99/articles/copyright.htm, access date: 14/09/2015.

[59]Ibid.

[60]'OMA's Race to Construct in China', http://www.bloomberg.com/bw/stories/2006-11-09/omas-race-to-construct-in-chinabusinessweek-business-news-stock-market-and-financial-advice/, access date: 14/09/2015.

[61]http://www.educity.cn/tx/928884.html, access date: 14/09/2015.

Founder Information Company is a pioneer of publishing industry in China, and Founder Apabi Technology Ltd., which provides digital publishing technologies and digital products, operates as a subsidiary of Founder Information Company. It has involved itself in digital publishing field since 2001. Apabi Company developed digital publishing technology, which has been treated as the solution strategy as a whole for digital publishing, based on Founder's domain position in China's publishing industry and traditional printing techniques.

The characters in Apabi (A-P-A-B-I) stand for Author, Publisher, Artery, Buyer and Internet respectively, which seems "claptrap" to its marketing strategy. As far as readers know, for Author, Publisher, and Buyer are the essential components in traditional publishing industry chain. Put another way, Apabi, linked by "internet", has combined with the traditional publishing supply chain for a full and novel digital publishing type. With respect to the digital technology (original style and streaming type) and the reading experience adopted and developed by Apabi would provide a secure platform for digital copyright protection.

As the core competences, data mining and knowledge indexing technology has further optimized its service. On the one hand, the whole publishing procedure has been presented online by Apabi to facilitate the publishing companies and periodical or newspaper offices to step inside of the publishing market. On the other hand, the websites involved can be equipped to be the digital electronic platforms for online reading. In this regard, traditional libraries are transposed to be the digital libraries. Apabi technology makes multi-win come true based on the each player's advantages and features in the digital publishing industry. Founder Apabi has offered a comprehensive solution concerning copyright for the presses, etc.

So far, Apabi has presented the digital books, digital newspapers, digital museums, other various specific databases, and mobile reading technical solutions. Even operation services regarding diverse digital resource products have been included as well. According to the statistics,[62] over 90% presses in China have been using Apabi's digital technology and its digital platform for online publications distribution. Around 120 thousand kinds of digital books, in total 700 thousand volumes of digital books are distributed through Apabi platform annually. Around 90% newspaper distributors and almost 800 kinds of newspaper and journals in China have adopted the digital newspaper system issued simultaneously by Founder Apabi. Globally, users from 8000 schools, governmental authorities, industries and public libraries have benefited from Apabi's digital resource and digital libraries' toolkit that afford the users online reading and professional knowledge retrieval service.

Digital rights management design under Apabi's technology system has been considered as the one of the most characteristic aspects as well. Of all the patented technologies Apabi owned so far, probably the most contributing of Apabi technology has been digital rights management technology. Apabi's digital rights management technology has stayed more leading position than other counterparties and

[62]http://gw.apabi.com/partners/press/.

shaped a systematic architecture for digital copyright protection. In Apabi digital rights management scheme, there are four mainstay products:

(1) **Apabi Maker:** various formats of digital files are transformed into e-book format through Apabi maker. E-book format is a format composed of "script" and "image" format. Transposed e-book format will still retain all the information (scripts and images included) that the former digital files contained without being constraint by the operation system and the internet environment.
(2) **Apabi Rights Server:** digital data will be copyright-protected and managed by this server. In addition, from the security identification for the encryption and transaction of digital books, to users' login to the online bookshop for consumption, this server, normally is fixed at the publishing terminate server, plays the basic, but the most important protection role in Apabi's digital system.
(3) **Apabi Retail Server:** as it mentioned above, issues a series of services for consumers who would like to buy the digital material, is located at the publishing terminate server as well.
(4) **Apabi Reader:** tools for reading digital books from Apabi's platform. Buyers could purchase, read and download digital resources through browsers, and create their owner electronic library, which has classified the management of e-books.

Above all, the most creative and crucial technology of Apabi, is no doubt, digital copyright protection technical system (digital rights management technology), which has been implemented by 168 digital encrypted technology.[63]

References

1. Farrand B (2009) The case that never was: an analysis of the Apple iTunes case presented by the Commission and potential future issues. Eur Intellect Prop Rev 31(10):508–513
2. Yang C-T, Chen C-J, Chen H-Y, Hsu C-H (2008) A Peer-to-Peer file resource sharing system for mobile devices. In: Conference: Grid and Pervasive Computing Workshops, 2008
3. Gasser U (2004) iTunes: how copyright, contract, and technology shape the business of digital media-a case study. Berkman Center for Internet & Society at Harvard Law School Research Publication No. 2004-07
4. Sharpe NF, Arewa O (2007) Is apple playing fair? Navigating the iPod FairPlay DRM Controversy. Northw J Technol Intellect Prop 5:331 (Northwestern Public Law Research Paper No. 07-18)
5. Rayna T (2009) The economics of digital goods: selling vs. renting music online. DIME Intellectual Property Rights Working Paper No. 13
6. Klebanow A, Wu T (2015) Is music the next eBooks? An antitrust analysis of Apple's conduct in the music industry. Columb J Law Arts, July 14 2015
7. Solo A (2014) The role of copyright in an age of online music distribution. Media Arts Law Rev 19:169

[63]http://www.enet.com.cn/article/2004/0907/A20040907341363.shtml.

8. Heald PJ (2014) The demand for out-of-print works and their (un) availability in alternative markets. Illinois Public Law Research Paper No. 14-31
9. Rowe EA (2009) Foreword, technology and intellectual property: new rules for an old game? J Technol Law Policy, vol 14. http://scholarship.law.ufl.edu/facultypub/66. Accessed 14 Sept 2015
10. Frost L (2006) French draft law threatens iPod's future. Associated Press. http://msl1.mit.edu/furdlog/docs/2006-03-17_apwire_french_interop.pdf
11. Fisher WW III (2004) Promises to keep: technology, law, and the future of entertainment. Stanford University Press
12. Ze Mer L (2006) Rethinking copyright alternatives. International Journal of Law and Information Technology. Springer
13. Larkey M (2015) Cooperative play: anticipating the problem of copyright infringement in the new business of live video game webcasts. Rutgers J Law Public Policy 13:52–109
14. Campbell T (2015) The E-Books conspiracy: crossing the line between applying and creating law. Univ Miami Law Rev Caveat 69:1, Chapman University, Fowler Law Research Paper No. 15-13
15. Lehdonvirta V (2012) A history of the digitalization of consumer culture: from Amazon through Pirate Bay to Farmville. In: Denegri-Knott J, Molesworth M (eds) Digital virtual consumption. Routledge, New York, pp 11–28
16. Hovenkamp HJ (2014) Antitrust and information technologies. In: Florida law review, Forthcoming. U Iowa Legal Studies Research Paper No.15-05
17. Desai DR (2014) The new steam: on digitization, decentralization, and disruption. Hast Law J 65(6):1469–1482
18. Deng M, Fritsch L, Kursawe K, Arenberg K (2006) Personal rights management: taming cameraphones for individual privacy management. In: Danezis G, Golle P (eds) Privacy Enhancing Technologies-Proceedings of the 6th workshop on privacy enhancing technologies PET2006, 29 June 2006

Part III
Proposed Digital Rights Management Model in China

Chapter 7
Predicament and Countermeasure

7.1 Necessity for A New Regulatory Model in China

The legislation and implementation systems of copyright protection aim to protect the legitimate rights and interests of authors, coordinate the relationship between author and users, and encourage authors to carry out creations as well as widespread promotions of creations for promoting the development of scientific culture. Copyright System emerges along with the issuance of *The Statute of Anne*, and the recent development history shows an ever-present contradiction between private right of author and public benefits. The balance of interest of various parties is the main issue remaining to be considered while it can be said that the copyright aims to show balance. However, the development of network technology has brought unprecedented challenges for the original balanced system. Both the circumvention of digitalization and technologically protective measures of copyright demonstrate the characteristics of the network: free information flow and information sharing, which are unprecedented challenges for the right of copyright monopoly. Besides, some people even vow that the copyright shall be overturned in the network era. On the one hand, there is about the precarious benefit of copyright holders; on the other hand, there are unprecedented requirements of information sharing. Network technology does not only provide powerful information and convenient communication approach, but also tools and channels for people to probe into other people's privacy, steal other's commercial secrets, carry out illegal transaction, obtain improper interests, and evade liability, etc. Accordingly, some copyright holders have to set up protective measures for their information and rights. However, some hackers try unremitting efforts, aiming to crack the protection technologies. In the network era, the development of digital technique and internet has brought with unprecedented challenges for the interest of copyright holders while traditional afterwards relief measures seem powerless facing modern infringement activities. Therefore, preventive copyright protection measures emerge as the times require. At present, popular measures refer to digital right management technology.

C. Xu, *Regulatory Model for Digital Rights Management*,
https://doi.org/10.1007/978-981-15-1995-6_7

Technologically protective measures of copyright substantially refer to technical protection measures, a historian called Arnold Joseph Toynbee believed that any power, including the power produced by advanced scientific technology is ethically neutral.[1] It can be right or wrong because of different methods of application. Judging from the nature, technical protection measures are compensated use methods, aiming to protect copyright. Furthermore, the legal sense of Technological Measures is to punish others from copyright infringement, and those equipment and services makers who deliberately provide techniques to carry out infringement activities. The new right of copyright holders in the network environment only shows in the controlling of spreading their work online. Digital works can completely free themselves from the psychical medium during the online dissemination, so traditional approaches used to prevent physical torts are not able to make a difference. Therefore, copyright holders cannot be adequately protected by law. Consequently, they have to seek to private remedies such as adopting technological measures to protect and achieve their right from unauthorized use and copy, etc. However, the barriers built by technology will quickly be cracked by new technologies and continuously advanced protection measures encourage hackers who are interested in hacking. Copyright holders match wits with anti-protection technology experts, and meanwhile appeal to the protection of law to strengthen their advantages in attack and defence actions.

Technological protection measures are introduced to protect the copyright in the digital era, which actually play the role. Then what is the legal nature of technological protection measures? How do these measures protect the benefits of copyright holders? Answers to these two questions are premises for correctly commenting on technological protection measures. From the perspective of legal nature, technological protection measures can be regarded as a private remedy for copyright. In terms of protected methods, technological protection measures are approaches to control the end consumers, which realize the protection based on controlling the activities of end-consumers.

7.1.1 In Terms of Legal Nature: Technological Protection Measures are Private Remedies to Protect Copyright

Copyright protection measures can be divided into public remedies and private remedies. Private remedies refer to the situation when they believe that their rights are being infringed, they solve the disputes to achieve their right independently without a third party or state officials. Characteristics of private remedies include: there is no third party; the disputes settlement process is non-programmable; when copyright holders adopt private remedies, they think that their rights are being infringed; the aim of private remedies is to achieve right and solve disputes; the

[1]Wilson [1].

channel of private remedies depends on private power. The key distinction between private and public remedies is the intervention of a third party. 'Private remedies are social-control models which are non-centralized, highly fragmented and private.'[2] On numerous occasions, people directly involved in disputes seek to solve problems by themselves. However, the institutionalization of private remedies does not mean that it will lose the nature. 'Because the key point to differ public and private remedies is the intervention of a third party, but not determined by legal rules.' Even though public remedies dominate in modern society, private remedies possess the necessity of existence because private remedies are always cheaper. Take three private remedies such as self-defence, avoiding emergency and self-help as examples; if they are not allowed and people have to wait for the help of public officials, then an extremely low economical efficiency will come to us. Of course, private remedies belong to spontaneous behavior, and it is individual but not the objective third party to comment on the necessity as well as limitation of remedy, which will inevitably bring along with benefit-orientation and randomness. Besides, its extensive range will also create negative effects. Therefore, legislation should have a prudent attitude toward private remedies. Furthermore, civil law has to make up for the potential shortages of self-defence, avoiding emergency as well as self-help in terms of remedy time, range and means.

In terms of legal nature, technological protection measures are no doubt approaches for copyright holders adopted to protect their copyright. The relevant copyright laws only define that anyone has the obligation not to evade technological protection measures. However, these laws do not have a clear declaration of the type and setting of measures, which are totally set by copyright holders. Moreover, judging from the process when measures are recognized by law, technological protection measures and anti-circumvention provisions are results that copyright holders are pursuing. It is the active promotion of copyright holders that protection measures and anti-circumvention provisions are finally introduced into the copyright. Accordingly, in terms of legal nature, technological protection measures can be regarded as private remedies ignited by copyright holders.

7.1.2 In Terms of Protection Methods: Technological Protection Measures Aim to Control and Consumers

As one of the important Intellectual Property Rights Laws, copyright law can be called Prohibited Law of Imitation or Hitch-Riding. That is to say, copyright law defines the range based on the range of prohibited behaviors. However in fact, the use of copyright works is more than that. Reading books, lending of audition works

[2]Gary T. Marx, "Technology and Social Control: The Search for the Illusive Silver Bullet Continues Encyclopedia of the Social & Behavioral Sciences", 2nd edition, 2001, http://web.mit.edu/gtmarx/www/techsoccon.html.

and exhibition of works also belong to copyright use, which are not included in the copyright law and are beyond law. The reasons why these behaviors are not included in the copyright law are: first, it is not efficient to carry out fully control. For example, it is hard to know how many times readers read the copyright books. Second, it may infringe the important interest of individual. For example, it may infringe the privacy when you supervise on the reading activities carried out by readers. Third, copyright works may be created for the public. Therefore, the full control on works may lead to a situation that the public is not willing to use these copyright works, and the benefit of copyright holders may thus rely on nothing. In the development course of copyright law, imitation activities, which should be prohibited, are changed with the development of social economy, culture and technology. Before the emergence of broadcast and televisions, works can be spread to the public by psychical mediums. Therefore, copyright holders obtain benefits by controlling the medium and selling activities. Copyright works have mediums, which possess consumption exclusiveness and competitiveness. In addition, the public are limited by space and time while using works, which are not beneficial to the benefits of copyright holders. The copying technology is not developed at that time, which also costs much and individual cannot carry out cost-effective copying. Consequently, copying activities are carried out by printing plant and publishing companies.

Therefore, it is for copyright holders to recoup the capital outlay and get benefits through controlling replication mechanisms.[3] After the emergence of broadcast and television, copyright works can be spread without mediums. However, relevant equipments are very expensive, and main disseminators concentrate on a few institutions. Not a large amount of individual communication and copyright holders are able to control these centralized disseminators to get back the outlay and obtain benefits. Overall, before the appearing of digital technology, copyright holders are able to protect their economical benefits through controlling centralized copying or major disseminators because copying and transmission are intensively carried out. At that time, copyright holders indirectly get their payment from the public or we may call them end consumers and the protection mode of copyright is a mode to control the intermediary, which does not only provide proper incentives but also give an enough space for the public. Even though the emergence of printing press grants individuals with the ability to have copying works, the restriction of private communication and quality of works cannot fundamentally change the copyright protection modes. However, the emergence of digital technology has changed everything, and its powerful copying ability and communication ability radically change the communication modes of copyright works. When a certain individual buys a book or a movie, he or she is able to upload it online. Afterwards, endless downloads and copying works shall occur. 'The use of copyright works change from copying to directly experience the contents of works', 'basic principles are no longer

[3]Dara Kerr, "Netflix purges 79 movies, say goodbye to 'Taxi Driver'", June 30, 2014, http://www.cnet.com/news/netflix-purges-79-movies-say-goodbye-to-taxi-driver/#!.

the buying and selling activities of property right in the market, but an access for providers and users to services in the network environment.' In a new environment, the market is giving a way to the network, and the property is gradually replaced by access. Then, the typical protection intermediary model cannot play its role. Experience and access have become the basic characteristics in the digital era and copyright holders begin to create various technological protection measures along with laws to change the intermediary model to an end-controlling model to change the protection mode that traditional model does not control the access to some extent. By the way, iTunes created by Apple is a typical case in the digital era to control the end consumers. Technological protection measures, which are similar to iTunes, have changed the copyright to an end-controlling mode of all of the activities. Meanwhile, the freedom of public casually dealing with copyright works in the pre-digital work has totally lost, and end users' behaviors are tightly controlled by copyright holders.

7.1.3 Rationality Analysis of Fair Use Under Digital Rights Management

A strong reality conflict in many aspects between the digital rights management and the Fair Use makes it possible for the copyright holder to strengthen the control on works at his will and even makes it hard for the continuity of Fair Use. However, Fair Use has its own necessity and value under the new digital media. First, as analyzed in Chap. 2 above, there is a conflict between the legal protection of digital rights management and the freedom of speech covered by Faire Use. Subject to the further analysis, the existence of Fair Use does have its own necessity because of the freedom of speech. The freedom of speech is a basic political right the Constitution entrusted to every citizen. From the perspective of the Copyright Law, the authors have the freedom to create, publish, access to and use works and communicate ideas. That the public can acquire ideas and information by accessing to and reading the works is just the legal way to realize their freedom of speech. To achieve the real value of works, it is quite necessary to entrust the public with the rights to access to and use the works while protecting the rights and interests of the copyright owner. The overemphasis on protecting the interests of the copyright holder not only distorts the interests balance of the Copyright Law, but also goes against the legislative purpose of the Copyright Law, which even prejudices the development of social and cultural industries. With respect to the legal protection system of digital rights management: first, it gives biased and unilateral comprehensive copyright protection to the digital copyright holder, which makes the digital copyright owner have over-strengthened rights and even seriously goes against the public; second, if the public want to access to and fairly use the digital works subjectively and expect to realize the freedom of speech objectively, they shall be restricted by not only the digital rights management but also the circumvention acts strictly forbidden in the

Copyright Law, so it is hard to realize the freedom of speech in the field of Copyright Law under such double barriers. Therefore, the existence of Fair Use is indeed necessary to fully safeguard the freedom of speech in the field of Copyright Law.

Second, from the perspective of the Western Classical Economics, the legal protection of digital rights management has corrected the market failure on the allocation of resources, which indeed has a necessity in existence. However, the Western Economics believes that the reason why the Technological Measure is feasible depends on the integrity of information, the zero transaction cost and the rationality of the act of party. In the practice, all the three conditions above are difficult to be achieved, so not all market failures may be corrected by the Technological Measure. First, the market information is asymmetric and incomplete. The digital rights management gives excessive rights to the copyright holder, which makes the other party not completely aware of work information and in a disadvantageous position before the completion of the deal and thus fail to make reasonable judgment or evaluation on the work, therefore the parties fail to act rationally under such conditions. Second, it is hard to realize the conditions precedent of the zero transaction cost. The transaction cost in the traditional field mainly includes the expenses to discover the work, to negotiate and contract, and to execute the contract. While under the digital rights management, the transaction cost mainly includes the expenses to identify the system, to acquire the permission from the holder and to conduct the Technological Measure, and those expenses are inevitable in the new digital media. Accordingly, even not all market failures may be corrected by the digital rights management, the existence of Fair Use is indeed necessary.

Finally, the need of public interests further clarifies the necessity and rationality of the existence of Fair Use. As described in Chap. 2 above, there is a strong conflict between legal protection of digital rights management and the public interests involved in Fair Use, and the main reason is that traditional Copyright Law is always aiming at safeguarding the public interests and serving the public. The formulation of laws and the modification of provisions require us to fully estimate the interests of others and consider the public interests while protecting and claiming for our rights. The new laws are formulated or modified not to create new rights or realize the benefit monopolization, but to achieve another equilibrium state of interests by another orderly allocation based on the original balance of interests. The public interest is mainly embodied in the right of social public to access to information and to receive new ideas, which is different from the freedom of speech above; from the public's general point of view, the public interest is aiming at fully safeguarding the social and cultural order, and realizing the sharing of social information and the cultural progress. The legal protection of digital rights management has overemphasized on the individual private rights of digital copyright holder, which is focusing on "promoting" the prosperity and development of the new digital media to narrow the gap with the developed countries and strengthen the stimulation for the re-creation by digital copyright owner; or aimed at "expanding" the interests of the new media service providers to rapidly spread new media and quickly replace the traditional simulation of copyright. However, whatever the purpose is, the biased protection given by digital rights management to the digital copyright owner has over-compressed the application of Fair Use and seriously damaged the public interests.[4]

7.2 Digital Rights Management Rules in China Against the Socio-Cultural and Economic Matrix: Theoretical Basis for Conflict Regulation

7.2.1 Based on the Theory of Copyright Benefit Balance

Benefit balance is a relatively compatible and equilibrium status for the benefits under a certain benefit pattern and system, which is not only a legislative but also a judicial principle. From the perspective of theoretical jurisprudence, benefit balance refers to the "reasonable optimized state of the benefit of the parties involved based on coexistence and compatibility, which is achieved by the legal authority to coordinate the conflicts in all aspects". In fact, the benefit interests balance is a dynamic regulating process, a process in which the holders selecting and allocating the interests under certain rules, accompanied by the conflicts of interest regulated by multiple autonomous acts under the admissible conditions of the law. From the perspective of the jurisprudence and philosophy, although balance is the ultimate goal everyone wants to reach in all aspects, but in the real world, the interest is so one-sided, narrow and blind that nobody will "pay attention to the interests of the whole" or "think over carefully", so it is inevitable to cause imbalance and conflict. The law is aimed at safeguarding the general security of the society, and its primary purpose is to safeguard and recognize the benefits of all parties at the minimum cost, including personal interests, social interests and public interests; clarifying the boundaries of the various interests to follow; making the balance of interests effective as far as possible from safeguarding the interests recognized above within the jurisdiction of law. It is the so-called theory of benefit balance sought on the jurisprudence and philosophy. From the perspective of game theory, balance is the spirit of the law, and it is a game to reach a balance that often reflects the balance of power between the parties. The legislation of laws is just a game for the interests of various parties and the embodiment of the will of the interests community, which is the basic thought to decide the legislation result and to dominate the legal value orientation; however, if the legal orientation is completely depended on the power of game parties, it will certainly make the interest scale tilt to the stronger party who will get more interests and further develop stronger laws, thus leading the society into such vicious circle. Therefore, the perfect rules are required in the gaming process to provide security, which is the so-called theory of benefit balance. The equalization of the interests of the parties involved referred to in the law will only be

[4]Gladney [2].

realized if the game parties play under the premise of open, transparent and efficient argument order and debate efficiency, and for the purpose of benefit balance.

With the creation of thought as the target, copyright is the intellectual property right. The purposes of copyright law to advance the knowledge and learning, to preserve in the public realm and to facilitate the public in accessing to works are realized by inspiring authors to create works and encouraging the transmission of works. The realization of the purposes above requires a great balance of rights between the author and the work users, and a balance between monopoly and sharing. The key of the balance mechanism is that the grant of proprietary rights by the copyright law to the author and other copyright owners is determined at an appropriate level. Although the international community and countries overseas protect the copyright as a private right, which is also the legislation foundation of copyright law, the protection the private rights of the owner is just the direct purpose of copyright law, namely the superficial benefit protected by copyright law. The basic requirements and the final goals of copyright law are to expand the diffusion of knowledge information, to promote the cultural innovation and to develop the cultural industry by protecting the private rights of the copyright owner. As the law to dominate the subject acts of all interest activities and even allocate the social resources, the copyright law redistributes social resources in related fields by clarifying the profit distribution; all articles and all modes stipulated by the copyright law are for the allocation of resources (such as setting the specific protection type of rights for the copyright owner, setting the Fair Use system, etc.) to make the interests of all parties balanced and to achieve the ultimate goal of laws.

Under the legislation purposes above of copyright law and its connotation of the benefit balance, the main reason for the conflict between the legal protection of digital rights management and the Fair Use is the contradiction between exclusive rights of right holder and the legitimate concern of the public to the knowledge. If the rights granted by copyright law to copyright owner are too wide, it will damage the rights and interests of the public to access to and to use the digital works, thus making the fundamental aim of copyright system unachievable; if the rights granted by copyright law to copyright owner are too narrow, it will make the author's innovativeness and creativeness insufficient, thus making the direct purpose of copyright system unachievable. Therefore, the conflict must be coordinated with the principle of copyright benefit balance as the core and the basis.

For the conflict between the protection of the private rights for the copyright holder and the public interests, there is a great benefit balance system in the traditional copyright law. From the perspective of overall copyright system, the interests of all parties in the field of copyright is considered broadly to be balanced, namely between the primary author and the secondary, and between the real authors and the service providers at the creation level; between the copyright owners and users, and between the authors and investors at the transmission level; the interests of the representatives of all parties involved are in a dynamic balance.[5] The

[5]Preamble of WIPO Copyright Treaty, http://www.wipo.int/treaties/en/text.jsp?file_id=295166.

introduction of the legal protection system of digital rights management undoubtedly moves the balance point between the rights of copyright owner and the public interests from the angle of the whole legal system of copyright law. Although the copyright law covers the rights given to copyright holder, and the relevant terms and conditions are written into the international copyright convention, the benefit adjustment mode is outside of the copyright system. In an era when the new digital media develops rapidly and both the computer penetration and the network coverage are greatly increased, the basic principle of benefit balance maintained by the copyright law shall not be changed furthermore, which is also the necessary premise for the copyright law to continue playing its effect. Under the legal protection of digital rights management, the principle of benefit balance is to promote the development of social and cultural industries while maintaining the balance between the individual interests of copyright holder and the public interests, namely: on the one hand, maintain an incentive mechanism by protecting the exclusive rights of the creators of digital works within a certain period to further promote the innovation and creation of works and the generation of more knowledge; on the other hand, restrict the rights of copyright owner to promote the wide spread of intellectual achievements, allow the public to make full access to and fairly use the digital works, and maintain the public interests, thus promoting the progress of the whole social economy and culture, and the development of new digital media.

7.2.2 *Oriented by the Coordination of Rights and Obligations*

The law often adjusts the objective behavior of peoples by setting the rights and obligations of the counterpart, and balances the interests of all parties by adjusting their behaviors, so the legal performance of interest coordination mechanism is usually the relationship between rights and obligations. The rights stipulated by the law are actually the interests protected by the law, which induce people change their own selfish motives into legal acts with the peculiar interest guidance and motivation guarantee mechanism acting on the daily behaviors of people to generate the interests conducive to themselves; the obligations stipulated by the law are actually to restrict the interests of a particular object, which are essentially the interest burdens or the responsibility consequences preventing a particular object from the acts prohibited by law and not conducive to his interests to protect the interests of the opposite party from another side and thus making for the public. The balance of interests referred to in the law is just the result of the bi-direction and balance stipulated by the rights and obligations in law.

In the field of the traditional copyright law, rights and obligations are often paired; the traditional copyright law sets various rights of the copyright owner, such as the property right of the copyright owner and the neighbouring right of the work disseminator to safeguard the interests of holder due to his intellectual labor, and regulates the corresponding obligations while promoting the innovation and recreation of works, such as the obligations without permission of statutory license and the obligations unable to ban the public of fair use; it is conducive to the promotion of works, the spread of the author's thought and even the social progress. Therefore, the matching of copyright rights and obligations plays a leading role in the process of interests balancing. From the perspective of value function, the rights and obligations are complementary. While setting various rights of the copyright owner, the traditional copyright law also regulates the obligation from another side that the public shall never infringe the private rights of copyright owner; the fair use right of the public regulated by the copyright law also indicates the obligation that the copyright holder shall not prohibit the public to exercise their rights. No any rights will exist if there is no obligation, and vice versa no rights, therefore the pure right will only get its interest value through its matched obligations. Under the new digital media, all countries are formulating laws for the digital rights management, all giving biased legal protection to digital copyright owner from contact, right protection, right management information protection and other aspects, but there are only enumerative and limited provisions completely unmatched with rights in the "Exception" with respect to the obligations to be undertaken by the users. The rule that so blindly emphasizes the unilateral rights of digital copyright owners but ignores the social obligations to be undertaken will affect the rights of both the digital copyright owners and the public, finally resulting in the conflicts of interests. For this reason, the conflicts may be settled with the coordination of the rights and obligations as the guidance to realize the legislative purpose of the copyright law.

To sum up, although there is strong conflict with the Fair Use, there is necessity and rationality in the existence of digital rights management. In terms of legal nature of Technological Measure, it is actually a means to protect the digital works, with the final purpose to protect the works. The cases cited further prove that the Technological Measure has played a strong restriction role in the infringement contact and use of digital works and has played a great role in the protections digital works, so the legal protection of digital rights management does have its necessity. However, the Fair Use also has rationality in its existence based on the freedom of speech of the public, the public interests and the social and cultural development. Therefore, in my opinion, the key to solve the problem is to grasp the essential root of conflicts between the legal protection of digital rights management and the Fair Use, with the benefit balance principle of copyright law as the theoretical basis and oriented by the coordination of rights and obligations.

7.3 Legal Protection of Digital Rights Management and Present Situation of Conflict Coordination in China

7.3.1 Legal Protection of Digital Rights Management in China

The *Copyright Law* was revised for the second time in February 2010 in China, which introduced an exclusive right of copyright holder to protect the Digital Rights Management, namely Article 48 (6), (7) of the *Copyright Law*. The general protection clauses of digital rights management only allow the holder to take the Technological Measure for protecting his copyright and other relevant rights, or he will be punished, and there is a certain difficulty and uncertainty in the application of these clauses in practice. The general provisions on the legal protection of digital rights management are to some extent caused by the passivity of relevant legislations on the digital rights management in China, when compared with the *Digital Millennium Copyright Act* and the European Union *Copyright Directive 2001/29/EC of the Information Society*, the *Copyright Law* in China does not specifically describe in detail the Technological Measures, the rights management information and the relevant circumventions. Although further detailing the punishment for the infringement acts including the circumvention and destruction of the Technological Measures, and the deletion and change of the rights management information in Article 36, the *Copyright Law Enforcement Regulations* still formulates no specific application rules for the protection of the Technological Measures.

With the constant improvement of socialist legal systems and the continuous perfection of copyright law systems, China has successively published and implemented a series of laws and regulations such as the *Regulations for the Protection of Computer Software*, the *Measures for the Implementation of Copyright Administrative Penalties* and the *Explanation on Some Issues of Laws Applicable to the Trial of Copyright Disputes Involving Computer Network by the Supreme People*'s *Court*. In July 2006, China began to implement the *Regulations for the Protection of Right of Communication through Information Network* containing the terms and conditions of the digital rights management; in June 2007, China became the contracting state of WIPO Copyright Treaty and WIPO Performances and Phonograms Treaty, thus further strengthening the protection of anti-circumvention legislation for the digital rights management in China. In Article 26 (2) and Article 26(3) of the *Regulations for the Protection of Right of Communication through Information Network,* the meanings of "Technological Measure" and "electronic rights management information" of digital works are described in detail. Starting from the definition, the *Regulations* has laid a solid foundation for the protection of anti-circumvention legislation for the digital rights management in China; from the perspective of the definition of Technological Measure, although the Technological Measure is not specifically classified as the contact control type and the rights protection type, it can still be seen from the expressions of "prevent unauthorized browsing work" and "prevent unauthorized provision of works to the public".

The *Regulations* has stipulated the corresponding protection articles respectively for the Technological Measures and electronic rights management information of the digital works. Among them, with respect to the legal protection of the Technological Measures, the *Regulations* comprehensively forbids the direct infringement acts of circumvention and destruction and the indirect infringement acts to manufacture, import and provide the public with the devices, components and services mainly used to avoid or destroy the Technological Measure. With respect to the electronic rights management information, the *Regulations* also regulates in detail from both directly deleting or changing the rights management information and mistakenly providing the works with deleted or changed electronic rights management information. Therefore, compared with the legal protection of digital rights management in the *Copyright Law*, the *Regulations* is more objective, more concrete and more operational only in terms of the general provisions of the infringement acts and the responsibilities to be undertaken. With respect to the responsibility and punishment for avoiding the Technological Measure of digital works or deleting the electronic rights management information, the *Regulations* also specifies the detailed applicable specifications. Among them, with respect to a series of direct infringement acts such as the deliberate circumvention and destruction of Technological Measure, the intentional deletion and change of the electronic rights management information, and the mistaken provision of the works with deleted or changed electronic rights management information, the infringer shall bear not only the civil liability but also the administrative responsibility such as the confiscation of illegal gains and the penalty in huge amount as per the illegal business revenue if the interests of the public are damaged, or even the criminal responsibility in case of gross violation. The *Regulations* also specifies the detailed and concrete protection rules for the indirect infringement acts of Technological Measure, and those who purposely manufacture, import and provide the devices or components mainly used to avoid or destroy the Technological Measure or who intentionally provide technical services for others to avoid or destroy the Technological Measure shall also bear the corresponding legal responsibility. Compared with Article 48 of the *Copyright Law*, the provisions on the legal protection of digital rights management in the *Regulations* are more specific, more standard and with stronger applicability and practicality only in terms of the direct infringement acts stipulated from the responsibility to be undertaken.

In Article 24 of the *Regulations for the Protection of Computer Software* and Article 6 of the *Explanation on Some Issues of Laws Applicable to the Trial of Copyright Disputes Involving Computer Network by the Supreme People*'s *Court,* the detailed specifications have been given for the legal protection of computer software and digital works. The computer software is the special digital work with universality, well-received and easy to be infringed, so the *Regulations* has given concrete legal protection to the Technological Measure and the electronic rights management information of the computer software, and has raised the upper limit of infringement penalty compared with other infringement acts, thus further clarifying the importance of protecting the Technological Measure. With respect to the booming of digital network and the increasingly serious infringement phenomenon by network service providers, the *Explanation* has specified from the directly mistaken infringement acts by network service providers, thus to further expanding the coverage of legal protection for the Technological Measure.

The *Copyright Law (Revised Draft)* released at the end of 2013 has greatly modified and adjusted the existing copyright law in China. The *Copyright Law (Manuscript of Revised Draft)* has set separate chapters and made detailed and specific provisions for the paragraphs related to the Technological Measures and rights management information of digital rights management. Based on absorbing and mirroring the *Regulations for the Protection of Right of Communication through Information Network,* the *Manuscript* has formulated more specific provisions for the legal protection of Technological Measure from its definition, the interest scope of the holder, the limitation of rights and the liability for tort. In terms of the definition, the "radio and television programs" have been added up to the use object of the Technological Measure in the *Manuscript*; the "reproduction", "operation" and "adaptation" have been added up to the use purpose of the Technological Measure in the *Manuscript*. The "radio and television programs, radio and television stations" and the "holder of radio and television programs" have been added up to the use object of the electronic rights management information in the *Manuscript*. The contact control type and the rights protection type Technological Measures covered in the legal protection have been further specified. In terms of the protection scope of rights for the holder, highly consistent with the *Regulations*, the *Manuscript* still follows the detailed and specific right contents. In terms of the liability for tort, Article 78 in Chapter 7 of the *Manuscript* specifically describes the liabilities for tort such as the circumvention and destruction of technical protection measures and the deletion and modification of rights management information. Compared with the *Regulations*, the *Manuscript* not only integrates the liability clauses on direct and indirect infringement acts, but also expands the indirect infringement manner of electronic rights management information to the behaviors including "copy, distribute, lease, show, broadcast, spread through the network to the public the rights management information even if aware of that the information is deleted or changed".

Although without legal effect, the *Deliberation* is likely to be the formally launched copyright law as the first draft of the copyright law modification draft. It can be seen from the substantial measures to define the rights of the holder and to define the liabilities for tort by setting separate chapters for the legal protection of Technological Measures and specifying the concept of Technological Measure that, the legal construction is increasingly perfected for the legal protection of digital rights management. At the executive meeting of State Council on January 16, 2013, the penalty amounts was modified in the four administrative regulations including the *Regulations for the Implementation of Copyright Law*, the *Regulations for the Protection of Right of Communication through Information Network* and the *Regulations for the Protection of Computer Software*, which has further strengthened the crackdown intensity on the circumvention and destruction of digital rights management, thus further protecting the digital copyright. In addition, before the National People's Congress and the Chinese People's Political Consultative Conference in

2013, the Democratic Progressive Central had organized some members of the national committee of Chinese People's Political Consultative Conference to carry on the thorough investigation and research for the digital piracy, and submitted the *Proposal on Strengthening the Digital Copyright Protection and Constructing the National Unified Public Service Platform for Digital Copyright.* The Democratic Progressive Central proposed to perfect the legislative works for digital publishing laws and regulations, to complete the "notification" and "deletion" systems, to lighten the burden on the rights of the copyright owner, to further protect the rights and interests of the holder, to clarify the tort compensation standard of the copyright law, and to strengthen the administrative law enforcement and focus on publicity and education of digital copyright. Therefore, the protection of digital copyright has received considerable attention, and China is certain to establish a more complete and perfect protection system for digital copyright in the near future.

7.3.2 Present Situation of Conflict Coordination in China

In Article 48(6) and Article 48(7) of the *Copyright Law* and Article 4(2) of the *Regulations for the Protection of Right of Communication through Information Network*, there is a restriction that "except as otherwise specified by laws and administrative rules and regulations" while entrusting legal protection to the holder for the Technological Measure. Similar to the exceptions in Section 1201(d)-(J) of the *Digital Millennium Copyright Act* and the restriction on Technological Measure and rights of the European Union *Copyright Directive 2001/29/EC of the Information Society*, Article 12 of the *Regulations for the Protection of Right of Communication through Information Network* also specifies the exception clauses on prohibiting the circumvention of Technological Measure. From school classroom teaching or research, provision of works for the blind, performance of official business by the state organs and computer safety performance test, the *Regulations* has made exception rules for the anti-circumvention legal protection of Technological Measure, and there is a strong limitation on its application: it is not allowed to provide any technology, equipment or component used to avoid the Technological Measure; it is not allowed to infringe upon others rights the holder entitled to enjoy; the first exception is only applicable when the relevant works are provided through information network; the first two exceptions are only applicable to the works acquired through information network. Article 71 of the *Copyright Law (Manuscript of Revised Draft)* has extended and supplemented six aspects based on the exception clauses of the *Regulations*: on the basis of making the extension and complement of the six aspects: 1. the broadcasting and television programs are supplemented as the exception object for classroom teaching and scientific research; 2. the works provided to the blind in the manner they can perceive are not limited to written works not for the purpose of making profits; 3. the restricted condition that the works involved in the above two exceptions "can only be acquired through information network" is modified to be "are unable to be acquired in normal way"; 4. the provision is deleted that the works involved in the above two exceptions can only be provided "through information network"; 5. the restrictive provision that "by the institution with security testing qualification" is added to the safety performance test of the computer and its system or network; 6. item (5) shall be added, namely the exception of encryption research or reverse engineering research of computer program regulates that compared with the United States, Germany and other Western countries with developed digital media industry, although not specific or concrete in terms of the application rules and the exception clauses in the legal protection of digital rights management in China, it is actually the substantive progress of the legal system construction from the perspective of the integrity of copyright protection law. Facing with various stresses from the growing competition of intellectual property rights by the Western developed countries since joining in the World Trade Organization, the biased and strict copyright protection system implemented by the United States and other developed countries, failure of the system construction in the developing countries to keep pace with the integration of global digital network and the rapid development in new digital media industry, China has actively performed the duties of the developing countries, formulated the domestic copyright legal system strictly conforming to the WIPO Copyright Treaty and WIPO Performances and Phonograms Treaty, comprehensively considered from various perspectives the legal protection of digital rights management, strictly formulated anti-circumvention legislation provisions for the Technological Measure, and improved the exception clauses for the wider adaptability and practicality of the rules. It follows that full affirmation shall be given to the active behaviors by China to explore and formulate the anti-circumvention legislation of digital rights management.

7.4 Coordination Approach of Conflicts

7.4.1 Technical Considerations

From the perspective of technology, digital rights management takes an indifferent attitude towards the Fair Use, and even the copyright law defines the Fair Use vaguely. It can be seen from the analysis above that there is indeed a reasonability and necessity for the Fair Use under the digital rights management, so it is actually prior to settle the conflicts between them from the procedures, language, machine expression and other technical means.

The authorization of use of digital works by the traditional digital rights management is realized by the pre-implemented system in which the right holders adopt the Extensive Markup Language, the Open Digital Rights Language and other rights expression languages. The rights expression language can formulate restrictions on the permission object, the permission scope, the use time and territory and the payment standards with respect to the work users according to the unilateral demands of the users of digital rights management. Although the Fair Use can be

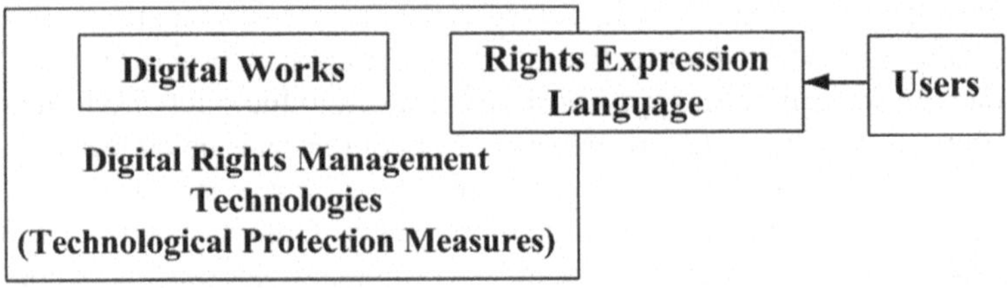

Fig. 7.1 Default Mode of Right Holders System

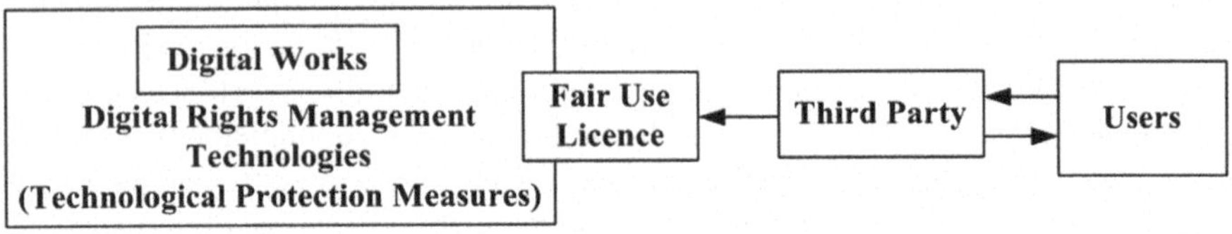

Fig. 7.2 Third Party Licence Model

realized immediately through a certain pre-implemented system, the demand on further Fair Use of the public is difficult to be fully expressed under the condition that the exclusive rights of holders are too broad and the system may recognize and reject any acts of the Client beyond the expressed authorized use mode (Fig. 7.1).

The third-party licensing mode may relatively solve the disadvantages of the unilateral licensing mode by the holder. It is mainly solved by the independent third-party mechanism selected and trusted by the transaction parties to undertake the demands on the acceptance, review and approval of Fair Use, thus avoiding restricting the Fair Use by the public for the inflexible and rigid conditions or the abuse of permission right by the holder of digital rights management in case of only using the preset mode of Rights Expression Language. In the era of the rapid development of the information society and the industrialization of new digital media, the major defect of this mode is the delay of information utilization caused by the long authorization period for the Fair Use (Fig. 7.2).

The Fair Use mode of digital works under the protection of digital rights management is developed to not only allow the public to exercise the fair use right without permission, but also not make the digital copyright owner lose the monitoring of public infringement acts; this new mode is consistent with the fair use characteristics of the traditional copyright, and is defined as the mode of "fair use process control" (see Fig. 7.3) by some scholars. While retaining the system preset mode and the third-party licensing mode of the holder above, the mode of fair use process control has established the unilateral claim mechanism for user rights as a supplement based on a certain usage rights to ensure that the public may fairly use the digital works without the permission of the right holder of Technological Measure. Within the specified authority, the user may freely, anonymously and in real time enjoy the fair use right of the personal non-commercial use conditions preset in the digital rights management and automatically defaulted to be determined

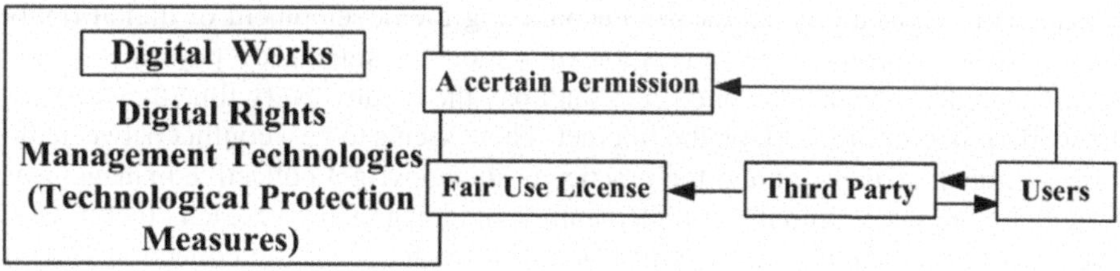

Fig. 7.3 Fair Use Course Control Model

by the existing laws, regulations and trading habits; with respect to the fair use beyond the system preset scope, the user may obtain license from a third party by bearing the risks of the inconvenience caused by the authorization delay.

7.4.2 *Administrative Intervention*

The state and the respective local governments shall encourage the innovation in digital rights management, give full play to and extend the functions of copyright collective management organizations, actively explore the new channel to establish the digital rights management organizations, and strive to perfect government management of digital copyrights and coordinate the conflicts between the two from the perspective of administrative management. First, a new mode shall be fully explored by combining the copyright collective management organizations and the digital rights management. The interest conflict between the copyright holder and the users is caused by the development of private reproduction technology, which is a international issue faced by many countries in the late twentieth century, and copyright collective management system is adopted by many countries due to providing a thought and solution for this issue, especially the European civil copyright law countries. At present, the copyright collective management organizations in China are China Audio & Video Copyright Association and China Copyright Society of Literary Works, are mainly responsible to collect copyright allowances from voice recording equipment, blank audio tapes, copying equipment, Karaoke and other media and manage and assign these copyright allowances to the authors, publishers, performers, producers and other holders, which cannot only compensate for the loss of the copyright holder, but also ensure that the consumers have free and unrestricted access to the copyrighted works. However, these copyright collective management organizations shall not collect copyright allowances from the media copying the works anymore since the copyright holder manages his works by the digital rights management. The digital rights management can provide a more efficient copyright management and licensing approach with lower cost and more equitable in distribution, which makes the reasonableness and necessity of the existence of copyright collective management system more questioned. United States, Europe and other countries and regions have established digital rights management legislations, all clearly encouraging the development of digital rights management to promote the formation of a more personalized "pay as you go" business mode, in which the end users shall pay the royalty every time they acquire the work or part of the work on the Internet. There seems to be a conflict between the digital rights management and the practice in the copyright collective management system, but they are mutually complementary and integrated with each other in fact. The copyright collective management organization has a classic collection system for copyright fee, which can be used to receive a license fee, eliminate the pain of selling to consumers, encourage the innovation and creation of copyright holders, and balance the interests between the public and the copyright owner. The digital rights management cannot only provide a good new copyright fee collection and distribution system for the copyright collective management organization, but also create favourable conditions for the healthy development of digital media. For example, the copyright fees of Karaoke entertainment industry may be collected on demand with the help of the copyright collective management organizations and the digital rights management in the network environment to realize a more accurate royalty payment manner, thus making it possible for the music creators to profit from their works. The administrative law enforcement departments in China shall encourage the copyright collective management organizations to fully develop and use the collection technology of digital rights management based on the original perfect collection system of copyright licensing fees to give full play to the advantages of the two, which cannot only firm the benefit balance in the field of the traditional copyright, but also lay a compacted foundation for the development of new digital media, the interest protection for the copyright holders of digital works and the supply for the legitimate demands of the public on digital works.

Second, the establishment of industry self-regulatory organization shall be urged, and the innovation of digital rights management organizations shall be encouraged. It is clearly stated in the *Cultural Industry Revitalization Plan* issued in 2009 in China: "All cultural industry organizations shall carefully perform market coordination, industry self-regulation, supervision services, rights protection and other functions in accordance with the laws and regulations to promote the healthy development of the industry. China Federation of Literary and Art Circles, the Chinese Writers Association, All-China Journalists' Association and other people's organizations shall actively play a role of industry self-regulation and rights protection. China Radio and Television Association, the Publishers Association of China, the Books and Periodicals Distribution Association of China, China Written Works Copyright Society, China Association of Performing Arts, China Film Producers' Association and China Film Distribution and Exhibition Association shall effectively change their functions, strengthen self-construction and improve the service functions. Efforts shall be made to construct and renovate various industry organizations in the culture field, so as to separate the government departments and the industry organizations".[6] Therefore, various cultural organizations are required at

[6]《文化产业振兴规划》, http://www.gov.cn/jrzg/2009-09/26/content_1427394.htm.

the policy level to actively explore ideas and make innovation in the construction and renovation various industry organizations in the culture field while maintain their own functions.

It is clearly proposed to construct the national uniform public service platform of digital rights in the *Proposal on Strengthening the Digital Copyright Protection and Constructing the National Unified Public Service Platform for Digital Copyright*[7] submitted by Democratic Progressive Central during the National People's Congress and the Chinese People's Political Consultative Conference in 2013. At present, the copyright trading platforms across the country are mostly located in one region, usually shorter in establishment time, smaller in scale, and imperfect in trading norms and standards. Therefore, to provide a comprehensive basic and guidance service for the digital publishing industry, the national uniform public service platform of digital rights shall be constructed through the integration of the copyright trading platforms across the country as soon as possible; in the meanwhile, a national digital rights trading market shall be established to further standardize the transaction order and reduce the transaction costs, thus promoting the healthy development of the industry. The digital rights management organization is the basis to further protect the interests of the digital works, and the business alliance self-organized by the service providers is just like an industry self-regulation organization; in the organization, all operators comply with a common management rule and cooperate with each other to jointly safeguard the copyright market to make the new digital media market larger and stronger. China shall fully learn from the domestic successful innovation examples of digital rights management organizations and the experiences in the countries abroad with developed digital media industry, and actively explore in the road of digital rights management, which cannot only implement the copyright term system of the Technological Measure or restrict the unfair competition behaviors of others by using the Technological Measure, but also balance the rights between the copyright holder and the public.

7.4.3 Judicial Expectations

Because our legislation is relatively conservative and the legislative process is too slow, it is generally difficult to make a quick legal response to new things, even if there are legitimate proposal as a basis. Therefore, it is preferred to coordinate the conflicts between the legal protection of digital rights management and the Fair Use relying on the judicial practice of intellectual property. The legal protection of digital rights management is directly aimed at fully protecting the private interests of digital copyright owners and encouraging the innovation, but its fundamental purposes are to benefit the public, to promote the dissemination of new knowledge and new ideas,

---

[7]《关于加强数字版权保护,构建国家级统一数字版权公共服务平台的提案》http://www.sipo.gov.cn/mtjj/2013/201303/t20130306_787114.html.

and to enhance the development of new digital media, rather than giving extensive monopoly rights to the copyright owner of digital works. The fundamental purposes can also be reflected in the judgment that the Defendant is not constituted an infringement by avoiding the Technological Measure of the Plaintiff in the Lexmark International vs. Static Control Components in the judicial practice for U.S. intellectual property and the Chamberlain vs. Skylink in the similar nature. Under the traditional environment of "judge-made law" among the judges of intellectual property rights, in the cases concretely involving the conflicts between the Technological Measure and the Fair Use, it seems to be well-reasoned and easier that our courts will finally control and regulate the social harms against the abuse of digital rights management implementation and coordinate its conflicts with Fair Use by adopting the legislative intent, spirit and original intention of the legal protection of digital rights management, and by understanding the substance and nature of the conflicts between the two.

Both the object and the impact are large in the judicial cases involving digital rights due to that the digital works are easy to be reproduced, well-received and easy to be infringed, and that the relevant legal issues are difficult and complex. Although legitimate judicial decisions may be made by the collegiate bench after careful investigation and cross-examination, the dispute between the partied involved may not be settled fundamentally, and the rancor may even be deepened to damage the interests of hundreds of millions of internet users because there are many holders of the digital works involved, or there are a lot of digital works of the related holders, or the infringement scope is broader, or the loss is larger. Therefore, the court with judicial adjudication and the Internet Society, Association for Computing Machinery and other third-party organizations with technical backgrounds, like new digital media technology and digital technology shall establish mutual trust relationships or mediation centre to develop mediation mechanisms for the hard cases above related to the digital rights, which cannot only effectively resolve the disputes of the parties involved, but also improve the judicial efficiency and save the judicial resources.

7.4.4 Legislation Suggestions

The construction of the legal system is the final safeguard, and the final "release agent" of conflicts is that there are laws to abide by. In the analytic chapters above for the conflicts between the digital rights management and the Fair Use, the objective manifestation of the conflicts between the two are discussed in detail, including: the existence of Technological Measure objectively narrows the application space of Fair Use, and makes the protection period of digital works extended infinitely, thus leading to the vicious cycle of the "no term of protection" for digital rights; because of the lack of restrictions on the finiteness principle of Technological Measure, the digital copyright owners or service providers may abuse the Technological Measures to excessively protect the private rights, which will further infringe the freedom of speech and restrict the public interest covered by Fair Use; the digital rights management holders may use the protection means of the Technological Measure to excessively collect and utilize the personal information of consumers, which may infringe consumer privacy and indirectly influence the safeguard of Fair Use; the digital rights management holder may use the legal protection of the Technological Measure to conduct the unfair competition or monopolistic competition, which may endanger the legitimate rights and interests of consumers, users and the public and even indirectly endanger the implementation of Fair Use by the public. The harmonious coordination of the conflicts of the two can be fundamentally ensured only by specifying the specific coordination rules from the perspective of legislation.

References

1. Wilson DCS (Fall/Winter 2014) Arnold Toynbee and the industrial revolution: the science of history, political economy and the machine past. History and Memory, Indiana University Press, 26(2)
2. Gladney HM (1999) Digital Dilemma: intellectual property: synopsis and views on the study by the National Academies' Committee on Intellectual Property Rights and the Emerging Information Infrastructure. IBM Almaden Research Center, D-Lib Magazine, 5(12). http://www.dlib.org/dlib/december99/12gladney.html

Part IV
Suggestions on the Improvement of Relevant Legal Systems in China

Chapter 8
A Comprehensive Regulatory Model

We become what we behold. We shape our tools, and thereafter our tools shape us.—Marshall McLuhan

The social consequences of a technology cannot be predicted early in the life of the technology. By the time undesirable consequences are discovered, however, the technology is often so much part of the whole economics and social fabric that its control is extremely difficult. This is the dilemma of control. When change is easy, the need for it cannot be foreseen; when the need for change is apparent, change has become expensive, difficult and time consuming.[1]—The Colllingridge Dilemma *The Social Control of Technology*

Digital rights management could be thought of as the "dot" in Lawrence Lessig's "Four Modalities of the Regulation" theory,[2] *if decisions regarding digital rights management regulatory models had been promoted by ever-changing digital technologies. Examples of social behaviour in cyberspace described in Lessig's book more emphasize how to integrate each modality and how these modalities interact with each other.*

Lawrence Lessig articulated in his book the dimensions of regulation structure should be acknowledged by the current society, although he explored his research upon a real life under a hypothetical environment. Four modalities could be regarded as four approaches by which the actions would be regulated in networking or non-networking situation: (1) the law, (2) social norms, (3) the market, and (4) the architecture.[3]

Lessig further explores how these four elements interact with particular actions in digital environment. Examples of social behaviour in cyberspace described in Lessig's book more emphasize how to integrate every modality and how these modalities interact with each other. These issues regarding intellectual property,

[1]The Colllingridge Dilemma The Social Control of Technology and also see Liebert and Schmidt [1], pp. 55–71.

[2]Lessig [2], p. 501.

[3]Lessig [3], pp. 122–123.

C. Xu, *Regulatory Model for Digital Rights Management*,
https://doi.org/10.1007/978-981-15-1995-6_8

privacy, in his mind, would be influenced by these formalities. Finally, he brought one thought-provoking question, though:

> How much control should we allow over information, and by whom should this control be exercised? There is a battle between code that protects intellectual property and fair use; there is a battle between code that might make a market for privacy and the right to report facts about individuals regardless of that market; there is a battle between code that enables perfect filtering and architectures that ensure some messiness about who gets what.[4]

If we took Lawrence Lessig's influential work on regulation as a research angle, then digital rights management matter could be thought of as the "dot" in his "Four Modalities of the Regulation" regime, if decisions regarding digital rights management regulatory models had been promoted by ever-changing digital technologies.[5] In a sense, the establishment of digital rights management regulatory model could be justified from the starting point at these four aspects.

It is regulated of various parties' behaviour in digital environment rather than digital rights management technology itself. If "four modalities of the regulation" theory was adopted in digital rights management regulation scheme. In fact, the four elements included in normative regulatory of digital rights management mentioned above, more or less, aim at the governance of people's actions in digital environment.

Also, the critiques on "digital rights management technology, is still working, though be taken"[6] are considered to be the obstacles for proceeding digital rights management substantive rules on the internet.

"The market" factor should be treated as the lubricant or lever in a profit diagram. However, regarding "the market" restraint, digital rights management system has been challenged by the all participants in digital industry business.[7] On the one hand, the economic benefit motivations for each parts (content owners/consumers/internet service providers) concerning digital rights management system has not been consistent. On the other hand, profitable copyrighted material subscription has been encountered with numerous piracy and non-profit employment.

As such, we might say, digital rights management market, at least, digital technology market is not fuelled by any anticipated common benefit of all participants. It is not easy for the content owners to abandon their interest gained from digital copyrighted works distribution to the public. In this regard, they cannot accept more of rampant piracy activities in digital world, not only out of "defending copyright dignity", also for "considerable revenue". Being in this situation, the divergence of economic position has definitely not put the regulatory model for digital rights management in before yet. Marketing impact obviously matters.

"Architecture" issue about digital rights management system has been protested as well. Architecture in Lessig's "four modalities theory" is regarded as a decisive

---

[4]Ibid.

[5]Lessig [3], pp. 122–123.

[6]See Chapter I, 3.1.2.4.

[7]Ibid 402.

formality in which norms and certain market characteristics are determined by the actual architecture under network circumstance.[8] In addition, architecture is deemed as a kind of law since "it determines what people can and cannot do".[9]

The architecture of digital space, more or less, makes people's activities or actions difficult to regulate.[10] The distribution scale/speed of copyrighted works has been more than large/rapid as people can imagine. In cyberspace, the digital technology seems not untouchable and unrecognisable by our cognition. Since the very intangible material was the only resource of network, and the computers manipulated by specific digital programming brought us to a wonderland, in which we even have no idea upon what we are using and what we are watching.

In terms of "norms", there are many differences between those which are in physical world and in cyberspace. As mentioned above, norms, to a certain degree, are determined by the "architecture" feature in digital world. In this regard, the negative influence initiated by the architecture, like the technology, has distorted the consumer's consumption decision.[11] The meaning of digital rights management technology has been narrowed down theoretically and yet in practice has been extended to almost all kinds of technology, which misaligned the users' reasonable or legal behaviour. Likewise, users are apostate to the technology since the traditional norms in physical environment cannot be the prohibition tool in digital era.[12]

It is embarrassing that what we called "piracy" in copyright scheme, in pirates' mind, was entitled as "freedom". However, it is even much more common in digital copyright world, since the internet facilitates copyrighted works' distribution and reproduction. Piracy issue has been more pressing especially in developing countries or nations. "The more one gets, the more one wants". Internet users favor this "free meal" (like download music for free or P2P file sharing) under digital copyright architecture, and absolutely they are insatiate all the time. So-called "piracy freedom" in this circumstance indeed need to be regulated by the "norms".[13] However, norms are likely not working in the intricate digital environment. It makes sense that the users are not tolerated to "norms" in network times, since they get used to enjoy "free" copyright. The norms in digital world hardly work.

According to Lessig's "four modalities", the position of "law" has been more vital than the other three.[14] The "law" formality, which at least as it was, is the most controversial element in digital rights management regulatory model. For the laws, especially anti-circumvention regulations that restrict the users' access to copyrighted works illegally actually have been treated as the biggest abhorrent factor

[8]Ludens [4].

[9]Lessig [3], p. 77.

[10]Ibid, p. 23.

[11]PPT (LEC).

[12]Weber et al. [5].

[13]Ibid 402.

[14]Ibid 256.

against technology innovation and creation.[15] Although the limitations and exceptions (fair use or fair dealing doctrines) can provide the certain room for the public interest, however, it seems impossible that these basic rules in copyright system could be applied in digital copyright architecture. Digital rights management technologies are updated along with ever-challenging circumvention technology. Hence, laws are not amenable to technological implementation, which is kind of entrenched issue in digital times.[16]

"Like a force of nature, the digital age cannot be denied and stopped."[17] Nicolas Negroponte stated the trend of digital world development almost 20 years ago in his classic work, "Being Digital". When his previous prediction has been proved true so far, the worries from human beings could be seen not merely on the "technology" aspect, but also upon regulatory level. Although we witnessed Nicolas's words, still, more than anything, the concern comes based on the elusiveness of digital environment, or, alternatively speaking, the elusiveness feature of technology. The complex of digital rights management architecture and the regulatory four modalities have pressured the current regulatory way of digital rights management to find itself an innovative and specific model to handle all risks.

8.1 Legislative Suggestions on the Direct Coordination of Conflicts

8.1.1 Establishment of Effectiveness Principle for Digital Rights Management

The relevant laws of the United States and the European Union have defined the effective Technological Measures, and it is believed by the United States that only the Technological Measures "which may allow the copyright owners to prohibit, restrain and restrict others" are effective.[18] In the European Union *Copyright Directive*, it is believed that only the Technological Measures "which may allow the holders to control the use of the protected works" are effective. It is simply mentioned in the definition of Technological Measure in the *Regulations for the Protection of Right of Communication through Information Network*[19] that the Technological Measure shall be effective, but no specific standard is specified. With respect to the effectiveness principle for digital rights management, those outdated Technological Measures or those too easy to be circumvented shall not

[15]Ibid 402.

[16]Wolfgang [6], pp. 9–29.

[17]Negroponte [7], p. 229.

[18]Directive 2001/29/EC of the European parliament and the Council of 22 May 2001 on the Harmonization of certain aspects of Copyright and Related Rights in the Information Society.

[19]《中华人民共和国信息网络传播权保护条例》.

be protected reasonably, as it may lead to the abuse of "protection of Technological Measure" and even severely restrict the social and cultural development. The digital rights management system adopted by the copyright holders must constitute a barrier to the illegal access and use of their works, which may not be cracked by ordinary users with the help of the general skills they have mastered and the general legal tools. Therefore, I propose that clear explanation and definition shall be made to the effectiveness of Technological Measure in the legal provisions.

In the *Interpretation on Regulations for the Protection of Right of Communication through Information Network*[20] by the State Council Office of Legislative Affairs, it is believed that the Technological Measures protected by law must be legally effective from the legislative spirit of the *Regulations*. However, in the *Interpretation*, the wording of "must be legally effective" only excludes the illegal Technological Measures, and no explanation is made to what is "effective"; in addition, the complexity of the audience determines that the standards vary with people in terms of whether the protection of the Technological Measure to works is effective; for example, the standards are certainly different between the ordinary users and the network professionals. Therefore, in light of the provisions of U.S. Digital Millennium Copyright Act, I believe that the definition of the effective of Technological Measure shall be aimed at the ordinary users rather than the network professionals, and whether the Technological Measures are effective shall be against the normal operation of works. The *Copyright Law* and the *Regulations for the Protection of Right of Communication through Information Network* in China only make provisions for the legal responsibility by deliberately evading or destroying the technical protection measures, rather than the legal responsibility of the holder due to the abuse of Technological Measures or how to undertake the legal liability. The fact that rights and obligations are not well matched at the legislative level has strengthened edgewise the rights of digital rights management uses, and has provided a "safeguard" for the private business interests and the narrowing of Fair Use.[21]

8.1.2 Supplement of Exception Clauses to Coordinate the Conflict with Fair Use

The appearance of digital technology only changes the resource adjustment mechanism rather than people's demands for intellectual achievements within the scope of copyright.[22] The essential purpose of digital rights management is to prevent unauthorised use or infringement of digital works in accordance with the copyright owner's intent to manage and protect the private property rights of copyright

[20]《中华人民共和国信息网络传播权保护条例》释义.

[21]Aretz [8], p. 1357.

[22]Sinnreich and Aufderheide [9].

holders. The legal protection of the Technological Measure is in essence a kind of benefit adjustment mechanism related to the use of works, namely the conversion of direct management mode to indirect management mode for rights.[23] The Fair Uses of the two are established on the configuration of intellectual achievements within the same specific range, but the specific adjustment mechanisms are different due to the different media of intellectual achievements. Therefore, the digital rights management and its legal protection can be traced to the same origin with the Fair Use in terms of the concept, and the two management modes can be regarded to jointly constitute the generalised copyright law. Furthermore, the infringement of Technological Measure will constitute the copyright infringement in a broad sense. Therefore, I believe that, it is actually in line with the true spirit of the limitation system of rights in Copyright Law to extend the Fair Use to the anti-circumvention exceptional range of digital rights management based on the balance principle and oriented by the coordination of rights and obligations.[24] The *Regulations for the Protection of Right of Communication through Information Network* provides only four circumvention exceptions with too narrow exception types, and the *Regulations* further specifies that the circumvention exceptions are only applicable to the works acquired through information network, excluding other works not communicated through information network, which severely expels the fair use right of the public. In the Article 1201(c)(1) of U.S. Digital Millennium Copyright Act, the rights of Technological Measure are restricted on the whole: "nothing in this section shall affect rights, remedies, limitation or defences to copyright infringement, including fair use, under this title".[25] The provisions also make detailed exception regulations from many aspects such as the disclaimers of the non-profit library, archives and educational institutions, the reverse engineering, the disclaimers of the protection of minors, the protection of personal information and the security testing, which has provided an important reference value for the perfection of copyright legal systems in China.[26]

From the perspective of fair use, referring to the traditional copyright law, the anti-circumvention exception clauses shall be further complemented and expanded to coordinate the conflicts between the legal protection of digital rights management and the public interests from various aspects such as individual learning, study and appreciation, the application of current events, the fair use by libraries and other utilities, the study on encryption and decryption technology for research, the law enforcement and intelligence activities, and the reverse engineering research.[27]

[23]Birnhack [10], pp. 264–284.

[24]Ibid.

[25]Loren [11], p. 685.

[26]Ibid.

[27]Ibid.

8.1.3 Introduction of Copyright Term System for the Technological Measures

If there is still technical protection measures for the digital works beyond the protection term, the ordinary public shall be restricted by not only the Technological Measure but also the *Copyright Law* in case of hoping to access to and use the digital works. It is pointed out by some scholars, the Technological Measures are not worthy of unconditional recognition and protection by the law, and it just conforms to the public interest and justice requirements to crack them in some cases.[28] The U.S. Digital Millennium Copyright Act, the European Union Copyright Directive and the relevant laws of Japan and Australia shall be attributed to the "fair use" and "limitations and exceptions of copyright protection"; I believe that the behaviour "to crack the protection of Technological Measure of works beyond the copyright term", shall also be excluded from the infringement act and included in the circumvention exception clauses of Technological Measure. If the works with knowledge and information in the public domain are beyond the statutory protection period, the Technological Measure is just to protect the copyright in essence; but the copyright does not exist now. "Mutually dependent, usefulness of having a buffer state in between",[29] therefore it is the inevitable requirement and necessary path to realise the public interest by cracking the Technological Measure of digital works beyond the protection term, which is also the manifestation of social justice. In addition, the works in the public domain are the most important part for the public to access to the works, to exercise the fair use right, to learn the cultural knowledge, to spread the social culture, and to develop the cultural industry; if this circumvention behaviour becomes the infringement act for the application of anti-circumvention provisions in the *Copyright Law* and the *Regulations for the Protection of Right of Communication through Information Network*, it will be not only contrary to the legislative intention of the *Copyright Law*, but also not conducive to realisation of benefit balance principle of the copyright law, which will ultimately damage the protection of the public interest.[30] Therefore, the copyright protection period system of Technological Measures has its necessity in the substantial sense.

Furthermore, in the *Copyright Law* and other relevant laws and regulations, the copyright holder shall be required to actively provide the cracking and circumvention manner for the corresponding digital rights management measures at the expiry of the protection term of digital works, which is essentially the obligation undertaken by the copyright holder while enjoying the copyright protection.[31] However, in

[28]Ibid.

[29]Aufderheide et al. [12].

[30]Martin [13].

[31]Netanel [14].

practice, it is impossible to require the copyright holder to fully relieve the Technological Measure due to the wide distribution and huge storage of work carriers.[32]

Therefore, another balance mode shall be taken into consideration so as not to affect the public's access to and use of digital works, namely the author shall submit the cracking manner to the copyright authority or competent authorities with targeted digital rights at the expiry of the copyright protection term of digital works.[33] If the copyright owner does not submit the cracking manner to the competent authority, the public shall be exempted from the use of works through self-circumvention of the Technological Measure.[34] The copyright holders shall further actively cooperate with the legality inspection for the network digital works in the administrative law enforcement.[35] The digital rights may be managed more effectively to coordinate the conflicts in the interests between the copyright holder and the public by regulating the existing copyright authorities, integrating their business systems, expanding the management scope and manner of digital works, or establishing the appropriate digital rights management organisations to deal with the digitisation and mediumisation trend. It is thus clear that, the term system of Technological Measure is compatible with the existing specific rules of copyright law.[36]

8.2 Legislative Suggestions on the Indirect Coordination of Conflicts

8.2.1 Establishment of Legal Protection System of Privacy Involved in the Supporting Technological Measures

The analysis above on the conflict between the digital rights management technology and the Fair Use does not rule out the capability of the Technological Measure to collect, store and handle the personal information of consumers, so the protection of internet privacy for consumers faces great challenges and threats under the environment of widely used Technological Measures.

More attentions are paid to the protection of personal information in the developed countries: the United States has implemented the *Privacy Act* as early as in 1974; the *Federal Electronic Communications Privacy Act*, the *Children's Online Privacy Protection Act*, and the *Computer Contrast and Privacy Protection Act* also have been continuously added into the protection legal systems of privacy right in the United States. In Article 57 of the Preface of the European Union *Copyright Directive in Information Society*: "The system can handle the personal data and

[32]Ibid.

[33]Lloyd and Mayeda [15], p. 59.

[34]Lloyd and Mayeda [15].

[35]Ibid.

[36]Ibid.

allow the tracking of online activities, and functional design of Technological Measure shall be consistent with the provisions related to the protection of personal privacy in the 1995 *European Union 95/46/EC Directive on the Protection of Personal Data*." Thus, the personal information has already been protected involved in the digital rights management in the United States and Europe. After the *Copyright Directive in Information Society*, the EU also issued in April 2004 the *E-Privacy 2002/58/EC Directive* which took effect in the EU Member States. Meanwhile, the Japanese government has enacted the *Copyright Law Amendment* in 1999 in the Internet age and implemented the *Personal Information Protection Law* in 2005,[37] and more efforts are made to the public education to make the awareness of personal information security penetrate into the life of the Japanese. It is worthy to be imitated by China that the personal information is protected and safeguarded by strengthening the education and popularisation of individual self-protection. Although the privacy protection laws and regulations in China at this stage have provided some principle articles and protection directions for the protection of privacy right, no provision has been made to the protection of personal privacy of consumers caused by the digital rights management. Before the development of specialised laws and regulations, we can only hope that the existing regulations will realise their potential.

The *Law on Protection of the Rights and Interests of Consumers* in China[38] has its exclusive coordination domain, so it has not been considered an important part of privacy protection. However, it is still expected that the rules in the *Law on Protection of the Rights and Interests of Consumers* may play a role of expansibility in the era of new digital media when there is no specific legislation to the protection of information privacy. The extended application of the *Law on Protection of the Rights and Interests of Consumers* may establish the minimum standards that must be followed for the protection of personal privacy involved in the digital rights management. In the *Law on Protection of the Rights and Interests of Consumers,* Chapter II stipulates the consumer's right to know, the right to choose, the right to fair trade and many other rights, while Chapter 3 also provides many obligations for the operators such as the observation of laws, the receipt of supervision and the informing of real information. The infringement of digital rights management on the personal privacy of consumer or user is mainly reflected in the irrational collection and unreasonable utilisation of personal data.[39] Therefore, the extended application of the *Law on Protection of the Rights and Interests of Consumers* may be specifically considered from the following aspects: 1. The collection and use by the digital copyright owners or providers of Technological Measures of the personal information from the consumers of digital works or other public shall be limited to the protection of copyright in the digital goods and the demands to complete the

[37]The Personal Information Protection Act (Law No. 57 of 2003) (hereinafter referred to as "Act") http://mondaq-business.vlex.com/vid/personal-information-protection-law-japan-56695004, access date: 26/09/2015.

[38]《中国人民共和国消费者权益保护法》.

[39]Sinnreich and Aufderheide [9].

transaction, without expanding the collection scope of information; 2. The other party shall be fully informed of the purpose and application on the collection and use of personal information; 3. The personal information shall not be disclosed or sold in any form without the consent of the consumer, or shall not be used for the purpose different from the previous one; 4. The information collectors shall take reasonable measures to ensure the integrity and security of personal information, and to prevent the information from loss or disclosure; 5. The privacy right involved in the Technological Measure of the consumers of digital works shall be safeguarded as far as possible through right relief under the relevant regulations of the *Law on Protection of the Rights and Interests of Consumers,* once the privacy right of consumer is threatened or infringed.[40] Learning from the experience of the developed countries, it is certainly necessary for China to develop special laws and regulations to protect the personal information, which can be legislated from the following aspects:

1. Distinguish the security and the collection of personal information.
   It is inevitable to collect the personal information in the network era, the legislation on protection of personal information shall not only allow digital rights management to collect certain personal information, but also ensure the security of those personal information collected[41]; the government departments and other organisations in good faith shall serve as the third party if the third-party program is adopted.
2. Prevent the excessive collection of personal information.
   Although the digital rights management is allowed to collect certain personal information, but the information must be related to the authorisation, tracking and other necessary functions of the copyright, which shall be clearly defined when developing new personal information protection act.
3. Completely ban the bargaining transaction of personal information and promote the corporate self-regulation.
   In face with the liquidation or bankruptcy, some companies often sell the personal information as the last batch of resources for benefits, or even make profits by selling personal information completely regardless of the user wishes. The harmfulness of such phenomena is so great that it has seriously threatened the personal security and the social stability.[42] The legislation on protection of personal information must completely ban such phenomena and promote corporate self-regulation, so that the corporate will consciously assume the relevant responsibilities.

The *Personal Information Protection Act (Draft)*[43] in China has been submitted to the State Council in September 2008, and the government shall promulgate and

[40]Cohen and Murphy [16].

[41]Ibid.

[42]Clinton [17].

[43]《个人信息保护法》(草案).

implement the draft in a timely manner after it is mature. With the development of digital rights management, taking example from the Europe, America, Japan and other countries, China shall pay attention to the protection of personal information, promptly revise and update the relevant laws and regulations, and constantly improve the legislation on protection and security of personal information, thus laying a compacted foundation for the coordination of conflict between the legal protection of digital rights management and the Fair Use.[44]

8.2.2 Improvement on the Laws and Regulations of Anti-Unfair Competition to Prevent the Unfair Competition

It can be seen from the analysis above that the user of the Technological Measure may conduct the unfair competition or monopolistic behaviours under the legal protection umbrella, which will further affect the legitimate rights and interests of consumers or even infringe the fair use right of the public. To limit unfair competition of some enterprises related to the digital rights management, while enacting the Digital Millennium Copyright Act, the United States also improves its Anti-trust Law, which clearly defines that the abuse of rights by the intellectual property holder shall be regulated. In addition to the formulation of provisions prohibiting the circumvention of Technological Measures in the copyright law, the Japanese government also revised and enlarged in 1999 the *Anti-Unfair Competition Law* to prevent the unfair competition caused by the Technological Measure and indirectly protect the rights of the creators and the legitimate users. Given to the promotion of technology updates and anti-monopoly, *Loi sur le Droit d'Auteur et les Droits Voisins dans la Société de l'Information*[45] is passed in France on June 30, 2006, which clearly requires the dealer to disclose his digital rights management format to his competitors, and the regulations shall be set up to prevent any kind of media player system from monopolising the digital music market.

In the laws and regulations in the field of digital rights in China, no response has been made to the threats towards the competition in the new digital media caused by the digital rights management and its anti-circumvention legislation.[46] In the judicial practice, although the judicial interpretation from the Supreme People's Court may reduce the side effects of anti-circumvention legislation to suppress the industry competition, these competitive threats may not be completely settled by just the judicial interpretation; in addition, it will still take a long time to construct the legal systems for the threats caused by the unfair competition. Therefore, the legislators in China shall actively respond to the unfair competition beyond the legislative intent

---

[44]Armstrong [18], p. 49.

[45]Gitton [19].

[46]Handke and Towse [20], pp. 937–957.

of digital rights management, and develop or expand the appropriate laws and regulations by adopting the legislative experiences from the United States, Japan, European Union and other countries and regions.

In Chapter II of the *Anti-Unfair Competition Law*[47] in China, detailed and specific prohibition provisions have been made for many unfair competition behaviours of the operators such as the deceptive trade, the mandatory transaction, the administrative monopoly, the false propaganda, the tying sale or the addition of unreasonable conditions. In the meanwhile, in Chapter 2 "Monopoly Agreement" and Chapter 3 "Abuse of Dominant Market Position" of the *Anti-Monopoly Law* in China, detailed prohibition provisions have also been set up for the market monopoly by the operators with the help of their dominant market positions. With the respect to the abuse of digital rights management, the tying sale, mandatory sale and deceptive sale of digital works and media with the help of the digital rights license agreement or the digital matching technique, and the mandatory tying sale of digital products by the operators in digital industry with the help of their dominant market positions, the nature of these behaviours are completely consistent with the unfair competition and market monopoly behaviours such as the deceptive trade, the mandatory transaction and the tying sale in the commodity exchange in the traditional market.[48] Therefore, the application scopes of the *Anti-Unfair Competition Law* and the *Anti-Monopoly Law* shall be extended, and the corresponding clauses on abuse of digital rights management are added in the unfair behaviours and the abuse of dominant market positions to prevent the unfair competition or market monopoly caused by the unreasonable or unlawful use of Technological Measure, thus further protecting the rights and interests of creators and the legitimate users of the works, and indirect coordinating the conflicts between the legal protection of the Technological Measure and the Fair Use.[49]

8.3 Far More Than Judicial Regulatory Model

Based on the analytical research above, I have proposed a variety of specific and practical coordination approaches in this chapter. From the perspective of the technology, I believe that the conflicts of the parties may be coordinated effectively from the technology containing certain Fair Use and the third-party authorisation mechanism[50]; the effective manner to coordinate the conflicts is to give full play to the copyright collective management organisation and motivate the innovation of industry associations from the interventions of national and local administrations; from the view of the judicial practice point, I believe that the key to settle the conflict

---

[47]《中华人民共和国反不正当竞争法》.

[48]Yu [21], pp. 13–77.

[49]Ibid 442.

[50]Wilson [22], pp. 2–7.

is to grant the judge with discretion at a certain degree in the judicial practice for the legal protection of the Technological Measure.[51]

The legislation on protection of Technological Measures starts late in China, and the specific provisions are still not enough for the relevant laws and regulations. Based on the aforementioned theoretical analysis, I have explored some detailed and practical legislative proposals from the perspectives of the direct and indirect coordination of conflict between the legal protection of digital rights management and the Fair Use. For the former insight, I believe that the effectiveness principle shall be further determined for the Technological Measure to rule out the malignant and illegal Technological Measures; the copyright term system shall be developed for the Technological Measure to avoid the "perpetuation" of digital copyright protection term; the "anti-circumvention exceptions" shall be extended and detailed to ensure the realisation of fair use right. For the later perspective, the legitimate rights and interests of consumers of digital works shall be protected to indirectly coordinate the conflicts of the two by the establishment of the protection mechanism of privacy involved in the Technological Measure and the expansion of application scope of the Anti-Unfair Competition Law and the Antitrust Law.[52]

8.3.1 Technology and Law of Social Norms

Comparing to simulation technique, digital technology makes pirated copying with tiny payment which have little differences comparing to original editions. Moreover, with the development of technology, the role of law shines out.[53] In addition, there is a mutual complement and interaction relationship between copyright law and technology. If the law fails to prevent infringement acts, technology shall be adopted to make up for it; and if technological techniques are cracked by advanced technologies, the law plays the role to prevent the technology cracking.

To conclude, law and technology can be regarded as two sharp swords to protect their own works. If legal sanctions for infringement act refers to the afterward remedy, then the approach adopted by copyright holders to prevent their work from being checked, copied, spread are precautionary measures. As the saying goes that, "mend the fold after the sheep have been stolen is not smart as keeping something for a rainy day". Therefore, in the opinion of people of various countries, technological protection measures should be properly adopted and at the same time, they have to conduct anti-circumvention activities against evasive actions.[54]

Technology produces a far-reaching and profound effect on people's life. Comparing to science, technology plays more direct and important roles in people's

---

[51]Bird and Jain [23].

[52]Ibid.

[53]Weber et al. [5].

[54]Ibid 449.

behaviour and real life.[55] Moreover, concerning the relationship between technology and law, the development of technology shall directly drive the growth of wealth to further push the growth of right as a vital factor in economic relations, which also leads to the changes of allocation principle and rules of both right and power. Therefore, as realistic productivity, technology fundamentally determines the contents of social norms with right and power as the core. Friedrich Engels believes that economic relationship is a critical base for social history, which includes all techniques of manufacturing and transportation. Furthermore, it also determines the exchange, distribution means and class division after the disintegration of the clan society, the relationship between politics and servitude, national law, etc. During the progress of copyright law, the growing sophistication of printing technology ignites the emergence of copy law and the advancement in terms of copy and communication field continually break its equilibrium which impel the constant changes.[56]

Technology appears as social norms in real life to directly and compulsively regulate people's behaviour. In addition, it has countless forms, among which morality, behaviour, discipline and law are commonly known. However, we can rarely see the role technology plays in social function as social norms in traditional societies which are popular in nowadays and have profoundly affected people's behaviour manners.[57] As social norms, technology and law are mutually independent, regulating people's behaviours throughout the whole society, and participating in the allocation of property, benefits, right and power.[58] Moreover, this kind of technology should be acknowledged and supported by law and is subject to law. Moreover, technology is able to provide assurances for the implementation of law. Comparing to law, technology has a glittering array of advantages in terms of social norms because the implementation of law depends on public force to a larger extent and common resources, which is effective within the certain scope of national compelling force. On the contrast, technology is capable of working directly, accurately, efficiently and economically because it is not only capable of building up behaviour standards, but also helping to realise the normative contents.[59] For example, CD with anti-copy function will restrain customers with infringement willing from copying which force them to obey relevant laws. Moreover, under the condition that people can protect their rights with technical approaches, they shall inevitably ask more requirements in terms of technology than law. Besides, the role technology plays is not confined to countries, which attracts right holders coming into the network environment. It is based on this condition that scholars have pointed out that the most obvious change in network policies is the role transition of technology: technology is law.[60]

---

[55]Ibid 449.

[56]Kleinsteuber [24], pp. 61–75.

[57]Ibid.

[58]Ibid.

[59]Nwogugu [25].

[60]Lessig [3], pp. 122–123.

Legal assimilation is a phenomenon of different laws embracing and affecting each other under global economy. Meanwhile, the application of computers and internet technology has generated the international law request because internet space has no border and the legal mechanism of online trading has to break national boundaries. Therefore, the law of cyberspace is asked to have global technological standards and trading rules.[61] At the same time, the digital trading of copyright works is also required to carry out in a relatively unified framework of international law protection. Therefore, intentional legal assimilation is to be imperative. However, legal assimilation is not simply putting each part together and embracing different laws. The country in a hegemonic position or a leading position is the promoter of legal assimilation which mainly shows in a phenomenon that the strong nations in terms of politics, economy and technology conduct one-way communication to promote its legal idea and systems to other countries with different presentation patterns of propagation paths.[62]

China could bite the dust when referred to most IP battles; the increased ability to share and distribute information, knowledge, and entertainment in the cloud age has also provoked a series of issues in China. Digital-era business models in China exploit some perceived gaps in copyright architecture to creatively include technological elements and thereby fulfil the demand for access to content.[63] Core objectives of cloud storage service (CSS) are to provide large amounts of storage space for users and to enable other functions such as file sharing. These added functions allow users to store their files and to share them with friends as well as with other users spreading across the internet. However, with the provision of these functions, CSS models represent a double-edged sword. By enabling access to sizeable free storage spaces, data storage security and reliability, convenient retrieval and ease of sharing stored data,[64] cloud storage service providers (CSSPs) are typically internet service providers (ISPs) who also make it easier for users to share copyrighted materials illegally.[65] In other words, large, secure storage spaces make it possible for users to easily store the cloud multimedia information in various forms of texts, images, movies and videos.[66]

---

[61]Ibid.

[62]Carbado and Mitu Gulati [26], pp. 1757–1828.

[63]"We Need to Talk About Aereo: Copyright-Avoiding Business Models, Cloud Storage and a Principled Reading of the 'Transmit' Clause" (Columbia Public Law and Legal Theory Working Paper, 1 June 2014, p. 43).

[64]Soghoian [27], p. 370.

[65]Xiao and Zhengcao [28], p. 26.

[66]On internet trade platforms, many users put their cloud storage space up for sale, and typically, there are huge amounts of copyrighted materials stored in these accounts, available at http://www.cs.com.cn/xwzx/201704/t20170427_5261009.html (visited 5 December 2018).

Widespread copyright infringements in China[67] related to cloud-based service inexorably give rise to the question where should CSSPs go? Cloud-based service relies heavily on technology, and its profound influence covers vast dimensions. The cloud storage industry of China is always stranded despite its avowed adherence to fight against copyright infringement. It hardly makes a liability refinement other than reforming with a "one size fits all" circumstance when dazzling CSSs regularly boom, and the corresponding technical devices do little to support its legislative basis.

8.3.2 Assimilation of Anti-Circumvention Provisions Based on Internationally Multilateral Treaties

Digital copyright works are easy to be illegally replicated and propagated and copyright owners in countries with intellectual property provisions and powerful information technology adopt technological protection measures to limit the access to their works without being authorised.[68] Nevertheless, these protection measures are cracked by new technologies and therefore copyright owners ask laws to protect technologically protective measures of copyright. *The WIPO Internet Treaties* of WCT and WPPT were forged in 1996 leading by America and driven by European Union, which defined that 'Contracting parties have to provide appropriate legal protection and effective legal remedies to technological circumvention means, which are adopted when creators are granted with the right of this treaty or *Berne Convention,* aiming to limit the copy of works, performance and sound recording without being authorized.' However, the formulation process of the treaty is difficult and complicated, which reflects the conflicts of interests between America, European Union and other countries. To conclude, the safeguard clause for Technological Measures is the result of compromise and its expression adopts principle text with flexible words determined by southern African nations, which does not define effective Technological Measures. Therefore, we cannot ensure whether access control technological measures are within the range of anti-circumvention provisions or not. Besides, these measures do not clarify exceptions and limitations, and the condition whether to provide dodging device, services or preparative acts for abandoning circumvention is also not clarified. The flexibility and principle of anti-circumvention provisions of technological measures in internet treaty lead to the illegibility of standards of legal protection, which leave a considerably large space for anti-circumvention duties. When various contracting parties formulate or revise the domestic law for technological measures, they explain and implement

---

[67] In recent five years, the National Copyright Administration of China (NCAC) has shut down 3908 pirate websites involving infringement cases, available at http://news.sina.com.cn/sf/news/fzrd/2018-02-26/doc-ifyrvspi1857037.shtml (visited 26 February 2019).

[68] Ibid.

Table 8.1 Protection standards comparison of technological measures in terms of assimilation of internationally multilateral treaties

	Access-control circumvention	Copy-control circumvention	Anti-circumvention exceptions	Protection level
United States	Forbidden	Not forbidden	Narrow range	Highest
European Union	Forbidden	Forbidden	Narrower range	Higher

anti-circumvention provisions from the aspect of their individual interests. Therefore, different domestic laws are generated to implement technological measures, and different countries work out different domestic laws to protect their own interest based on the product competitiveness of network copyright (Table 8.1).

8.3.2.1 Assimilation of Anti-Circumvention Provisions Based on Bilateral Free Trade Agreements

Copyright is definitely a favorable property for international trading in America. The emergence of internet has provided a world-level open market for American copyrighted products, which also face a great threat and huge losses in the network environment.[69] Therefore, it is the common wish to develop serious mechanism against digital privacy. Moreover, Technological Measures of protection clause in *The WIPO Internet Treaties* have not reached the requirement of the edition requested by American copyright owner and software industry organisations. Meanwhile, the U.S. Congress explained and understood the Technological Measures in accordance with the highest standards of protection information content industries based on its flexibility and principle to meet the information content industry's demands, and worked out *Digital Millennium Copyright Act* in 1998. This act creates a series of rights which are completely different from traditional editions, and the anti-circumvention right in the act is described as super copyright: allow the controlling of non-copyrighted materials, grant information owners with a new right, which do not only control the access to works protected by Technological Measures but also control the attached technology involving information protection. America, as the biggest exporter of intellectual property products is trying unremitting efforts to clear the range of intellectual property and expand the executing intensity.[70] The standards all contracting parties adopt in implementing *The WIPO Internet Treaties* are lower than the standards stipulated in *Digital Millennium Copyright Act.*

Intellectual property protection under the network environment should transcend geographic and political boundaries, and its international convergence has become an irreversible tendency. Concerning international legal rules, China is not able to

[69]Ibid 299.

[70]Ibid.

become the absolutely dominant player who always plays the role as a participant or executor.[71] Therefore, China should correctly choose the paths for the convergence of network copyright law. The above path shows that the final result of convergence is to present the legal ideas and systems of powerful countries, yet sky rocketing contracting parties are granted with opportunities to demonstrate their appealing in international law mechanisms; besides, strong states find it difficult to unify the different wills of various negotiating states and therefore international legal mechanisms which are finally formed are always in shortage of inflexibility and clarity. Consequently, we can draw up regulations or executive modes in accordance with China's legal environment and in line with the fundamental interests in the premise of fulfilling international obligations under the principle and ambiguity of internationally multilateral treaties. Concerning the second convergence mean, it is acceptable if China is able to obtain full and reciprocal benefits.[72] However, it is hard to implement in real life because China is a big country with enormous profits and extensively divergent interests so reciprocal benefits exchange is difficult to be realised through one concrete legal mechanism. Accordingly, China ought to focus on the first approach while participating in the convergence of international network copyright law with the second approach as supplementation.[73] Different countries have diversified copyright advantages and various international trade positions. The construction of legal system for a nation's internet copyright should be law localisation instead of law globalisation, which adjusts global laws to make them adaptable for their own nations.[74] The convergence of internet copyright law must be accompanied by interest games between nations, and the relationship between law globalisation and national interests have to be appropriately dealt with to obey the global legislative trends and protect national politics and economic benefits, namely to obey the following rules: Global thought and local focus. China has a stronger protection intensity comparing to America and Japan, mainly showing in the conditions that there are few statutory exemptions and open terms and forbidding exceptions.[75] Obviously, legislators for anti-circumvention law of Technological Measures do not take the status of China in International Copyright Trade System into consideration and do not take fully use of the principle and ambiguity of internet treaties to draw up anti-circumvention provisions adapted to national interest in the premise of fulfilling international obligations; they only conduct simple and cursory imitation of America's laws with the absolute superiority in terms of information technology and knowledge economy.[76]

[71]Cunningham [29].

[72]Ibid 162.

[73]Ibid 163.

[74]Ibid 162.

[75]Välimäki and Oksanen [30].

[76]Ibid.

8.3.2.2 Technical Protection and Anti-Technique Circumvention in Copyright Relations: Lessons and Experience of America and Europe

Technological protection measures and anti-circumvention rules are two important approaches to adjust each party's behaviours under digital environment and their relationship embodies the relationship between technology and law in field of copyright. It is not strange for Chinese and foreign copyright owners to have the exclusive right endowed by copyright law through technological protection measures. In an emulated environment, copyright owners prevent pirates from obtaining the same quality as authentic products based on unique printing methods. The approach of stopping the infringement according to technological protection is rarely seen in an emulated environment but is common in information age. In the digital environment, copyright infringement is easy and cheap and even everyone has the ability to implement it on the one hand, which will cause greater losses than in an emulated environment; on the other hand, traditional judicial remedy is helpless in protecting copyright owners, especially their interests. Technological protection measures enable the remarkable decrease of infringement and owners do not have to take on the expensive counsel fee because of copyright action, a lengthy process undefined verdict and judgment enforcement. Therefore, more and more copyright owners adopt technological protection measures to regulate consumer behaviour and at the same time protect their own interests.[77]

Copyright owners can guide most of people to obey the rules in the consumption of copyright works through technological protection measures, yet they are unable to order those who are not willing to obey the rules and have ability to take evasive action. Therefore, they hope to have a guarantee by coercive force of state. Under such circumstance, anti-circumvention rules emerge as the times require, which refers to legal norms of forbidding avoiding, getting around, eliminating and damaging technological protection measures. Provision of anti-circumvention of copyright law can be traced back to the prohibition of manufacturing and spreading hacking cable communication equipments issued in 1984. Soon after, laws of abandoning manufacturing and spreading the equipments which can hack satellite communications were passed and *Family Audio Recording Method* was issued in 1992, which incorporated terms of control mechanism to abandon damaging copying digital audio and video equipment. After entering the era of digital time, two treaties issued by WIPO in 1996 set rules for anti-technique circumvention asking contracting parties to provide full law protection and effective legal remedies in response to the requirement of copyright owners calling for law recognition for technological protection measures. Afterwards, a large number of nations started to

---

[77]Copyright Law and Consumer Protection ECLG/035/05 – February 2005, Policy conclusions of the European Consumer Law Group (ECLG) based on a study carried out by Dr. Lucie Guibault and Ms Natali Helberger, academic researchers at the Institute for Information Law, University of Amsterdam. Available at: https://www.ivir.nl/publicaties/download/copyrightlawconsumerprotection.pdf. Access date: 17th/07/2018.

make and perfect their anti-technique circumvention rules. For example, the DMCA passed by America in 1998 and 2001/29/EC passed by European Union in 2001. The anti-technique circumvention rules in American digital copyright law and EC Directive mainly consist two parts: action items of anti-technique circumvention and equipment terms of anti-circumvention. Between these two parts, the former forbids avoidance behaviour for technological protection measures so that the avoidance behaviour shall cause legal liability whether these behaviours lead to copyright infringement or not. The latter forbids manufacturing and spreading any equipment or services to help the circumvention. To avoid the condition that anti-circumvention rules give excessive protection to copyright owners and damage the interest of consumers and benefits of public, both the American digital copyright law and EC Directive have set escape clauses that allow the avoidance behaviour under strict conditions.[78]

As an implementation tool for copyright policy, technological protection measures have reinforced and strengthened copyright law and have become important approaches to achieve their copyright rights in digital times.[79] Moreover, the application of technological protection measures has been common in America and European Union, especially for big manufacturers and almost every piece of product has been granted with protection measures. For example, Audio & Video Products widely adopt the technology of preventing unwanted copying, which greatly boost the sales of genuine copyright works, decrease the copyright infringement as well as improve the copyright industry's living environment. According to the data released by Records Industry Association of America, the sales of DVD and VHS of America music in 2004 increased by 51% compared with the former year,[80] which achieved 32 million sales with 610.7 billion dollars.[81] To conclude anti-technique circumvention rules legally provide security for the technological protection measures. For example, since the establishment of *Digital Millennium Copyright Act*, there have been a number of litigations based on these rules. Besides, technological protection measures have gradually become the consumer behaviour specifications of copyright owners, which constantly affected the right allocation of copyright owners and consumers. For example, with the geotagging LV, they are able to make certain playback devices have the access to read the copyright works in certain markets to confine the consumption to specific areas. Along with the advancement of technological protection measures and strengthening of law protection, copyright owners shall accurately control the access and usage of their work. The consumption rule of digital copyright work will clear the right division between copyright owners, consumers and the public, which is determined and revised by copyright owners to some extent and quite a few of them expect to expand their rights through

[78]Griffiths [31].

[79]Tang [32], pp. 852–871.

[80]According to a 2004 study by Jessica Reif-Cohen, media and entertainment Research Analyst at Merrill Lynch.

[81]Ibid.

technological protection measures. For example, they can limit consumers' fair use of their copyrighted works. Fair use can be divided into transformative and consumptive use.

Transformative use refers to the condition that users add their own creation while using, for example the news report, comment, criticism or imitation of a copyrighted work. Consumptive use is to grant the consumers with privilege. Private copying is a typical consumptive fair use. Besides, there have always been controversial in the jurisprudential circle for fair use, especially for the nature of consumptive fair use. Some people hold the opinion that fair use is a kind of right, and once they are jeopardised, they can bring it into court to ask the enforcement while other people think that it is a kind of privilege. Further, whether consumers are able to carry out full implementation or not depends on the limitation regulated by copyright owners. Moreover, some scholars point out that consumptive fair use is the result of market failure, which is different from the opinions of theory circle.[82] Fair use, including consumptive fair use is a common phenomenon in practice and the only difference is that some countries compensate for the damages of copyright owners and some do not compensate because in fact, copyright owners are unable to stop the emergence of fair use. However, nowadays, copyright owners can take consumptive fair use into their right scope which cannot be controlled before based on the advancement and implementation of technological protection measures. Therefore, technological protection measures, to some extent, determine the right allocation between copyright owners, consumers and the public.

By the way, technological protection measures also affect the benefit allocation of copyright owners to some extent and indirectly affect public benefits. The serious anti-technique circumvention rules of America and European Union contribute the digital blockade and some manufactures prevent others from manufacturing compatible accessories and other equipment under these rules and a digital competitive insulation is then set up. For example, the copyright owners of some file formats of digital information can implement technological protection measures to make these formats work on certain devices. Hence, if manufactures expect to produce certain products to read the file, they have to sign with copyright owners because the law bans technology circumvention, and they can control the market of playback devices and accessories. At the same time, various playback devices and file formats are incompatible, and most of consumers cannot afford the price to buy the devices. Consequently, they will become faithful users once they choose a certain device. Through this way, copyright owners can have fixed users and keep competitors away.

Of course, copyright owners are restrained while adopting technological protection measures in the social norm sense. As the most powerful social norm in legal ruling society, relevant laws have to carry out examination and regulation on technology playing the same role to ensure the implementation of the allocation scheme and principle. Although the main aim of anti-technique circumvention rules

[82]Lunney [33], p. 975.

is to provide guarantee to technological protection measures but not complete identification without resolution. Its aim is to guarantee the effective implementation of copyright law and balance the benefit between copyright owners, consumers and public. Therefore, under some circumstances, these kinds of rules have to limit technological protection measures. Both the anti-technique circumvention rules in American digital copyright law and EC Directive have set up exceptions against technological circumvention, which can be divided in two types: exceptions guaranteeing legitimate reverse engineering, encryption technology research and security testing; exceptions which are favorable for reasonable use contributing to public interest and public safety. However, relevant laws have to strictly prevent and control the conditions that copyright owners regard technological protection measures as tools to obtain illegal interests, such as collecting the private information of consumers. Technology also changes the way of people's protecting their own interests. For example, in simulation environment, the realisation of copyright depends on the force of law and copyright owners tend to seek judicial remedies once there should be infringement and they are in vulnerable positions being attacked.

Copyright owners can directly and forcibly realise the legitimate rights and interests though technological protection measures. In contrast, consumers are in weaker positions in terms of technology and capital and they have to seek the help of law when their legitimate rights are being eroded. When coordinating the relationship between technology and law, the anti-technique circumvention rules in America and European Union are successful as a whole. There is a lot for China to learn from them whether from the perspective of system or concrete legislative techniques of American or European rules, among which the most important key is that these rules are clear and mature with strong enforceability and certainty. These rules are comparatively new and people have a little knowledge without enough experience in terms of legislation and judicial practice. Therefore, it seems significantly important to work out detailed and perfect provisions. These rules do not allow copyright owners to randomly control their copyrighted works through technological protection works but respectively set up exceptions against computer scientific research and reasonable use contributing to public interest and public safety. China, as a developing country, ought to pay attention to the limits to scientific research and academic freedom caused by these rules. Meanwhile, China has a less-developed economy, people do not have rich living standards, and many consumers cannot always afford to buy copyrighted works. Accordingly, laws have to clear that the technological network measures of copyright owners should not hinder public interests and safety, especially reasonable use which can help to promote the development of social culture and education. However, these rules in America and European Union give excessive protection to technological protection measures that leads to a condition that copyright owners have overreliance on these remedy, which does not merely damage consumers and public benefits but also threaten the copyright law itself. In addition, digital blockade damages the market competitiveness, which also kills minor enterprises, and China should avoid it because it is in a weaker position in international copyright market.

8.3.2.3 Limitations of China's Anti-Technique Circumvention System

In China, more and more copyright owners start to obtain the rights though technological protection measures endowed by copyright law to change the rule of people's consuming their works and sometimes there are illegal phenomena when implementing technological protection measures. To ensure the legal rights of copyright owners and at the same time regulate the application in practice are the reason and goal of the emergence of China's anti-technique circumvention rules.

There are rare civil actions because of new anti-technique circumvention rules. The earliest case was that the defendant, World Magazine software released registration code generator of Ultra Edit 32 which made consumers who bought the magazine have access to illegally use this software. Afterwards, the copyright owner IDM Computer Solutions, Inc., along with its Chinese agent, Beijing Ruize Site Information Service center sued World Magazine Software to Beijing First Intermediate People's Court with the reason that it has violated the anti-technique circumvention rules. The rare cases of relevant legal proceedings are in remarkable contrast to the real fact because of people's recognition and major defects of the rules which bring along with many difficulties for implementation. To be concrete, these rules are too simple and blurred, which weaken the role technological protection measures play in certain matters as legal implementations, which also induce copyright owners take actions above the law with technologies.

At first, overall prohibition on various technology circumvention activities will go against computer scientific research, because not all of the technology circumvention activities should be banned, which do not necessarily bring along with damages for copyright owners and infringement. In some cases, the technology circumvention activities are essential to meet important legitimate interests. Different from most of the copyrighted works, the value of computer program does not lie in presentation but in running, selling machine-readable editions in most of the cases and the hidden principles are not familiar to consumers. Therefore, legitimate academic research and academic activities should involve avoidance behaviours. For example, computers experts have to turn the object code into the origin code to research how a computer program execute specific function, namely to carry out reverse engineering and inverse assembler, decrypt source program, etc. People engage in computer security testing can only find out the loopholes of certain programs whey they attack a system process and then make up for the loopholes. Consequently, reverse engineering activities are allowed in most of the countries and regions under some circumstances. Although the Chinese copyright law does not stipulate in explicit terms the legitimacy of reverse engineering can be indicated in the 17th item in Regulations for the Protection of Computer Software: 'In order to study and research on the design ideas and concepts of software, the following activities such as install, present, transfer and store software can be conducted without the permission of copyright owners and payment. However, decryption research and security testing cannot be included because they are not designed to study and research on its ideas and concepts.' Such rules will inevitably hinder the normal proceeding of decryption research and security testing and at the same time hamper further development in terms of technological protection measures.

Subsequently, the anti-technique circumvention rules do not clear the definition of technological protection measures, which will give opportunities for copyright owners seek right expansion and illegal benefits. (A case study on Jiang Min)

Besides, these technological anti-technique circumvention rules do not forbid providing circumvention devices or services, which greatly weaken the role technological protection measures play in helping copyright owners realise lawful interests. Thus, these rules have a big loophole. Evasion tools, especially those can be provided online will increase infringement risk because countless consumers can afford the evasion tools. Therefore, anti-circumvention device provisions are of vital importance to strengthen the protection on copyright owners under digital environment. Judging from a comprehensive perspective on the anti-technique circumvention rules of other countries and regions, anti-equipment articles are significant parts. For example, both DMCA and 2001/29/EC prohibit manufacturing, selling and promoting any devices or services in terms of circumvention technology. Some experts believe that activities of providing and instigate the infringement will be regarded with liability for infringement under the 1st term of item 148 in *Trial Implementation Several Issues of the General Principles of Civil Law of the PRC Regulated by Supreme People's Court.*[83] Besides, the item 1 in *Explanation on Several Issues Concerning Application Laws of Dispute Cases of Computer Network Copyright*[84] issued in 2000 also prescribed that liability for infringement of Internet service provider, other perpetrators and direct actor should be pursed based on the 130 terms defined in general provisions of the civil law if Internet service provider participate in the infringement activities or instigate and help them carry out infringement. However, I beg to differ from your opinion that it is not necessary to establish other anti-technique circumvention rules. There exist many different viewpoints between providing circumvention devices and common joint act of infringement and common violating liability cannot be applied to the activities of providing circumvention devices or services.[85] So increasing technology circumvention activities cannot be defeated. To begin with, in common joint infringement, contributory infringers instigate and help specific people who have an acquaintance with major infringers while the providers of circumvention devices or services help unspecified people who do not have to directly contact with direct infringers. However, they are able to help more people to carry out infringement activities. For example, providers expose the decode procedure of a certain specific technological protection measure. In the next place, liability shall be pursued with the premise that the major infringers constitute infringement activities yet the terms of anti-equipment are not conditioned

[83]《最高人民法院关于贯彻执行<中华人民共和国民法通则>若干问题的意见(试行)》第一百四十八条, 1988年4月2日.

[84]《最高人民法院关于审理涉及计算机网络著作权纠纷案件适用法律若干问题的解释》第一条, 2000年11月22日.

[85]Perry and Casey [34].

on the criteria of infringement. Once the circumvention devices are provided, perpetrators have to take on infringement liability whether the devices are applied to carry out infringement or not because the goal of anti-equipment terms is not to punish the joint liabilities but to prevent large-scale infringement activities. Universal City Studios, Inc. vs. Reimerdes in America[86] is a good example. The plaintiff adds a cryptographic system on his DVD to guarantee that his DVD can be only read by devices with his authorisation and display technology. Eric Corley, the defendant of this case published an evasion procedure called DeCSS written by Jon Johansen, a Norwegian in his quarterly publication and website.[87] Although the plaintiff did not provide any evidence that DeCSS can decrypt the DVD, the court decided that the defendant constituted actions to provide circumvention devices and asked him to eliminate related contents and website links.

At last, these anti-technique circumvention rules are not beneficial to standardising the allocation of rights between copyright owner and public, since they do not involve the technology protection measures and fair use.[88] Copyright has never been an absolute right, which is restricted by various kinds of limitations. Apart from the restriction of legal protection period, the most important restriction on copyright comes from fair use system. Copyright has been infringed by the employment methods contained in the rational employment system, but they are exempted by lawmakers to protect public's access to copyright materials. Therefore, the fair use principle is of vital importance to seek balance between copyright owner's limited monopoly right and protection of public's access to works. However, the implementation of technology protection measures has always been conflict with fair use system, which will expose its limitations as social norm.[89] Likewise, the usage behaviour of copyright work may have different legal property due to different enforcers. However, technology can only tell the concrete behaviours without an insight of actor's purpose, identity as well as other conditions.

Thus, while prohibiting illegal use of copyright work, technology protection measures will also inhibit consumers' fair use. As for fair use, people have different opinions towards it. There has not been a consistent view that it is on earth a right, a privilege or product of market failure. The most controversial and fierce part of anti-technique circumvention rules is the exception and limitation of technology protection measures in terms of legal protection, and thus many cases concerning anti-technique circumvention rules occurred in many countries have been involved. However, the anti-technique circumvention rules have been shunned in Chinese Copyright Law and Regulations for the Protection of Computer Software, which makes it a doubt that whether fair use can be a strong defense for technology protection measures in China or not.

[86]Universal City Studios, Inc. v. Reimerdes, 111 F. Supp. 2d 294 (2000).

[87]Ibid.

[88]Iwahashi [35], p. 491.

[89]Lessig [2], p. 501.

At the end of 2003, the Supreme People's Court had some amendments with *Explanation on Several Issues Concerning Application Laws of Dispute Cases of Computer Network Copyright.*[90] As for the judicial interpretation after the amendment, the previous 4th article which looks into the joint infringement responsibilities of network providers has been replaced by the newly added Article 7. It stipulates that if network service providers know particular methods, equipment or materials of technology protection measures which are used to shun or destroy others' copyright, they still upload, spread and offer them, and then network service providers will be asked to undertake civil infringement responsibilities according to the party's appeals and concrete cases by the provision 6 of the Article 47 of Copyright Law. This judicial interpretation standardises the offered equipment and service, which has supplemented the blank of China's anti-technique circumvention rules, so its purpose is positive. However, it is doubtful if the Supreme People's Court has surpassed its judicial interpretation right. Under Article 18 in the People's Court Organization Law,[91] the Supreme People's Court has the right to interpret how to apply laws to trial. However, it is illegal to prohibit circumvention equipment behaviour by law, so is it beyond its interpretation range with modification to the law? The second doubt is that the Supreme People's Court only stipulates whether network service providers are rational to undertake legal responsibilities for offering circumvention equipment.

8.3.3 Accountability & Liability

The Oxford dictionary defines liability as being legally answerable to their deeds or engagements. The same dictionary, *Concise Oxford Dictionary*, defines accountability as being able to justify their actions and decisions. As such, looking at the literal aspect of it, there is a difference between the two words. To start with, the definition of liability implies that one must be able to justify their deeds, from a legal point of view. To say, it is legally binding to an individual and hence is applicable to legal actions and steps. Accountability, on the other hand, is not legally binding but is more of a question of integrity. Though one may be subjected to legal steps for lack of accountability, it is not universal, according to this definition. In the social and literal aspects, therefore, liability and accountability may be used separately, and accountability can be interpreted as responsibility, while liability will still reflect the application of legal steps to the deeds of an individual on the condition that they happen to infringe upon the rights of other persons.[92] Bovens and Schillemans further described accountability as transparency and trustworthiness in one's deeds

[90]2003年12月23日最高人民法院审判委员会第1302 次会议《关于修改〈最高人民法院关于审理涉及计算机网络著作权纠纷案件适用法律若干问题的解释〉的决定》修正).

[91]《中华人民共和国人民法院组织法》第十八条, 2018年10月26日.

[92]Bovens and Schillemans [36], p. 228.

in a political and social aspect. They have also defined accountability as a virtue, because actors and public figures are usually expected to be accountable and to provide accounts for their actions. Perhaps, Lodge and Stirton define accountability, in a more precise manner, as obligation one has to clearly and concisely give details of and validate their deeds to other interested persons.[93]

In contrast, what are the legal meaning and implications of these two phrases? In his editorial, Ivo Giessen defines accountability as a process directed at assessing the conduct of an individual, evaluating the appropriateness of such conduct and eventually determining the liability this individual holds. In Giesen and Kristen's definition, they further expanded the concept of accountability as the ability to establish the position and function of the convicted or involved individual in the same act. Accountability is further used legally to establish the perpetrator's extent of engagement in the acts.[94] It is also from such a definition that liability was derived. They defined liability as the state of the perpetrator being linked to their accountability, but with reference to legal consequences.[95] This means that the attachment that arises from accountability of the individual to his conduct is thus his/her liability. If we were to analyse and observe it from a legal perspective as defined by Giesen and Kristen, liability thus arises from accountability and without accountability there would be no liability. Being accountable means a person is liable for his action. This means that if someone is accountable for his/her action, he/she will be held liable. However, without proof of accountability, one cannot be held liable for any conduct/act in question.

Liability is defined according to the damage or loss that individual acts cause to either an individual or the society.[96] According to this publication, liability is applied or enforced to get the offending party back to the original position to prevent the offense from happening. The paper, however, admits that liability leads to the question of accountability; to establish liability, the offending person(s) must be proven accountable for what he/she has perpetrated. This is where the issue of network service providers comes in negligence. To start with, it is the form of liability that arises when the responsible individual fails to do what he/she had the power to do and to prevent the occurrence of something that would infringe on the rights of other persons or would cause loss and damage to other persons.[97] In this definition, there must be proof that the responsible person did omit to do something that any prudent person would have done, as per the guidance of the ordinary governors of the general conduct of persons.[98] The duty of care is an inherent factor in enforcing this form of liability. The offending party must be proven to bear the duty of care to the plaintiff. As such, individuals are required to take care not to omit

[93] *Ibid.* and Baldwin et al. [37], p. 349.

[94] Ivo and François [38], pp. 1–13.

[95] *Ibid.*

[96] Reed et al. [39].

[97] Gilles [40], pp. 1291, 1295.

[98] See Reed et al. [39].

to act prudently, such that persons closely related or affected by his/her actions, because they are acts of negligence. If ISPs are held with this view, they will thus act to ensure that they notice the public of the copyrights in the information that is transmitted across the network. However, if they do so and the users still infringe on the rights of the right holders, then the network service providers should not be held liable.

Strict liability is slightly different. Taking YouTube, for example, the network service provider's strict liability is described as the form that requires the offending person to fully indemnify the offended person, without regard of how much this person had tried to act responsibly, to avoid the occurrence of the offense.[99] It means that the responsible individual is unconditional to blame for losses and damage that occur from his engagement in an event, an act or a possession. In this context of network service providers, e.g., one involved in YouTube services would be held liable for every transmission across YouTube. This would imply that in such a case in Spain,[100] where a user infringes the rights of the holder, even without the awareness of the network service provider, the network service provider would be held liable. However, the network service provider is only a platform to help the right holders enforce their ownership by helping notify the public of the existence of such rights.[101]

While the network service providers are provided with the information regarding media being shared over the internet, they may not be able to reach every user to which they provide access to over the internet. A case study would be, e.g., a case decided in Barcelona court that did not show the relevance and actual application of accountability vs liability in the context of internet usage, which is exactly the interest of this paper. In this case, the user was accused of infringing upon the rights of a Spanish Association of Music Producers by sharing files they claimed bore their copyright.[102] The network service provider was required to block the user from accessing the World Wide Web, as the Spanish Association of Music Producers demanded. While the user was eventually not disconnected from the internet, it is an application and indication of how then the ISPs were held accountable for the actions of the users. The case demonstrated what measures the network service providers were required to supply with the account of internet usage as well as how they should ensure the proper protection of copyrights. Though the network service provider was required to enforce the injunction upon its user's behaviour, the network service provider was not to be held liable but only accountable for the user's infringement.

As was put forward by Lodge and Stirton, being accountable does not require individuals to account to the public but rather the obligation that competent representatives have to be responsible for their conduct.[103] Taking this simple definition,

---

[99] *Ibid.*

[100] *Audiencia Provincial Barcelona Promusicae v X* (2013) 470/2013.

[101] Husovec [41], p. 10.

[102] *Ibid.*

[103] See Baldwin et al. [37], p. 361.

accountability is what is required of the ISPs, for they only need to provide a clear account of the activities running through their service. Following a deeper understanding of the phrases in question, accountability turns out to be more appropriate to network service providers than liability. Network service providers should only be held accountable but not liable for what their users share over the internet.

- Experience from Abroad
  Under the InfoSoc Directive and the Enforcement Directive, court orders that are issued based on liability to the intermediaries involved in a specific transaction involving the rights of individuals are not meant for these intermediaries, but rather the bystanders.[104] According to the InfoSoc Directive and the Enforcement Directive on the court orders, the network service providers should not be held liable. However, while holding them accountable may count in ensuring that they communicate the rights of persons and boundaries in using media and files over the internet; holding them liable will put them at a position that is reverse of what they are. Husovec mentions that intermediaries are only mandated with placing the right holder at a position closer to his/her desired position, regarding the protection of his/her property.[105] Assuming that liability was enforced in place of accountability, the network service provider involved in the Spanish case could not be held liable but only accountable for the rights of the holders. In this case, e.g., the network service provider was not held liable and was not demanded to cease his services but to disconnect the client. Network service providers are only a platform to enforce the rights of the right holders; therefore, they ought not to be held entirely liable.

  Another reason the ISPs should not be held liable is that they are operating in a business that brings about enormous social benefits and profitability. By providing a platform for advertisements and internet access, they create the possibility of industries reaching a wide range of customers and in large numbers.[106] It would be a great compromise to these benefits, holding network service providers strictly liable even they have tried preventing the violations to the rights of individuals. However, it will be irresponsible to do that because end users could be distances away from the network service providers and can have an easy time bypassing the ISPs with technology advancing, so the network service providers would have no powers over such clients. It is thus only prudent to maintain that network service providers are only liable to the use of the internet by their endpoint clients, as opposed to being liable for the same. In any case, they are accountable for the infringement of the rights involved.

  (i) United Kingdom
  The general tort theory and more precisely the tort-based doctrine of joint tortfeasance provide a more reliable and direct approach for dealing with

104 Husovec [41], p. 10.

105 Ibid.

106 Ibid, p. 12.

issues of intermediary liability, given the fact that copyright infringement is a tort. Besides, joint tortfeasance serves as the foundation of the codified concept of authorisation, and it has been portrayed as the English version of the American concept of "contributory liability." Several persons are held liable in the common law doctrine of joint tortfeasance where they are linked to or indirectly connected to the same infringement.

Joint tortfeasance is more advantageous than the overused and archaic concept of authorisation in the examination of the liability of online-based intermediaries for the violation of copyright laws perpetrated by others. An advantage it provides is concrete legal supports for the introduction of an element of accountability to the liability standard. The United Kingdom has traditionally avoided the "direct liability" approach for assessing the liability of intermediaries for copyright infractions but has rather given more attention to the legal weapons of "accessory liability." It is emphasised in the case law, on equivalent providers of support in violation, stating that there is a need to differentiate between the two concepts as well as that of "mere facilitation," which connotes that accessory liability cannot be linked to the act of merely abetting another to carry out an infringement.

In reality, the proscribing of the general monitoring by the intermediaries can hardly guarantee the prevention of future infringement. While the monitoring obligation is rendered due to the multiple postings of similar contents by different or the same users, the host service providers are obliged, under such systems, to expunge the remaining or reposted unauthorised copy to avoid probable liability on getting notified. However, all contents (including non-infringing contents) going through the servers of host service providers must follow the mandatory screening for copies with infringing properties (i.e., implementing general monitoring). To achieve this, practically, the only realistic way is to adopt certain automatic filtering technology such as fingerprint identification, which is likely to grow up at a fast rate. The broad coverage of the practical implications weakens the supposed specificity of the obligation, and this affects the liability of all hosting services that have been notified, for all work as regards a single infringing copy.

(ii) Germany

In Germany, it is very difficult to place a direct liability on an internet-based host unlike in France and the United Kingdom. The distinctive legal tool of Störerhaftung is primarily employed in dealing with intermediary liability in copyright in Germany. In English, this code is usually translated as an "interferer" or "disturber" liability, and it enables the imposition of injunctions against intermediaries as a preventive measure against infringement. Hence, a Störer (interferer) cannot be held accountable for damage. Two major conditions need to be satisfied to confirm the finding of a Störerhaftung, (a) They must have contributed immensely to that infringement; (b) Failing to carry out a reasonable duty to review (Prüfpflicht).

In German law, "accessory liability" arises based on the general principles of tort law just like that in French law. If damage is caused by a jointly committed tort instead of just one single party, then as documented in Art 830(1) of the German Civil Code (Bürgerliches Gesetzbuch),[107] each of them shall be held accountable for the damage. The same liability applies to accessories and instigators as contained in Art 830(2). In this light, the process of finding liability requires a reliable intent. In addition, it is required to acquire knowledge regarding the principal offence as well as awareness of their unlawfulness. Online intermediaries usually neglect this condition. Similarly, if a defendant keeps violating duties of care for an extended period, then the defendant may be held liable. However, in cases where service providers disregard specific notices of illegal activities and refuse to avert further infractions, such gross and constant violations of the duty to examine will be accepted. Actually, this type of behaviour gives rise to infringement by forbearance.

Limiting the legal duties of intermediaries to adjust the framework of the tort law would be myopic. Intermediaries are held responsible in most countries for some assistance given to right holders even when they are not responsible for harming their users.[108] The most critical example deals with a claim for information known as a subpoena, and there is a simple idea behind such a remedy. To enable them to enforce their rights, the right holders might still look for the help of intermediaries such as disclosing the identity of the infringing user although the intermediaries might carry out the recommended optimal care.[109]

In general, with years passing by, there has been a continuous increase in the level of additional claims for assistance. In Europe alone with recent times, it transformed increasingly from being an excellent tool of justice to a complete remedy against anyone who responds to the emergency call of right holders. The economics surrounding the basic principles of tort law is now being challenged by the remedy that was initially supposed to support it.

A German researcher, Joachim Bornkamm, has been trying to create a solution for the protection of network users' right. He propounded the Störerhaftung Mode (intruder prevention mode) in his bid, while an IT researcher from Holland, Martin Husovec, added in his research that the building and developing of inhibitions within the network service would utterly fix the apparent liability model of network services to create an

[107] § 830 BGB Mittäter und Beteiligte(1) Haben mehrere durch eine gemeinschaftlich begangene unerlaubte Handlung einen Schaden verursacht, so ist jeder für den Schaden verantwortlich. Das Gleiche gilt, wenn sich nicht ermitteln lässt, wer von mehreren Beteiligten den Schaden durch seine Handlung verursacht hat.(2) Anstifter und Gehilfen stehen Mittätern gleich.

[108] The German Federal Supreme Court (BGH) prescribed policing of external websites such as special search engines. In this regard, the notification burden related to external websites was shifted from right holders to search engines and it was obligated for those intermediaries to subsidize the enforcement expenses of right holders with no time or condition limit. See OLG Düsseldorf-I-20 U 59/10 – Entscheidung vom Urteil vom 21. Dezember 2010 Karlsruhe, den, 13. Juli 2012.

[109] Cooter [42], pp. 523, 536.

accountability model. A network injunction mode, built from the creation of the accountability system, goes a long way to build connection between users' rights and those of the network service providers to prevent infringement in that network. The impact of network service providers will therefore be strong and improved. Not only will their legitimate rights be maintained but also they will have a more transparent and defined sense of responsibility in their standing to help their users in protecting their rights from any infringement, fostering the latter to comply with the regulations binding them. They propose to improve the laws for network service in the *Book of Law*. Even if network service cannot investigate, they can learn how to take action and solve problems.

Although it is the most convenient way for communication circumvention equipment to offer circumvention equipment on the internet, it constitutes extremely large threat to copyright owner's benefits. However, it does not mean legislators can have discriminatory rules on network service providers so that other people who work on the same job can exempt themselves from punishments. The Software World Magazine was complained by IDM Computer Solutions Company and Beijing Red Jersey Information Service Center since the defendant published the registration code generator of the plaintiffs arbitrarily, which was obviously an offer of technology circumvention equipment. However, since the defendant in this case was not network service provider, it could neither adapt to the provisions of common infringement in the Article 4 of the judicial interpretation before modification nor adapt to the newly added Article 7 after the modification concerning prohibition of offering circumvention equipment and service, which was obviously against the Supreme People's Court's intention on cracking down copyright infringement behaviours. Besides, this anti-technique circumvention rules have no specific definition on circumvention equipment without pointing out technology, which can be considered as circumvention equipment by requirements. The deficiency of legal norms will cause differences on people's knowledge necessarily, while the different knowledge will probably result in different standards executed by court during trial, leading to uncertainty of some legal relationship.

8.4 Exception Rules of Technological Measures

The exception rules for technological measures is an important measure to prevent over-protection or the abuse of technological measures protection. The exception rules are closely related to the development of science and technology. With the social development, technological measures are constantly being reformed, which has led to the exception of technological measures that have been in the process of dynamic development. Under the current knowledge economy dominated by digital technology, countries have provided exception rules to technological measures. Although there are differences in regard of content, there are exception rules for encryption research; exception rules for reverse engineering; exception rules for library circumvention techniques; exception rules for personal information protection, etc. The exception rules for technological measures have been widely adopted by countries and regions in the world. In view of this, it is necessary to analyse the above basic rules to lay the foundation for the analysis of the exception rules for technological measures.

8.4.1 Encryption Research Exception

Encryption technology is one of the key and core technologies of copyrighted technological measures. Copyright technological measures anti-circumvention legislation was designed to prohibit the conduct of cracking technological measures, which to a certain extent affected the development of encryption research. At present, to reduce the negative impact of technological measures on encryption research, many countries set up exception rules for technological measures in the study of encryption in domestic copyright legislation. Although technical research measures for encryption research exception rules have become an integral part of the exception rules for copyrighted technological measures, our country has not reflected this in relevant laws. This section focuses on the following three parts of the technological measures encryption research exception rules connotation, debates triggered by the encryption research exception rules and the attitude of national copyright legislation on it to explore to formulate the corresponding exception rules to provide reference experience.

As an encryption technology research, it is of great significance to improve the development of encryption technology and promote the transformation of technological measures centred on encryption technology, and it is an insurmountable technological approach. However, due to in the specific implementation process of encryption research, the encryption technology contained in the existing technological measures will follow to perform copy, crack, analyse and other acts, which will undoubtedly violate the technological measures to circumvent the legislation. In practice, encryption research exception rules are strongly supported by scientific researchers. They criticise the anti-circumvention legislation and restrict the research on encryption. At the same time, they call for lawmakers to provide corresponding institutional space for "encryption research".

8.4.1.1 The Role of Encryption Research Exception Rules

The role of the encryption research exception rule is mainly in the socio-economic development and the need to protect consumer rights. Specifically, the role of the encryption research exception rule is mainly reflected in the promotion of innovation and dynamic development of encryption technology and the protection of the economic security of e-commerce and the legitimate interests of consumers. These are described as below:

First, encryption research plays an important role in promoting the innovation and dynamic development of encryption technology. The effectiveness of technological measures to prevent the illegal exploitation of digital works is largely dependent on the development of technology, and the "technology" category includes technological measures based on "encryption technology". The development of encryption technology requires scientific researchers to test and research the technological measures being used. Only on this basis can encryption technology improve and strengthen overall. In the process of testing encryption technology, researchers need to perform decryption or damage on encryption technology to discover the shortcomings of encryption technology and to research and develop more inclusive systems. However, under the anti-circumvention legislation of the existing technological measures, this kind of behaviour is prohibited. In summary, the technological measures to circumvent the provisions of legislation to some extent hinder the development of basic encryption technology.

Second, encryption research plays an important role in protecting the economic security of e-commerce and the legitimate interests of consumers. In many cases, its own problems only become apparent when the encryption system is officially used. Therefore, careful research on the crypto systems that have been put into use will not only identify defects within the system, but also protect personal information and economic security of consumers who are using the crypto system. The prosperity of the e-commerce economy relies heavily on legitimate encryption research. If we wait until the illegal "hackers" find loopholes in the encryption system, people will face more than just economic losses.

8.4.1.2 Specific Application Conditions for Exception Rules to Crypto Research

Under DMCA Article 1201, encryption research exception rules can be exempted from the following two behaviours:

a. Directly circumvent contact control measures
   Article 1201(g)(2) of the DMCA stipulates that if the perpetrator who conducts the encryption research in good faith complies with the relevant conditions, then the cracked technological measures to obtain copies, audiovisual products, and performances and broadcast the published works may not be The sanctions imposed by section 1201(a)(1)(A). The "good faith" researcher stipulated by the DMCA must satisfy the following conditions: First, the copy of the encrypted works obtained by the researcher, phonograms, performances and published works must be obtained through legal channels; second, the researcher's The act must be necessary for the encryption institute; third, the researcher must be able to prove that he had made a good faith effort to obtain authorisation before

the conduct of circumvention; in the end, the researcher must perform the act of encryption research must be a violation of the law.

In addition, the DMCA of the United States stipulates the conditions for verifying whether the encryption research exception rule can be applied. That is, when the encryption research behaviour implementer satisfies the corresponding conditions, the implementation of the encryption research behaviour complies with the law; the behaviour implements the avoidance technology. Measures can be exempted.

b. Acts to provide auxiliary equipment or services for circumvention

The encryption research exception of Section 1201 of the DMCA of the United States also exempts another prohibited act, namely the act of creating and providing auxiliary equipment or services to evade technological measures. In general, the encryption research exception rule provides legal support for the "development and dissemination of decryption software that is indispensable in the process of encryption research" so that it is no longer worried about the illegal nature of the act. Article 1201(g)(4) of the DMCA stipulates that applicable circumvention devices that meet the following conditions may be exempt from the provisions of Article 1201(a)(2): First, the well-meaning encryption research researcher defined in the preceding paragraph. Develop or use means to break technological measures; second, provide technical means to partners of good faith encryption research to conduct well-intentioned encryption research as defined in the previous article, or to third parties engaged in encryption research defined above to verify encryption research results.

8.4.1.3 Legislative Options for Exceptional Research on Encryption

At present, the provisions of the copyright laws of various countries on the technical research measures for encryption research exception rules can be roughly divided into three types:

The first is the country that has specified in the Copyright Law the detailed rules for encryption research exception rules for technological measures, mainly representing the United States, Canada, Australia, and South Korea. These countries generally have established American-style protection measures for technological measures and setting of exception rules in domestic copyright laws. There are two main reasons for establishing the exception rule in the above-mentioned countries in the domestic law: On the one hand, the e-commerce economy and the rapid development of the Internet technology, the demand for encryption technology is increasing. Encryption researchers call for the establishment of technical measure exception rules to mediate the conflict between the nature of their work and the anti-circumvention legislation. On the other hand, the US uses its own economic advantages and constantly utilises bilateral international trade agreements or multilateral international trade treaties to "sell" its own intellectual property protection models and technological measures. This includes the content of the "technological measures for Encryption Research exception rules".

The second is the country that has already set encryption research exception rules for technological measures in the Copyright Law. However, the rules of the encryption research exception rules that it provides are more abstract and not suitable for specific operations. Its typical representative is the EU in the Copyright Directive, the set encryption research exception. However, as the European Union's copyright directives were drafted earlier, most of the provisions therein have been unable to adapt to the current pace of the Internet economy. In September 2016, the European Commission released a new "Draft Copyright Directive" that provides new insights into the issue of the resetting of exception rules for technological measures. Although the encryption research exception rule is not discussed in detail in this draft, it should do an in-depth study of how to set an exception rule for encryption research in the process of revising the exception rule for technological measures.

The third is a country that does not provide for the encryption research exception rules for technological measures in copyright law, such as China. China's "copyright law" and related legislation have not made any provision for encryption research exception rules. The reason for this is that the intellectual property system as a Western import has always been in a state of coordination and integration with China's basic national conditions, and it has not considered the improvement of related institutional rules. Second, the development of China's economy and science and technology has not yet reached the status quo. The status of detailed regulations on the exception rules for encryption research is not high enough for social needs. However, with the rapid development of China's economy and the rapid advancement of science and technology, our country's scientific and technological workers are increasingly calling for exception rules to encryption measures for technological measures. Therefore, to respond to the appeals of scientific researchers and improve the exception rule system for technological measures, China has added an exception rule for technological measures for encryption research in the third revised draft of the Copyright Law.

8.4.2 Reverse Engineering Exception

Reverse engineering as a means of innovative technology has been controversial since its inception. Some scholars have elaborated on the controversy involved in the reverse engineering from the "trade secrets extended to the field of integrated circuit layout design and software." For the legality of reverse engineering, this article will not repeat them here. The academic community has reached an agreement on this issue: Under certain conditions, reverse engineering constitutes reasonable use of copyright and has legitimacy. However, as the WCT and WPPT have established the protection of technological measures, reverse engineering of software that originally had reasonable use of defence is once again facing the risk of legal sanctions. Faced with the conflict between technological measures protection and software reverse engineering, all countries hope to solve the contradiction between the two by setting up technological measures to reverse engineering exception rules.

8.4.2.1 The Meaning of the Exception Rules for Reverse Engineering

The reverse engineering exception rule is not a specific legal concept term, and it is more appropriate to regard it as a general description of a prescribed content. In other words, the reverse rule of technological measures for reverse engineering refers to the behaviour of circumvention technological measures implemented by reverse-engineering implementers who meet certain conditions from the anti-regulation regulations. Different countries and regions have different ways of implementing exception rules for reverse engineering because of their different legislative backgrounds and legislative techniques. For example, because the United States does not provide specific legislative protection for computer software protection, it is embodied in the "reverse engineering" exception clause in Article 1201 of the DMCA. The European Union's legislation presents a completely different style. In 1991, the European Community protected computer software by enacting a "computer program protection directive" special law. Furthermore, the EU's technological measures of reverse engineering exception rules are mostly incorporated into the provisions of the Directive along with the exception rules for fair use.

The exception for reverse engineering is established in the Copyright Law or related departmental law. Its function is more like a "bridge" or a key to the "digital fence". In other words, due to the protective protection effect of technological measures on computer software, others cannot access the software content or use software code without the authorisation or permission of the right holder. Even if the researcher satisfies the conditions for the fair use of the contents of the software works, due to technological measures, the researcher cannot evade the technological measures. This is because the system of proprietary rights and technological measures of the works is intended to be distinguished. Where the researcher has a reasonable defend of the copyright, it does not of course have the right to evade technological measures. There is a difference between the two in protecting the object. Therefore, the establishment of technological measures for reverse engineering exception rules can properly link reverse engineering and fair use, and give full play to the effectiveness of software's fair use of reverse engineering.

8.4.2.2 The Role of Reverse Engineering Exception Rules

It is reasonable and necessary to establish software reverse engineering exception rules in the exception rules of technological measures. To a certain extent, the necessity of creating technological measures for reverse engineering exception rules is also necessary to establish reverse engineering exception rules in the copyright restriction system. Both of them have common social needs at the practical level.

First, the establishment of reverse engineering exception rules can prevent computer software owners from monopolising software development, inspiring innovations, realising technological innovations, and promoting technological progress. If no strict distinction is made in the country, the implementation of strict prohibition and evasion technical measure standards will, on the one hand, encourage computer software owners to use technological measures to realise their exclusive control of the software, and further use the technical advantages of software to seek economic benefits. This has a negative impact on eliminating the adverse effects of the monopoly of the software market and promoting the pace of innovation in the software industry.

Second, the establishment of reverse engineering exception rules can promote the integration and matching of existing smart devices, improve the user experience of consumers, promote the prosperity of the Internet industry, and achieve social progress. Under the traditional copyright system, due to technical reasons, legislators did not realise the importance of reverse engineering. With the development of information technology, people began to enter the era of "smart devices", from mobile phones, computers to all kinds of household equipment, automobiles, medical equipment and other equipment have entered the "Intelligent Age". In summary, intelligent software has become an integral part of our lives today. If the use of anti-circumvention legislation to limit the implementation of reverse engineering software, it is very likely that a variety of intelligent software cannot be compatible with each other, smart device developers use smart software to limit consumer behaviour to achieve "interest zone." Although from the perspective of market development, this phenomenon will often occur, but from the perspective of promoting social development, it should be possible to reduce the duration of this phenomenon as much as possible. Because, the time cost and money cost that the mass consumer will pay for solving the problem that the above-mentioned intelligent apparatus produces will be enormous. Therefore, from the perspective of protecting the interests of consumers and promoting social progress, it is necessary to set up technical protection measures for software reverse engineering exception rules.

It should be noted that although software reverse engineering does not affect the economic benefits of the manufacturer of the software in the implementation process, once the result is leaked or propagated after reverse engineering, it would cause negative economic effects to the manufacturer. In view of this, all countries have set certain restrictions on the exception rules for software reverse engineering protection measures to protect the economic benefits of software vendors.

As mentioned above, the main difference between the major countries and regions in the legislative model of reverse engineering exception rules for technological measures is whether the computer software is protected by special legislation. Therefore, in accordance with the different legislative means, the legislative model of exception rules for reverse engineering of technological measures can be divided into two types: the first is a special legislative model, the main representative for the European Union's "Computer Program Protection Directive" and the European Union to develop The "Information Society Copyright Protection Directive"; the second is the specific provisions of the legislative model, the typical representative of the United States DMCA Article 1201 (f) provisions. This section will introduce the two legislative models one by one, compare and analyse the merits and demerits of their respective legal values, and on this basis, outline the reverse engineering exception rules stipulated in the current Chinese legal provisions.

A. Regulations of the European Community's "Computer Program Protection Directive"

Due to the EU's protection of computer programs through specific legislation, there is no clear provision in the EU Information Society Copyright Directive ("Copyright Directive") for the application of circumvention technological measures exception rules in the field of computer programs. It is only specified in Chapter 50 of the Preface to the Copyright Directive.

Therefore, judging from the combination of the "Copyright Directive" and the "Computer Program Protection Directive", the European Union deems the implementation of computer software reverse engineering activities and corresponding circumvention of technological measures within certain limits to be lawful, and sums up the restrictions on their establishment. The main points are as follows: (1) The entity that implements reverse engineering must be a legal user of computer software, that is, a licensee or a person who has the right to use a copy of the program or is authorised to represent the rightful person to engage in the act. (2) The "necessary information" obtained through reverse engineering should not be easily obtained from other sources; (3) Only the part of the computer program necessary to produce a compatible program can be reverse engineered.

At the same time, for the use of information obtained from software reverse engineering, the "Computer Program Protection Directive" also sets certain restrictions: (1) It must not be used for achieving computer compatibility; (2) It must not transmit information to others. Unless required for computer program compatibility; (3) Information shall not be used to develop, reproduce or market programs that are substantially similar to the computer program, or for other copyright infringement.

In summary, the European Union's affirmation of the legitimacy of software reverse engineering is limited to the purpose of reverse engineering "production compatible procedures" and the identity of the reverse engineering software implementation subject. In line with the purpose of "production-compatible computer software program", the use of software content behaviour and cracking technology measures implemented in the reverse engineering process are permitted.

B. United States DMCA Section 1201(f)

According to the experience of judicial practice in the United States, reverse engineering constitutes reasonable use when certain conditions are met. Article 1201(f) of the U.S. DMCA formally establishes the content of reverse engineering exception rules for technological measures through legislation. +There are provisions for obtaining restrictions on the dissemination of information.

Under the first provision, the exemption conditions for reverse engineering are respectively limited to the objectives of reverse engineering implementation and the source and route of the reverse engineering source program. Under the second provision: when technical means must be used to achieve compatibility of software, to achieve the above-mentioned identification and analysis or to achieve the compatibility of independently created computer programs and other programs, technical means can be developed and used Avoid technological measures or avoid the protection provided by technological measures. Under the third provision: for the purpose of achieving the interoperability of independently created computer programs with other programs, the information obtained may be provided to third parties, and the conduct of such acts within this limit does not constitute infringement in the sense of this Law, nor does it violate the law applicable outside this section.

Through the above listed analysis, it can be inferred that the U.S. and the EU views on the issue of the legality of software reverse engineering can be said to be consistent.

First, both of them impose restrictions on the subject of reverse engineering and require that the principal can only be a legitimate user or authoriser of the target program. The main purpose of this restriction is to ensure that the legitimate economic interests of software rights holders will not suffer losses due to the implementation of reverse engineering. Second, both of them have limited the implementation purpose of reverse engineering, that is, to achieve compatibility between computer software programs. Finally, both of them restrict the use of information obtained from reverse engineering. They only require that they implement the communication behaviour to achieve software compatibility.

However, the contents of the reverse engineering exception rule formulated by the United States and the European Union also fully reflect its own legal values and values. As the two most powerful economic entities in the world, the content of the stipulated legal rules also contains the high standard of intellectual property protection. Further, these high standard level protection rules are not necessarily applicable to all countries. Judging from the contents of the above-mentioned reverse engineering exception rules, there are two points in the EU's and US' practices that are not worth adopting in the developing countries' legislation:

First, the purpose of reverse engineering should not be limited to achieving compatibility between computer software. On the one hand, non-individual or profitable reverse engineering may be recognised as a reasonable use. If blindly limiting the purpose of exception rules for technological measures to reverse engineering is limited to software compatibility, it may cut off the bridge between the two and cause certain conflicts between legal rules. On the other hand, because of the arbitrarily limited implementation purpose, it will stifle the possibility of reverse engineering implementation for other purposes and increase the economic costs of software development companies. This is inconsistent with the industry concept that the software development industry is new and fast, which will have a negative impact on the rapid development of the software development industry.

Second, the nature of the dissemination of information obtained after the implementation of reverse engineering should be limited not transmitted. Both the European Union and the United States have limited the scope of the information obtained after the implementation of reverse engineering, and require that it disseminate information only for software compatibility purposes. In fact, the significance of this restriction is not great. The significance of reverse engineering is to create independent software works by analysing existing software to obtain useful information.

As a country whose software development R&D capacity is late, and whose R&D capability is lagging behind that of Britain and the United States, China should encourage software developers to learn advanced foreign software design concepts and improve the quality of China's software industry. At the same time, this also requires China to provide more free institutional space for software developers at the legal level, especially in software reverse engineering. However, China's current "Copyright Law" and "Computer Software Protection Regulations" lack the explicit provisions for software reverse engineering. Some scholars believe that in the "Computer Software Protection Regulations", you can vaguely find the software reverse engineering. However, this view was verified by another scholar and confirmed that from the perspective of legislation, Article 17 of the Computer Software Protection Ordinance does not include software reverse engineering. Therefore, considering the development needs of the software industry, it is possible to improve the software reverse engineering system by revising the computer software protection regulations and establish the implementation conditions for software reverse engineering. At the same time, it is also necessary to establish in the revised draft of the Copyright Law the status of software reverse engineering under certain conditions in the rules of fair use system and technological measures exception rules.

8.4.3 Library Evasion Exception Rules

When libraries are exerting their best efforts to fulfil their functions of "cultural heritage" and "knowledge dissemination", there is a conflict between the series of actions they implement and the legitimate interests of copyright owners and other related parties. For example, library interlibrary loan and document transfer activities conflict with the copyright owner's right to reproduce and the right to disseminate information networks. Another example is the preservation of information on libraries and archives, and the technological measures to break down digital works to convert storage methods. When copying, the behaviour conflicts with the copyright owner's right to copy, the legal rights of protection technology measures, and so on. To ensure that libraries, archives, museums, and other institutions can fully play their institutional functions, under the premise of balancing the interests of all parties, the copyright laws of various countries have given the library and other institutions the privilege of exception rules to the copyright law.

Since countries have affirmed the protection of technological measures in the copyright law, libraries are unable to circumvent technological measures during the dissemination of knowledge, and once failed to fully realise their institutional functions. Faced with the appeal of the library community and the criticism of the academic circles, legislators have established copyright exception rules in the Copyright Law to meet the needs of all parties. Based on this, the following section will analyse and discuss the specific meanings and effects of library exception rules for evading technological measures.

8.4.3.1 Meaning of Library Circumvention of Technological Measures Exception Rules

The exception to the library's circumvention of technological measures is that under the limited goal, the library can evade the technological measures set by the copyright holders and will not bear the corresponding legal liabilities. In other words, the library circumvention of exception rules to technological measures is a reasonable defence that libraries and other institutions face when confronted with illegal behaviours to evade actions under certain circumstances. Under the provisions of the current copyright laws of most countries in the world, exception rules to technological measures involve multiple situations. The circumvention of exception rules to technology measures by libraries specifically refers to non-profit libraries' circumvention of technological measures specifically designed to control the access or use of copyrighted digital works for legitimate purposes set out in the Copyright Law. Depending on the type of technological measures that the library circumvents, the exception rules for circumvention of technological measures in libraries can be distinguished as follows: exception rules for contact control measures, exception rules for copyright protection measures, and exception rules for providing technological measures to circumvent equipment or services.

Because of the large number of institutions such as libraries, archives, and museums, and the use of works, the economic benefits of copyright owners will be affected to a certain extent. Therefore, when countries set up exception rules for circumventing technological measures in libraries, they generally set stricter restrictions on the purpose of the behaviour, the nature of the actors, and the manner in which the behaviour is implemented. The question of whether the specific conditions for restricting exception rules for technological measures by libraries in various countries is reasonable is left for further discussion.

8.4.3.2 The Exceptional Role of the Library in Avoiding Technological Measures

Under the condition that the library's digital management is increasingly strengthened at present, the exceptional rules of the technological measures library play an important role in the library's social effect. Specifically speaking, libraries evade the role of exception rules to technological measures, mainly in the following three aspects:

A. To Make up for the Inadequacy of the Traditional Copyright Exception System
To ensure the effective realisation of the public's access to and use of the right to knowledge and information, the Copyright Law presupposes a series of limitations and exception rules. However, these restrictions and exception rules are mainly restricted to proprietary rights in works, and they are inconceivable when restricting the abuse of technological measures. In essence, technological measures do not fall within the scope of the traditional copyright system. It is not an exclusive right but a "legal benefit" related to copyright. In this regard, the protection provided by copyright law for technological measures has, under certain circumstances, formed a kind of "ultra-copyright protection", which is no longer covered by the traditional copyright law, but is a stronger protection method. This also determines that the copyright restriction and exception system based on the traditional copyright system is difficult to regulate technological measures effectively. On the contrary, the abuse of technological measures can seriously affect and limit the use of copyright restriction and exception systems. In other words, libraries and other institutions cannot rely on traditional copyright restrictions and exception rules to break technological measures to achieve their mission of spreading culture.
B. To Protect the Basic Functions of the Library
The basic functions of the library include, but are not limited to, preservation of civilisational achievements, dissemination of knowledge and information, development of social education, and development of intellectual resources. However, all these functions are based on the fact that libraries can effectively access and use various types of information resources. In the pre-network era, various types of information resources were presented in the form of tangible carriers. By acquiring tangible carriers that carry information, libraries can access various information resources. In the Internet age, information is often stored and disseminated in digital form. To protect the legitimate rights and interests of copyright owners, the law allows rights holders to set technological measures for their knowledge and information, and set up a relatively complete legal protection system for them. At the same time, more stringent restrictions have been set for the public to evade technological measures. For example, under China's Regulations on the Protection of the Right to Spread of Information on the Internet, libraries can only evade technological measures based on the following circumstances: first, to support classroom learning or scientific research; second, to meet the needs of the blind for obtaining written works. The legislative

choices of the Regulations on the Protection of Information Network Communication Rights have the following limitations: first, they limit the scope of the works that the library can provide; second, they limit the range of beneficiaries that the library circumvents technological measures and exception rules. The institutional arrangement of the existing copyright system in our country with respect to exception rules for library circumvention measures is obviously a serious constraint on the hands and feet of the library, it cannot meet the interests of the library, and it is not conducive to the basic functions of the library. Therefore, the creation of a library to circumvent the exception rules of technological measures helps meet the library's interests and helps to achieve the basic functions of the library.

C. To Achieve a Balance of Interests Among Right Holders

As a sophisticated system design, the copyright system protects a chain of intertwined interests. According to the analysis of scholars, in addition to the interests of copyright owners, there are still the following interests in the copyright system: first, the benefits of free information; second, institutional benefits brought about by the public domain in copyright law; third, cultural consumption and educational benefits; fourth, the benefits of technological innovation. However, the legislation of technological measures in the Copyright Law strengthens the protection of rights holders while ignoring the protection of the legitimate rights and interests of other related rights holders. This has seriously hindered the realisation of the goal of balancing the value of interests. Therefore, to reconstruct the balance of interests between right holders and other right holders in the field of technological measures legislation, copyright law is necessary to reform the exception rules of technological measures in the current copyright system to ensure that other rights holders have more freedom to use their works. This is also consistent with the original intention of the copyright law to protect technological measures. The purpose of the copyright law is to establish a technical measure protection system based on contact control, mainly to protect the business model based on price discrimination established by right holders, rather than to limit the use of works for the purpose of academics, reviews, etc.

Second, the library chooses to avoid the exception of technological measures.

Judging from the exception rules to library evasion technological measures in the copyright legislation of various countries, this exception rule presents three characteristics:

First, statutory exception rules and temporary exception rules coexist. Article 1201 of the DMCA of the United States stipulates that libraries can circumvent the technological measures to control the work in determining whether to purchase a certain copyrighted work. At the same time, the temporary every three years amendment rule stipulated in Article 1201 of the DMCA of the United States also mentions that the library can reasonably evade technological measures. For example, the new applicable exception rules announced by the Library of Congress on November 27, 2006 include the exception that libraries can circumvent technological measures, that is, computer programs that are outdated and require the use of original media or hardware to enable them. Games, libraries or archives may be circumventing their technological measures in preserving published digital works; the format is obsolete if the equipment used to identify the works stored in that format has been discontinued or cannot be obtained at a reasonable price.

Second, the library circumvents technological measures exception rules and sets strict restrictions. Nevertheless, whether it is the United States DMCA Article 1201 or the circumvention of technological measures in the EU's Copyright Directive", the applicable conditions for libraries to evade exception rules are strictly limited. For example, the exception rule stipulated in Section 1201(d) of the DMCA of the United States first restricts the retention time for libraries to obtain copyrighted works, and must not exceed the time for the good faith judgement of whether to purchase the works; second, the application of the rules is only possible in other ways. Applicable for obtaining copies of works reasonably, in the end, the rule also sets a violation of "non-profit".

Third, library circumvention technological measures exception rules are only exempt from liability for circumventing specific technological measures, regarding the provision of equipment or services to circumvent technological measures, there may be no exemption. For example. The American Digital Millennium Copyright Act (DMCA), rule 1201(d) only targets the disclaimer of contact-control-type technological measures that are circumvented only for the library's good faith in determining whether a copy of the work is required to obtain commercial development. Similarly, the European Union Copyright Directive only mentions exempt circumstances towards protective measures in copyrights. Yet, because of the lack of professional circumvention techniques, equipment and human resources, the library industry cannot effectively enjoy the privileges specified in the above rules of exemption.

In sum, the library is a place where the people obtain knowledge and information. The realised functions of the library can only be guaranteed by the Copyright Law via certain restrictions, thus ensuring the basic human rights for the public to obtain knowledge. In our current legislation, libraries can only exist as the applicable subject of the copyright exception system.

As far as China is concerned, whether the library can be used as the subject of the exception rule for circumventing technological measures or whether the current law is applicable is unknown. However, in judicial practice, the library can be tolerated as a technical measure to avoid exception rules. If the role of libraries, museums and other institutions as a process of cultural inheritance and knowledge dissemination is recognised, China's copyright-related legislation must seek to provide legal support for its institutional functions. First, establishing certain circumvention rules for measures in the copyright law through legislative pathways to protect the realised, institutional functions of the library from technological measures. Then, implementing reasonable circumvention of technological measures for libraries, such as providing equipment, technical support, or requiring right holders to provide alternative solutions. Currently, the legislation in China explicitly prohibits providing equipment or services for circumventing technological measures. If exception rules are set blindly for the library, then it would not match the legislative spirit.

8.4.4 *Personal Information Protection Exception*

With the haste expansion of information technology, the functions of technological measures have already far exceeded the setting of legislation in various countries. Whilst the copyright owner uses technological measures to protect their work(s), they also began to use the same measures to limit the way works are used and how they are disseminated. This not only affects the personal use behaviour of consumers, but also the information privacy of digital works consumers and threatens personal information security. To prevent the occurrence of cybercrime, multiple countries have begun to stipulate the implementation of the "(Network) Real Name System" for personal network usage. Personal online consumer activities are often tied to personal identification or mobile phone number, and all of this information is included in the information content that is collected daily via the aforementioned technological measures. Some scholars believe that "copyright holders collecting personally identifiable information, personal consumption information, and conducting data predictions through the above justification to identify individual behaviours risks infringing on information privacy rights."[110]

8.4.4.1 The Connotations of the Exception of Personal Information Protection

Copyright technological measures exception rules to personal information protection are provisions for privacy-related content in the exception rules. When copyright technology measures threaten the protection of users' personally identifiable information, technological measures can provide exception rules to maintain the important rule of keeping said information safe and secure.[111] Therefore, the following will discuss the specificity and necessity of creation of the personal information exception of technological measures in more depth.

---

[110] Futao [43].

[111] In the process of writing this article, the author asked the teachers and students about the issue of "personal information protection". Many academics believe that the issue of personal information protection or privacy protection is a problem in the scope of civil law and therefore should not be discussed in the field of copyright law. To respond to doubts, this article explains the exception rules to the personal information protection exception rules for copyright technology measures.

8.4.4.2 The Meaning of Personal Information Protection Exception Rules

Copyright technological measures Personal Information Protection exception rules encompass specific exception rules that are set in the technological measures system to ensure that individuals who evade technological measures for the purpose of protecting their own information security free from legal blame. Using the US DMCA Rule 1201(i) as an analytical blueprint in this instance, briefly, this exception is based on the need to protect the privacy of personally identifiable information and only allows for exception rules specifically regarding the technological measures. First, the article limits the circumventable technological measures and requires technological measures or protection thereof to have the function of collecting or disseminating personal information of network activity capable of displaying a user of these services. Second, the provision provides for the circumvention of technological measures - the technical measure collects the personal information of the user, but does not display the notice to the natural user. Finally, the provision states that circumvention is limited to the function of collecting or disseminating personal information that deactivates the technical measure. The original intention of the DMCA Article 1201(i) was to protect the privacy of personal network information and stipulates in the technological measures exception rule that its contents do not have a negative impact on the legal rights of others.[112]

It should be noted that the establishment of technological measures for the protection of exception rules for personal information is not the sole method to protect the privacy of personal information. It is only a common solution to the current legislative practice in various countries. Below is an analysis of other typical protection methods used in some developed countries.

ii. The necessity of personal information protection in the age of a digital environment

In the current climate of the digital environment, it is undoubtable that the collection of user information for technological measures goes hand in hand with the protection of personal information privacy. For example, a series of login passwords or registration requirements set on the website would be user information that is closely related to personal privacy, which is often collected through technological measures. This is the reason that is necessary to set personal information exception rules for copyright technological measures to ensure smooth and legal operation of technological measures. Specifically, the necessity of creating copyright information technology exception rules for personal information protection, which can be summed up in the following two points:

[112]Samuelson [44], pp. 5–6.

(a) Personal information has the risk of being illegally collected and illegally transmitted, which is a breach of privacy
As a specific subsection of human rights, privacy states that a person should be entitled to a private life, which includes sensitive information being protected by laws (including but not limited to; not illegally intruded, acquired, collected, exploited, and/or disclosed by others).[113] With the development of science and technology and economics in society, the contents of privacy laws are being updated and expanded constantly. Some scholars have classified the sub sections involved in privacy laws as physical privacy, decision privacy, psychological privacy and information privacy.[114] Of which, information privacy concerns are closely tied to technological measures.
Because the copyright owner wants to protect the spread and use of their work, it is standard practice to set up contact control technology measures and copyright protection technology measures to protect their own interests. This is particularly important regarding contact-controlled technological measures that collect personal information through certain procedures. For example, when a researcher wants to use a database to search for the documents needed, the database often requires login, including entering "username + password" information before proceeding to the actual contents of the database. These kinds of procedures belong to contact control type technological measures, which database service providers often use to authenticate the identity of users. In turn, by monitoring the user's search and download records when using the database, the user's behaviour of using the digital work is monitored. User-specific personal information, personal browsing history or consumption records are saved by the network service provider. Currently, the collection, storage, management and use of user information mainly rely on the self-discipline policy of Internet service providers and companies. Although China has enacted the "Network Security Law", since it was implemented on June 1, 2017, the specific regulations still need to be polished and tested in practice.

(b) Personal information protection is closely related to the protection of the legitimate rights and interests of consumers of digital works and services
This is because contact control technology measures can track the user's personal consumption record, bank account number and personal identity information through the user's consumption behaviour. In addition to this, if the copyright owner adds the digital watermark to the work, the owner can obtain information on the use of digital works through technological measures, including the method of access, location, time, number of uses, etc. Most information on the illegal use of software is tracked through digital watermarking. The user's behaviour, preferences, private information involved (above) fall into the category of personal privacy. However, most of the aforementioned tracking actions carried out by copyright owners are not notified to consumers of digital works

[113]Liming [45].

[114]Himma and Tavani [46], pp. 135–156.

clearly. Therefore, the protection of personal information and the protection of consumer rights of works are connected and closely related on some levels, and the comprehensive protection of personal information is the embodiment of protecting the legitimate rights and interests of consumers.

As mentioned previously, the technological measures for personal information protection exception rules specified in the US DMCA are not globally accepted templates for protecting personal information. Different economic, cultural environments and legal development backgrounds will enable different countries to propose different solutions to the same legal issues. The Law on Regulation of Copyright in the Information Society, revised and released by Germany in September 2003, was revised again in 2008. The law had already applied to the EU Copyright Directive and WCT Article 11 Incorporate regarding specific regulations. In addition to the requirements and exception rules for the implementation of international conventions and EU directives for the protection of technological measures, the German Copyright Law provides for enforcement restrictions (Article 95b of the German Copyright Law) and labeling obligations (German Copyright Law) to prevent abuse of copyright technological measures, Article 95d). Judging from the relevant provisions of the German Copyright Law, Germany has already found that beneficiaries in the implementation of technological measures are not equal. The mandatory provision of circumvention obligations and labelling obligations is extremely important for the beneficiary to effectively apply exception rules. First, the mandatory provision of circumvention obligations can help the beneficiary get rid of the technical shortcomings and push the beneficiary's "privilege" to be implemented. Compared with the anti-circumvention exemptions regulations of the United States and other countries, it stipulates that the copyright owner's obligation to provide circumvention means is more operable and worthy of reference. Second, the provisions of the label obligation guarantee the legitimate rights and interests of consumers, such as the rights of consumers of products like digital works, and improve the transparency of digital product transactions. In the end, the labeling obligations are very beneficial for promoting the healthy and orderly development of the digital product trading market. From another perspective, the combination of the label obligation and the beneficiary's claim can also achieve the effect of preventing the disclosure or spread of the consumer's personal information.

Article 15 of the French Law on Copyright and Neighboring Rights of the Information Society imposes a new obligation on the application of copyright technology measures to the stakeholders involved in technological measures, which is deemed as the information security compliance obligations.[115] The French copyright law determines the responsibility for information security compliance, primarily due to the threat of information security issues in the digital environment. With the continuous innovation of digital technology, the technological measures implemented by copyright owners have been endlessly upgraded to prevent others

[115]Article 15, LOI n° 2006-961 du 1er août 2006 relative au droit d'auteur et aux droits voisins dans la société de l'information.

from evading and contacting behaviours, and the accompanying information security issues have become more prominent. In addition, the 2005 Sony BMG CD scandal case also gave France a certain influence on the establishment of this clause in the Copyright Law.[116]

Setting technological measures for personal information protection exception rules is the main legislative model for countries to protect the privacy of personal information through copyright law. From the current state of legislation in various countries, it can be said the majority of countries that stipulate exception rules for personal information protection in the Copyright Law. On the one hand, this is because the method of exception rules to personal information protection enables consumers of digital works to obtain self-reliance and decide for themselves whether to use the law to protect their own interests. On the other hand, legislators set personal information protection exception rules, prompting users to maintain their own "active position" of rights and interests, and thus achieving a balance of interests between copyright owners and users.

The EU and German technological measures for the disclosure of copyright measures and the labeling obligation are powerful guarantees for the legitimate rights and interests of consumers of works.[117] In the age of the internet, due to the serious mismatch between the setter of the technological measures and the information held by the digital work consumers, the aforementioned methods of balancing rights may not achieve their original effect. Therefore, to protect the legitimate rights and interests of consumers and the privacy rights of consumers, legislators should stipulate the corresponding information disclosure obligations from the legal level to the technological measures setters to alleviate the problem of information inequality. A good example for references would be the EU's information disclosure and labeling obligations under the Consumer Rights Directive as well as the German Copyright Law.

8.4.5 *Exception Rules for the Benefit of the Visually Impaired*

Although the development of digital network technology has accelerated the speed of copying and disseminating works, the visually impaired have not had more help in obtaining information and reading works. On June 27, 2013, the WIPO Diplomatic Conference adopted the "Marrakesh Treaty to Facilitate Access to Published Works for Persons Who Are Blind, Visually Impaired or Otherwise Print Disabled" to facilitate the acquisition of published works for the blind, (hereinafter referred to as "Marrakesh"). The treaty is the first international treaty of its kind in the world to include limitations and exception rules to copyright, and is the first international

[116]Szuskin et al. [47], pp. 157–158.

[117]Lili [48], pp. 125–130.

treaty to explicitly set exception rules to technological measures for the visually impaired.

8.4.5.1 Details of Exception Rules of Technological Measures for the Benefit of the Visually Impaired

The circumvention of technological measures for the benefit of the visually impaired means that the authorised entity does not provide the published works to the visually accessible version that can perceived for profit, and can circumvent technological measures. In accordance with Article 7 of the Marrakesh, parties must take appropriate measures to ensure that the legal provisions protected by technological measures provided by the contract do not prevent the visually impaired from enjoying the rights under the Treaty. The specific conditions involved in the exception rule are discussed in depth, below.

8.4.5.2 Defining Elements of Exception Rules to Technological Measures for the Benefit of the Visually Impaired

Specifically, in determining the specific meaning of the exception rule, it is necessary to define the meaning of the four defined elements under the provisions of the "Makkaresh". These four defining elements include (but are not limited to): works, accessible format versions, beneficiaries, and authorised entities.

First, under the provisions of the "Makarresh", works refer to literary and artistic works in accordance with the provisions of the Berne Convention.[118] As for the specific form of the work, the treaty provisions allows for words, symbols or illustrations. It should be noted that audio books are also included in the scope of the work. This means that visually impaired people can obtain audio books in a specific way to meet the needs of contact works.

Second, the accessible format version refers to a version that enables visually impaired people to use the work "as practically" and "as comfortably" as other non-visually impaired audiences.[119] It can be seen that the treaty does not limit the accessible format version by way of enumeration to prevent restrictions on the emergence of new ways in the future.

Furthermore, the beneficiaries mainly include blind people including; those with visual impairments, sensory impairments or dyslexia; those who are unable to hold books with their physical disabilities and are unable to concentrate or move their eyes.[120] The range of beneficiaries specified in "Makarresh" is relatively broad, which will greatly expand the protected interest groups.

[118] Art.2(1), The Marrakesh Treaty.

[119] Art.2(2), The Marrakesh Treaty.

[120] Art.3, The Marrakesh Treaty.

Finally, the authorised entity can be described as a very important concept in "Makarresh". It is the main implementer of the copyright exception rule and the exception rule for circumventing technological measures. It also guarantees for the beneficiary to obtain an accessible format. From the above definition, the treaty puts forward two requirements for the authorised entity: (1) it needs to be authorised by the government,[121] recognise or accept the government's financial support; (2) it needs to operate in a non-profit manner.

First, the establishment of an exception to the technological measures for the benefit of the visually impaired is conducive to the realisation of human rights. This means protection for the visually impaired to realise their right to education and participation in cultural life. Article 30, paragraph 1, of the United Nations Convention on the Rights of Persons with Disabilities, adopted in 2006, also regulates the rights of persons with disabilities to participate in cultural life, recreation, leisure and sports. Therefore, it is a human rights protection for the visually impaired to ensure that visually impaired people can access works and read works like seeing people. The establishment of exception rules for the circumvention of technological measures for the visually impaired can help the visually impaired and the authorised subjects to break through the limitations of technological measures and help them apply the copyright restriction and exception system stipulated in the "Makarresh" to help achieve protection of human rights of the visually impaired.

Second, the circumvention of technological measures exception rules for the benefit of the visually impaired can help emphasise the importance of copyright protection for stimulating literary and artistic creation and achieve the goal of the copyright system. The establishment of this technical measure exception rule provides an opportunity for the visually impaired to "read" the works, help them participate in the cultural life of the society, enjoy the art and share scientific progress with the rest of society, and finally achieve the goal of the copyright system.

Third, circumventing technological measures exception rules for the benefit of the visually impaired can help achieve the balance of interests in the copyright system as well as maintaining a balance between the protection of the work and the education, research and public access to knowledge. The balance of interests is the goal that copyright law has been pursuing. At present, there is a "book shortage" phenomenon of the accessible reading version of works in the world. The performance of the unbalanced interests between the official copyright owner, the relevant rights holders and the public become seriously. Therefore, it should be facilitated for the visually impaired to obtain works by setting corresponding effective and timely copyright restrictions or exception systems to achieve a balance of interests with copyright owners and related rights holders. The circumvention of technological measures for the benefit of the visually impaired can effectively assist the authorised subject to obtain the work and create a corresponding accessible format version for the visually impaired.

[121] Agreed statement of Art.2(3), The Marrakesh Treaty.

Fourth, the circumvention of technological measures exception rules for the benefit of the visually impaired can help achieve cross-border exchange of accessible format versions and reduce waste of resources in various countries. Some scholars have concluded that most developing countries hope to obtain accessible formats from developed countries at no cost or at lower cost for use by their visually impaired. The cross-border exchange of content in the accessible format version specified in the "Marrakesh" allows the visually impaired to obtain an accessible format version of the work. The circumvention of technological measures for the visually impaired benefit exception rules can be exchanged between countries for technically accessible accessible format versions, so that authorised entities are not held accountable for circumventing technological measures. At the same time, the creation of this exception rule is also conducive to saving national resources of countries.

"Marrakesh" is the first international convention to limit copyright and its limitations. At present, many countries including China have signed the "Marrakesh". Once the treaty is approved for implementation, the relevant content of the domestic copyright law of the parties must be consistent with the provisions of the "Marrakesh". This means that once a party to the "Marrakesh" has signed the treaty and approved its entry into force, the contracting party will need to make changes to the relevant provisions of the domestic copyright law, that is, to set or amend the technological measures for the visually impaired. Under the insistence of the developing countries, the developed countries have made concessions on the issue and finally passed the provisions of Article 7 of the "Marrakesh". This article provides for State Parties to prevent technological measures from restricting or impeding beneficiaries from enjoying copyright limitations and exception rules.

Due to the backwardness of legislative technology and the lack of localisation of the legal transplantation process, the exception rules to the technological measures rules established in China's current laws are ambiguous. This is also largely due to the lack of basic legal principles of exception rules to technological measures. The basic principles of law are not only the basic norms governing a specific social relationship and solving certain types of specific social contradictions, but also suggesting a general proposal for situations that are not clearly defined by law, and are the basic norms of various legal rules.[122] Therefore, when the legislators reconstruct the technological measures exception rules, it is necessary to establish the corresponding basic principles to provide basic norms. This paper believes that the basic principles of improving the exception rules of technological measures in China should be proposed from the following four aspects.

The balance of interests has always been regarded by the theoretical circles as the value goal of the intellectual property system and the spiritual core of the entire copyright system. Under the effect of the balance of interest mechanism, the interests of various bodies of conflicting interests can always be coordinated. Specific to the field of copyright technology measures, the conflict of interest mainly protects the

[122]Hongyi [49].

conflict of interest between the copyright owner and the public; the conflict of interest between the information communicator and the public. For the former, the conflict of interest between the two is akin to the conflict between copyright and freedom of speech. Some foreign scholars compare the conflict between copyright and freedom of speech to "gates of a canal", which can promote the flow of knowledge information, and can set obstacles to hinder its flow. The conflict of interests between the interests of copyright owners and the public to obtain information is essentially at opposite ends of the spectrum. The relationship between the two sides is both unified and antagonistic. On the one hand, by constructing a copyright technology measure system, the legitimate interests of copyright owners can be protected, thus stimulating the author's creative enthusiasm and increasing social and cultural reserves. This leads to the total amount of cultural wealth in society is rising. At the time, the amount of information available to the public increases. From this perspective, the copyright technology measures system is beneficial to the public to acquire knowledge. On the other hand, in some cases, the two will may not have such conflict. If the digital works in the Internet environment are not protected by technological measures, the legitimate interests of the copyright owner will be infringed by the illegal use of works. Although in this case the public will have access to more works that can be accessed or utilised. However, at this time, the legitimate interests of the copyright information network environment are not guaranteed (for example, distribution rights, copyrights, information network communication rights, etc. in the digital environment). In the end, the enthusiasm and drive of the author to create works will diminish and ultimately affect the total amount of information that the public can obtain, hindering the progress of society. At this point, the conflict between the two requires technological measures exception rules for coordination and mitigation.

Under the effects of the interest balance mechanism, the technological measures exception rules cannot only meet the needs of the public to access and use the works, but also stimulate the creation of literary and artistic and scientific research and development, and promote scientific realisation and scientific and technological progress. In addition to this, technological measures exception rules help the public to obtain works while helping communicators to disseminate information and increase their economic returns. In summary, the copyright technology measure exception rule constructed under the concept of interest balance can effectively mediate the conflict of interest between related topics caused by excessive protection of copyright technology measures.

When American copyright experts commented on US copyright law, they noted that copyright law cannot only focus on the protection of authors' exclusive rights, but also on the interests of individual users. Therefore, when legislators in China improve the exception rules for copyright technology measures, they should not only pay attention to the protection of the public interest, but also protect the relevant interests of the authors, so that the two are in an equilibrium. Specifically, when legislators in China improve the exception rules for copyright technology measures, they should pay attention to two aspects: First, to rationally formulate the qualification conditions for exception rules for copyright technology measures, and fully protect the legitimate rights and interests of copyright owners from infringement; Second, to accurately locate the development status of relevant industries in China and related interest needs, and make full use of the exception rules of technological measures to adjust the level of protection of high-standard technological measures currently established in China.

Considering everything mentioned above, it is important for the public, copyright owners and related rights holders to establish the concept of "strengthening the balance of interests" when perfecting the exception rules for copyright technology measures in China.

From the perspective of social development, with the development of digital technology and network technology in mind, the carrier of works has changed from paper to digital form, and the speed of copying and spreading has also made a qualitative leap. Humanity has officially entered the age of an information society. Information has become one of the important resources that affect human survival and development. Some American scholars pointed out that the acquisition of knowledge information is the key in the information society. On the one hand, knowledge information has become the main driving force for social development and progress; on the other hand, knowledge utilisation can effectively promote scientific and technological progress and achieve social development. It can be said that in the information society, the acquisition of knowledge information has been closely related to human development and has important significance. From the perspective of citizens' political rights, the right to access knowledge has been embodied in human rights conventions and is now a citizen's "right to seek and accept information".[123] Presently, many countries have adopted legislative activities to protect citizens' "right to accept information."[124] This right is the right to access knowledge. At the same time, some scholars have argued from many aspects that the right to acquire knowledge belongs to the essence of human rights: first, the right to acquire knowledge is the right enjoyed by everyone; second, to satisfy people's need for knowledge, to realise the subjectivity of human being belongs to the right to acquire knowledge. Third, human rights focus on life and dignity, and access to knowledge can satisfy the demand for knowledge and help individuals achieve dignity and value.[125]

The copyright system itself is an alien ideological product from the Western system.[126] The establishment of China's copyright technology measures system is also derived from the signing of the WCT and WPPT treaties under the framework of the World Intellectual Property Organisation. It is necessary to fulfil the obligations

[123] International Covenant on Civil and Political Rights, G.A.Res.2200A(XXI), U.N.GAOR, 21st Sess, Supp. No. 16, U.N. Doc. A/6316, at 16 (Dec. 16, 1966).

[124] Li [50].

[125] Ibid.

[126] Hu [51].

of the two treaties on the protection of technological measures. Some scholars believe that "the law can only be closely related to a particular country, region, or nation, and conforms to the norms of behaviour of the country, region, and nation."[127] Therefore, in the process of legal transplantation, legislators need to fully consider the economic development of the country, the socio-economic development environment of the country and the policy environment.[128] If the legislators do not fully consider the relevant interest factors in the process of legal transplantation, then the functions and benefits of the transplanted legal system cannot be fully realised. Some scholars have suggested that in the process of legal transplantation, the intellectual property system often has insufficient measurement of interests, which leads to the "declining effect of intellectual property law transplantation."[129]

With that in mind, during the process of perfecting the technical rules exception rules, Chinese legislators should respect China's national conditions and national interests and make appropriate choices for relevant international legislative experience. As far as the copyright technology measures system is concerned, China has chosen a higher level of protection mode in fulfilling its international treaty obligations. When countries fulfil their international treaty obligations, the choice of the level of protection reflects the interests of the country. For example, the reason why the EU chose a higher level of protection stems from the identity of the countries that export cultural products within the Union. However, the high standard of protection of technological measures in China is obviously inconsistent with the identity of its major importers of cultural products, and even undermines China's economic interests. Therefore, in fulfilling its obligations under international treaties, China should give full consideration to China's basic national conditions and formulate a legal system that can maximise the national interests of our country.

In other words, when legislators of China improve the exception rules for technological measures, they should establish the basic principles of "respecting China's national conditions and national interests" from two aspects. On the one hand, legislators should make legislative choices based on China's basic national conditions. In the theoretical research work, some scholars are keener to introduce the legal system content of developed countries and ignore the local climate of the legal system, and fail to consider whether the system is consistent with China's basic national conditions. Chinese legislators should abandon this research paradigm in the process of perfecting relevant legislation, and should study the feasibility of foreign advanced legal system in China from the perspective of China's indigenous resources. On the other hand, when implementing the obligations stipulated in the corresponding international treaties, legislators should, from the protection of our national interests, try to create a legal system that maximises the national interests of our country. For example, when Chinese legislators set up corresponding copyright restrictions and exception rules and exception rules to copyright technological

[127]Jingwen [52], p. 140.
[128]Zhiguo [53].
[129]Ibid.

measures in the implementation of the Marrakesh Treaty to protect the interests of visually impaired persons, we should maximise the benefits of our visually impaired. Depart, modify or improve the corresponding legal provisions. In summary, when perfecting the exception rules for copyright technology measures in China, Chinese legislators adhere to the principle of respecting China's national conditions and national interests. When fully understanding China's basic national conditions and the needs of relevant stakeholders, learn from the advanced experience of international legislation and compare with China's economy. The status quo of legislation in developing countries with similar development status, and timely legislative choices should also be considered. Only through this way can legislators establish a scientific and reasonable system of exception rules for technological measures.

The three-step inspection test, from the Berne Convention to the WCT and WPPT under the WIPO framework, constantly changes its contents and to cope with is constantly expanding scope of application. With the change of technology, the scope of the three-step test has expanded from traditional copying rights to all proprietary rights, neighbouring rights, and new and emerging types of communication rights. With the strengthening of bilateralist copyright protection, the importance of the three-step test is further enhanced. This is mainly due to the existence of the principle of MFN treatment in Article 4 of the TRIPS Agreement. The effect of the TRIPS Plus clause in the Free Trade Agreement between the two countries has been further expanded and gradually become a global unified protection standard. Among them, the US-led free trade agreement usually uses the three-step test in the TRIPS Agreement, WCT, and WPPT. With the increase of free trade agreements, the importance of the three-step test is also fortified.[130]

Since the aforementioned international conventions are subject to the "Member States" as the premise of the three-step test, member states must abide by the obligations under the Convention, that is, they need to implement the mentioned obligations through domestic legislation. From this perspective, the primary function of the three-step test is the legislative code function. Some scholars have concluded that as a legislative preparation, the three-step test principle function is embodied in two aspects: the additional guarantee function and the new exception function.[131]

In the current legislative and judicial practice of various countries, the three-step test method also appears as the referee's standard. The two representative legal documents are: the EU Copyright Directive and China's Copyright Law Implementation Regulations.[132]

The European Union's Copyright Directive does not state whether the provisions of the three-step test are aimed at the courts and the general public in member

[130]Jianbang [54].

[131]Li [55], p. 147.

[132]Ibid, p. 149.

countries or governments. Some scholars believe that this, in and of itself, shows that at least the member governments are not the main targets. This marks the directive to transform the three-step test from legislative norms into judicial standards. A three-step test can be applied to every case in the court that is related to limitations and exception rules.[133] Some foreign academics further this belief that the three-step test is not the test standard of the legislative text but the standard of practice between the parties.[134] Therefore, in the "Implementation Regulations", the object of this regulation is obviously only the public and the court. It becomes the standard of conduct of the public and the court's referee standards, and further makes it a general rule of the copyright system.

Article 43 of China's "Copyright Law (Revised Draft for Review)" adds a clause to the bottom, and absorbs the three-step test to the specific rules for fair use. The provisions not only reflect the requirements of the "three-step test" in international conventions, but also the factors of "reasonable use" in the United States. On the one hand, because of the international obligations under the three-step test, China can only impose restrictions and exception rules on copyright for specific and special circumstances, and the formulation and interpretation of corresponding provisions should be appropriate and reasonable, and should not affect the normal use of works. This has serious harm on the legitimate interests of the right holder. The civil law countries often stipulate the limitations and exception rules of copyright in an exhaustive way, and the provisions of Article 22 of the current "Copyright Law" in China follow this style. On the other hand, China's "Copyright Law (Revised Draft for Review)" stipulates the provisions of the slogan and further integrates the provisions of Article 21 of the "Implementation Regulations of the Copyright Law", which is similar to the open-ended fair use system of the United States.[135] Some scholars have concluded: "According to this, the restrictions on the rights of copyright law in China will be adjusted by the 'open list' supplemented by the 'general principle'.[136]

Although the current revision of the Copyright Law has not yet been completed, it is self-evident that the three-step test has officially entered the legal system of copyright in China according to the content of the review. Thus, the introduction of the three-step test method in the technological measures exception rule just happens to make the technical measure exception rule and the copyright restriction and exception system agree on the legislative norm and the evaluation criteria,

[133]Ibid.

[134]Jehoram [56], p. 364.

[135]The fair use and three-step test are two sets of theoretical and institutional systems are sometimes independent, but sometimes overlap. Although the original intention of both theories is to balance the private interests of the right holders and the private interests of the users, there is a significant difference between the two in terms of specific norms. According to the existing theoretical theory in China, many scholars do not understand the difference and connection between the three-step test method and the fair use, and then misunderstanding and confusion when discussing relevant theoretical content.

[136]Chenguo [57].

forming a complete set of integrated systems. If the three-step test method is established solely in the copyright restriction and exception system, the application of the standard in the reconstruction of the technological measures exception rule is abandoned. This will result in the formation of two different sets of restrictions and exception rules in the copyright law system. Since the protection object of the anti-circumvention clause is different from the copyright protection object, the technical measure protection system and the copyright exclusive rights system are independent of each other, and the beneficiary of the copyright restriction and exception system cannot evade technological measures based on the legitimate reasons for reasonable use. The copyright owner relies on technological measures to prevent circumvention of the legislative provisions, and can still be responsible for the reasonable use of beneficiaries to evade control of contact-type technological measures. Therefore, when the copyright technology measures exception rules are reconstructed, the same standards are introduced into the reconstruction standards and the copyright restriction system legislative standards, which form a mutual cooperation relationship between the two systems, which is conducive to giving full way to the functions of the two and realising the benefits; balanced value goals.

References

1. Liebert W, Schmidt JC (2010) Collingridge's dilemma and technoscience: an attempt to provide a clarification from the perspective of the philosophy of science. Poiesis Prax 7:55–71, Springer, 24/03/2010. https://www.axelarnbak.nl/wp-content/uploads/2014/01/Liebert-2010-Collingridge%E2%80%99s-dilemma-and-technoscience.pdf
2. Lessig L (1999) The law of the horse: what cyberlaw might teach. Harv Law Rev 113:501. http://www.yalelawtech.org/wp-content/uploads/lessig-horse.pdf
3. Lessig L (1999) Code and other laws of cyberspace. Basic Books, New York, pp 122–123
4. Ludens P (2012) Digital architecture and online behavior: a study in Pinterest, June 28, 2012. https://puellaludens.wordpress.com/tag/lessigs-modalities/
5. Weber RH, Grosz M, Weber R (2010) Shaping internet governance: regulatory challenges. Springer, Berlin
6. Wolfgang K (2008) Multi-stakeholder internet governance: the governments. In: Benedek, Bauer, Kettemann (eds) Internet governance and society. Utrecht, pp 9–29
7. Negroponte N (1996) Being digital. Hodder & Stoughton, p 229
8. Aretz YL (2015) The subtle incentive theory of copyright licensing. Brooklyn Law Rev 80 (4):1357
9. Sinnreich A, Aufderheide P (2015) Communication scholars and fair use: the case for discipline-wide education and institutional reform. Int J Commun 9
10. Birnhack M (2015) Judicial snapshots and fair use theory. Queen Marry J Intellect Prop 5 (3):264–284
11. Loren LP (2015) Fair use: an affirmative defense? Wash Law Rev 90:685. Lewis & Clark Law School Legal Studies Research Paper No. 2015-12
12. Aufderheide P, Milosevic T, Bello B (2015) The impact of copyright permissions culture on the U.S. visual arts community: the consequences of fear of fair use. New Media & Society, Online First, March 10, 2015
13. Martin KE (2015) Understanding privacy online: development of a social contract approach to privacy. J Bus Ethics, April 25, 2015

14. Netanel NW (1996) Copyright and a democratic civil society. Yale Law J:106
15. Lloyd FW, Mayeda DM (1986–1987) Copyright fair use, the first amendment, and new communications technologies: the impact of Betamax. Fed Common Law J 38:59
16. Cohen M, Murphy J (eds) (2001) Exploring sustainable consumption: environmental policy and the social sciences. Pergamon (Elsevier Science Ltd), Oxford
17. Clinton H (2013) Internet rights and wrongs: choices & challenges in a networked world. http://www.state.gov/secretary/20092013clinton/rm/2011/02/156619.htm. 15 February 2013
18. Armstrong TK (2006) Digital rights management and the process of fair use. Harv J Law Technol 20:49. University of Cincinnati Public Law Research Paper No. 07-10
19. Gitton A. Analyse du projet de loi français sur « le droit d'auteur et les droits voisins dans la société de l'information » (y compris les créations des agents publics). http://www.droit-technologie.org/upload/dossier/doc/106-1.pdf. Accessed 26 Sep 2015
20. Handke C, Towse R (2007) Economics of copyright collecting societies. Int Rev Intellect Prop Compet Law 38(8):937–957
21. Yu PK (2006) Anticircumvention and anti-anticircumvention. Denver Univ Law Rev 84:13–77. MSU Legal Studies Research Paper No. 04-05
22. Wilson A (2010) Digital rights management-an overview. Legal Journals Index, Bus Law Rev 31(1):2–7
23. Bird RC, Jain SC (eds) (2009) Reviewed by John A. Tessensohn, The global challenge of intellectual property rights European Intellectual Property. Edward Elgar Publishing
24. Kleinsteuber HJ (2004) The internet between regulation and governance. In: Möller, Amouroux (eds) OSCE representative on freedom of the media. The Media Freedom Internet Cookbook, Vienna, pp 61–75
25. Nwogugu M (2008) Economics of digital content: new digital content control and P2P control systems/methods. Comput Telecommun Law Rev. https://doi.org/10.2139/ssrn.1134407. Accessed 14 Sep 2015
26. Carbado DW, Mitu Gulati G (2003) The law and economics of critical race theory. Yale Law J 112(7):1757–1828
27. Soghoian C (2010) Caught in the cloud: privacy, encryption, and government back doors in the Web 2.0 Era. J Telecommun High Technol Law 8:370
28. Xiao S, Zhengcao L (2015) Copyright infringement regulatory countermeasures on network cloud drive. China Copyright 6:26
29. Cunningham M (2014) Next generation privacy: the internet of things, data exhaust, and reforming regulation by risk of harm. Groningen J Int Law 2, Ed. 2
30. Välimäki M, Oksanen V (2006) DRM interoperability and intellectual property policy in Europe. SSRN Electron J
31. Griffiths J (2009) The 'Three-Step Test' in European Copyright Law - problems and solutions. Queen Mary University of London, School of Law, Legal Studies Research Paper No. 31/2009. Available at: http://ssrn.com/abstract=1476968. Accessed 17 July 2018
32. Tang P (2005) Digital copyright and the "new" controversy: is the law moulding technology and innovation? Res Policy 34(6):852–871
33. Lunney GS Jr (2002) Fair use and market failure: Sony revisited. Boston Univ Law Rev 82:975. Available at: https://scholarship.law.tamu.edu/facscholar/504. Accessed 18 June 2018
34. Perry M, Casey MC (2000) Copyright and anti-circumvention: growing pains in a digital millennium. N Z Intellect Prop J
35. Iwahashi R (2011) How to circumvent technological protection measures without violating the DMCA: an examination of technological protection measures under current legal standards. Berkeley Technol Law J 26:491
36. Bovens M, Schillemans T (2008) Does public accountability work? An assessment tool. Pubic Adm 86:228
37. Baldwin R, Cave M, Lodge M (eds) (2010) The Oxford handbook of regulation. Oxford University Press, Oxford, p 349

38. Ivo G, François K (2014) Editorial – liability, responsibility and accountability: crossing borders. Utrecht Law Rev 10:1–13
39. Reed C, Kennedy E, Silva SN (2016) Responsibility, autonomy and accountability: legal liability for machine learning. Legal Studies Research Paper No 243/2016
40. Gilles SG (1992) Negligence, strict liability, and the cheapest cost-avoider. Va Law Rev 78:1291, 1295
41. Husovec M (2016) Accountable, not liable: injunctions against intermediaries. Tilburg Law and Economic Center Discussion Paper, 2 May 2016, p 10
42. Cooter R (1987) Torts as the union of liberty and efficiency: an essay on causation. Berkeley Law Scholarsh Repos 63(523):536
43. Futao S (2017) Analysis of privacy infringement risk of copyright technological measures in the era of big data. China Publ J
44. Samuelson P (2000) Towards more sensible anti-circumvention regulations, 5 NO. 5 Cyberspace Law 2:5–6
45. Liming W (2012) Redefining the concept of privacy. Jurist (Chinese Version), vol 1
46. Himma KE, Tavani HT (2008) The handbook of information and computer ethics. Wiley, New Jersey, pp 135–156
47. Szuskin L, Szczygiel J, Kevin C et al (2008) When information security meets intellectual property in France and in the United States: requirement applicable to certain DRMs. Priv Data Secur Law J 2:157–158
48. Lili Z (2016) Research on information security compliance system of copyright technology protection measures. Wuhan University Press, pp 125–130
49. Hongyi G (2002) The position and function of legal principle in legal reasoning -- a comparative study. Legal Research (Chinese Version), vol 6
50. Li P (2014) The proof of knowledge acquisition right—from the perspective of due rights. The rule of law research (Chinese Version)
51. Hu K (2011) Perfect the principle of our broadcasting organization right system. Review of political science and law (Chinese Version), vol 5
52. Jingwen Z (2006) A country ruled by law under the condition of globalization. Ren Min University Press, p 140
53. Zhiguo S (2006) Analysis on the reasons of diminishing effect in the legal transplantation of intellectual property rights in China. Politics and Law (Chinese Version), vol 5
54. Jianbang Z (2011) On the formation and characteristics of MFN treatment system of intellectual property rights. J Int Econ Law 18(1)
55. Li Z (2011) The boundary of copyright—research on the limitation and exception of copyright in information society. Peking University Press, p 147
56. Jehoram HC (2005) Restrictions on copyright and their abuse. Eur Intellect Prop Rev:364
57. Chenguo Z (2016) Interpretation of "three-step test law" and "fair use" —research on Article 43 of copyright law (revised draft). Global Law Review (Chinese Version), vol 5

Part V
The Room for Perfecting China's Digital Rights Management: Some Experience Can be Learned from Europe and America

Chapter 9
Status Quo and Foreground

Although laws may be restricted by national borders, the relationship between technology and laws can surpass the border universally, which obviously manifests in the system of anti-technique circumvention rules due to the infinite of network. Since the EU and America have accumulated quite a lot of experience and lessons regarding anti-technique circumvention rules of legislation and judicature with an early start, we can learn from their anti-technique circumvention rules to perfect China's relevant legislation, which can provide enough guarantee for technology protection measures first, and then, copyright owners will be stopped to realize interests beyond laws by technology. From my point of view, the current Copyright Law in China should be changed by including it to the Article 47 of copyright infringement.

9.1 Clear the Definition of Technology Protection Measures

The definition of technology protection measures should be included into the anti-technique circumvention rules. The definition can be expressed as follows: technology protection measures mean effective technology, equipment as well as parts that copyright owners adopt to protect their execution right of materials for which they have copyright or neighboring right by *Copyright Law*.

The technology protection measures protected by anti-technique circumvention rules should be effective because it will be nonsense to protect ineffective technology protection measures by law. Therefore, whatever American Digital Copyright Law or European Copyright Orders, they only offer legal protection to effective technology protection measure by giving definition for its effectiveness. As for the judgment standard of technology protection measure's effectiveness, a lowest standard scheme has been adopted by DMCA, which stipulates that technology protection measure will be considered effective as long as consumers have no access to the work without permission of the copyright owner or execute certain copyright. This

C. Xu, *Regulatory Model for Digital Rights Management*,
https://doi.org/10.1007/978-981-15-1995-6_9

method is worthwhile to be learned by China. There is no absolutely effective technology protection measure in the world; otherwise, anti-technique circumvention rules are unnecessary to exist. Moreover, notwithstanding how effectively technology protection measures can protect the interest of copyright owner, they are still execution tools of laws. It is law instead of technology that gives final relief to copyright owner. Therefore, although copyright owners aim to protect their copyright from infringement by employing technology protection measures, the realization of the aim cannot be seen as the criteria for judging the effectiveness of the technology protection measure. Besides, technology protection measures are implemented for common consumers. Therefore, the technology protection measure can be seen effective as long as common consumers without professional techniques have no access to copyright materials by the measure.

9.2 Distinguish Legal Technology Circumvention Behaviors from Illegal Ones

The technology circumvention behaviors have diversified purposes with different consequences as well. Therefore, anti-technique circumvention rules should be told from technique circumvention behaviors by giving different legal status to them. For example, without permission from copyright owner or right holders related to copyright owner, no one is allowed to deliberately shun or destroy technology protection measures that hold owner adopted to protect their copyright or rights related to copyright for their works as well as sound and video recordings. However, this article will be inapplicable if the technique circumvention behavior is necessary to reach a legal goal without damaging the interest of copyright owner. Science and research workers can have technique circumvention behaviors for their research, but information gained from the research cannot be applied to other purposes beyond academic exchanges.

At first, anti-technique circumvention rules should set up common object clauses exempting from technology circumvention, namely certain avoidance behavior can be free from responsibility investigation for certain purposes which grant the court with discretionary power to determine whether technology circumvention activities violate the law or not. In digital era, technology especially the digital technology is rapidly developing. Thus, if laws carry out closed list for legal technology circumvention activities there should be some left out or eliminated because of technology development's follow-up. Besides, along with the emergence of digital environment, there may be problems which are not included in or not prominent in the digital environment with various circumvention situations. For example, technical failure may occur to a certain kind of technological protection measure and cause irregular operation that further causes the unavailable use of these works and even other works. Under some circumstance, consumers have to adopt avoidance behaviors for those good running techniques. For example, the technology renewal process is rapid and a certain technology will be quickly obsolete. Therefore, consumers have to adopt technological protection measures circumvention to understand the antiquated works. Under such circumstance, law should support the technological circumvention. Based on this circumstance, both American digital copyright law and EC Directive have authorized to set up a committee to discuss on the effects of anti-technique circumvention rules and at the same time adjust technology circumvention which can exempt from blame. In China, to make common objective clauses for legal technological circumvention shall provide regulations for Supreme People’s Court to abide by in the course of making judicial interpretation or directive opinion and enable the rules become more flexible and fair. As far as I am concerned, common objective clauses should include the following contents: First, technological circumvention aims to obtain a legal objective. Second, technology circumvention activities are necessary for completing the objective. Notwithstanding the subjective aim of an actor, technology circumvention activities will increase the risk of being infringed for copyright owners. Only necessary technological circumvention activities to which can achieve legal goal are exempted from being punished by law to avoid technological circumvention activities to the best advantage and prevent copyright infringement. Third, the technological circumvention activities will not cause damages to copyright owners. The aim of anti-technique circumvention rules is to protect the benefits of copyright owners, so these rules should only punish those cause damages for copyright owners. The practices of America and the European Union also proved that the prohibition of technology circumvention activities would shackle scientific research, academy change and market competition. We can punish those intentional circumvention activities carrying out copyright infringement.

Second, those avoidance behaviors, which are conducted by researchers only for research purpose, should be ruled out of anti-technique circumvention rules. Moreover, researchers and related colleagues should be equipped with circumvention devices while they are carrying out avoidance behaviors, allowing them to discuss information obtained in avoidance behaviors. Of course, if they implement infringement activities based on the above conditions or create convenience for infringement, they have to take on responsibilities of infringement and providing circumvention devices.

9.3 Add “Anti-Equipment” Items in Regulatory Architecture

Anti-circumvention devices are of vital importance for the protection on copyright owners in digital environment. Therefore, China’s anti-circumvention provision should incorporate this item. However, the legitimacy of anti-circumvention devices provisions explained by Supreme People’s Court is suspected because it is beyond permissions, which is also blurred with discrimination and is not suitable to be implanted into copyright law. I suggest making a clear definition for anti-circumvention devices provisions: Anyone cannot manufacture, spread, input, lease approaches, equipment, accessories, services or constituent parts which are able to carry out avoidance behaviors or damage the benefits of copyright owners. Laws should prohibit everyone, not only Internet Service Provider from manufacturing or providing circumvention devices. Technology is neutral, which is able to obtain illegal profits and legal interests as well. Devices themselves cannot distinguish it is infringing use or not. Therefore, abandoning everyone from manufacturing and transferring circumvention devices is helpful to protect the rights of copyright owners and is more feasible. Those activities such as reverse engineering for legal objectives can be set down with exceptional approaches.

Anti-technique circumvention rules should clearly define the connotation of circumvention devices, and the word device makes a general reference, including tangible machines and accessories and intangible services, technology. I think simple devices services or a part of them, which can independently complete avoidance behaviors, should be included. Furthermore, anti-technique circumvention rules should also set up standards of judging the circumvention devices, in other words which kind of equipment should be regarded as circumvention devices. Both American digital copyright law and EC Directive have worked out a quite low standard. Not only equipment which are subjectively designed, manufactured or promoted to evade certain specific technological protection measure but also those equipment which have limited commercial significance besides circumvent technical protection measures are banned by anti-equipment provisions. In my opinion, judgment standards for circumvention devices in American digital copyright law and the EU Directive are to be questioned. To begin with, if we prohibit those equipment which have limitless commercial meanings besides circumvent technical protection measures, there should be a wide attack and technology development shackle because those equipment with limited commercial meanings may be applied to non-commercial yet legal activities. Second, it is not reasonable to determine the fate of a certain technology based on the will of the producer or seller. Whether the equipment is applied to carry out infringement action depends on the will of the user but not the producer. We cannot deny a certain technology when manufacture and distributors produce or promote it because they expect to circumvent it. For example, the first person who produced audio and video equipment does not mean to illegally copy audio-visual products and we cannot ban the audio and video equipment. Furthermore, it is rarely seen that equipment are used for other purposes while producing for another purpose. Finally, America and the European Union have always adopted a serious standard to judge whether the equipment belongs to circumvention devices or not with good effects. The substantive non-infringing use standard determined in a case of Sony[1] judged in U.S. Supreme Court said that people have to ban the avoidance behavior but not the equipment itself when it can be used for technological circumvention with practical substantial

[1]Sony Corp. of America v. Universal City Studios, 464 U.S. 417, 442 (1984).

non-infringing uses, such as reasonably use certified copies. However, in the EU Directive only those equipment that are used to help technological circumvention should be ruled out. Laws ought to fight against the legal activities through technology but not the technology itself. Consequently, China has to adopt substantive non-infringing use standard to assess circumvention devices.

There are always conflicts between technological protection measures and consumers' fair use in the digital environment. Therefore, anti-technique circumvention rules should make it clear under which condition there should be priority. It hereby could be summarized from the following explanation of the relationship between technological protection measures and fair use: when state organs use works which have been published in a reasonable range while performing official business or copy works stored in the library, archives, memorial hall, museum, art gallery and copyright owners have to provide copies without technological measures or technological circumvention tools or approaches. In principle, anti-technique circumvention rules do not have to be involved in interventions on consumptive fair use. Transformative fair use is an important part of free speech with significant meaning for modern democratic society, which should be preserved in digital times. Besides, transformative fair use does not have damages because of technological protection measures, which may not be convenient as digital technology requires. However, comparing to the expectation that consumers hope to implement fair use with the most convenient way, the will that copyright owners hope to stop infringement activities should be paid attention in law. Concerning the nature of consumptive fair use, I tend to approve the idea of market failure model. Because of technology limits, there are always limitations when the law implemented actions and things just go as the same in terms of consumptive fair use. In principle, copyright owners are granted with rights to have compensations while other people using their works. However, previous technology cannot exactly stop and punish the private copy on the premise of not violating privacy and not consuming huge financial resources. Thus, people have to sacrifice the justice of copyright law to win the stability of social democracy.[2] What is lucky is that current technology is able to overcome the market failure to fairly allocate social benefits, properties, various rights and power, which expands the breadth and depth of the justice laws aspire for. Accordingly, laws have to adjust objectives and it is not necessary to emphasize the consumptive fair use, which is supported by the theory circle and judicial practice circle in Europe. Concerning consumptive fair use, anti-technique circumvention rule should be granted with priorities. That is to say, consumers conducting consumptive fair use depends on the condition that whether copyright owners adopts technological protection measures or not. Fair use set for protecting public interest should not be affected by technological protection measures. Comparing to copyright law, the public safety and other public interest of state organs using works, which have been published in a reasonable range, should have priority. Libraries, museums, and educational agencies are public organs for people to obtain information and technology, promote the

[2]Jiang and Zhao [1], p. 203, p. 4.

development of science and culture, which are beneficial owners in a simulated environment and should be granted with priority. Because the public interest they show is the ultimate goal, copyright law is longing for. To not repeat the same mistakes of American digital copyright law and the EU Directive, and prevent the condition that some public interests are not implemented because of the block of technological protection measures, laws have to allow the avoidance behavior of library, museum and educational agencies for the purpose of public benefit.

9.4 Comparison Between China and Europe and America

The ideological base of copyright comes from the theory of natural rights, and protection of copyright is actually the respect for human creations. In the early days, protection of copyright aimed to protect the rights and interests of author and publisher; while in recent years, with the expansion and communication of knowledge, public has an increasingly greater need for knowledge, and then the relationship between copyright owner and user has been developed during the development of copyright protection system. Besides, the development trend of copyright is to seek balance between copyright owner and public appeals, which is the sociology of law's penetration in copyright system.

Cultural globalization is the concomitant of economic globalization.[3] "Cultural globalization does not mean global integration of culture only, but it is also accompanied by cultural conflict." The national cultural security and world cultural diversity are expressions of social risk in cultural field. In today's society of cultural globalization and cultural industry globalization, we are faced with "an era of risk culture".[4] Scott Lash once warned people that "unexpected risk and danger will be new risks and dangers coming from information field, biological technology field, communication and software field instead of risks and dangers produced from material production process in industrial society".[5] The "cultural risk" in contemporary society manifests in weakness of national culture and marginalization of traditional culture. The traditional culture as well as the so-called mainstream culture or powerful culture of many tribes and nationalities have always had certain tension state worldwide, which not only exists between Eastern and Western cultures, but also manifests inside European and American culture. Cultural globalization, the concomitant of economic globalization, cannot eliminate the nationality and diversity of culture. In fact, there are over ten thousand different social groups living in about two hundred countries, so for each country, they belong to multi-culture and multi-nations country. To protect cultural diversity is mainly to respect the rights of minor groups. However, as for international society, cultural diversity means

[3]Ibid.

[4]http://www.riskcultureinsights.com/, and also see Adam et al. [2].

[5]Lash [3].

differences in language, religions as well as ways of life. To admit the cultural diversity is to admit the independence and autonomy of cultural sovereignty in different countries. It is theoretical basis to realize cultural diversity and legal requirements of national cultural sovereignty principles to "respect equal status, diversity and rich vitality of different cultures, and to respect their different development routes".[6] The system deficiency of international protection system focusing on TRIPS lies in that it manages to protect the originality and novelty of cultural forms while the diversity of cultural forms has been overlooked. We can see that the world has been basically dominated by European and American culture which is characterized by its "modernity".[7] From the perspective of culture, while assimilating native culture and traditional culture all over the world, European and American culture has also nibbled the world cultural diversity gradually. From the perspective of laws, the legal spirit and system principles advocated by Western countries have become guideline of international social life. In the domain of intellectual property, intellectual products of European and American culture types have been perfectly protected in various forms of "intellectual innovation" by international intellectual property system indexed by European countries during modern production. On the contrary, the system of intellectual property right lacks necessary legal conservation for "intellectual source" of different cultural types. The system can "only protect property rights of intellectual property without extension to the coexistent cultural interest".

9.5 The Development of American Network Copyright Law: Dominated by Government Under the Promotion of Practitioners

The United States has had almost two hundred years' development history since its establishment of copyright in its early years of the new nation. The protection range has been developed from the early books to afterward arts and musical electronic from weak to strong. The development history of American copyright system contributes a lot to the copyright owners in each field.

The development history of copyright before network age: The development process of American copyright in the early years is mainly as follows. Copyright regulations were issued successively by each state. In 1789, articles and clauses of copyright were defined by Constitution. In 1790, the first Copyright Law was passed by the Congress. The copyright system in early America was mainly affected by Great Britain. After the Independence Movement, British laws and regulations were abandoned in America without establishing corresponding copyright protection

[6]http://portal.unesco.org/culture/en/ev.php-URL_ID=34321&URL_DO=DO_TOPIC&URL_SECTION=201.html.

[7]Giddens [4].

system; besides, issues related to copyright was not mentioned in the Articles of Federation passed in 1781 as well. Publishers, represented by Noah Webster, persuaded among states, which greatly promoted the issuance of copyright regulations in each state afterward. Actually, both the content and language completely copied the Statute of Anne or made a tiny change on its basis in terms of legislation in each state. The articles of copyright in each state manifest the protection of authors' ideas to stimulate authors' further innovation, enlarge knowledge communication, and further increase publishers' interests. However, it caused great inconvenience because of the disunity of copyright regulations in each state, so a united law needed to be formulated within federation urgently. Thus the eighth item, eighth clause, the first article of the Constitution was passed on constitutional convention in 1787. It claimed that "authors and inventors have exclusive rights for their works and inventions in a certain period in order to promote the development of scientific and practical technology", which is generally considered the foundation of American copyright law and patent law.

The first Federal Copyright Law, Copyright Law in 1790, was passed by the Congress in 1790. It has seven articles in total, which are almost the copy of the Statute of Anne, aiming to protect the copyright of native citizens and residents. In 1990, the Copyright Law was revised again, and the prominent feature was that work concept became mature with large protection range. Although authors were entitled with copyright under the Copyright Law in 1790, the protection object was book without the concept of "work". After over one century, the stipulations of Copyright Law in 1909 was further expanded because of publishers' constant appeal to courts and persuasions to the Congress, by which the right of reproduction was increased based on the previous print, reprint, sales and import. Network technology was early developed in America, and thus America was the earliest country who protects network copyright. In the network era, under the traditional copyright law, copyright owners have lower control the capability of copyright, so right holders managed to seek new legal provisions to protect their interests and status. In 1993, the National Information Infrastructure Task Force was built by Clinton Administration who began to study copyright policies in digital age. The Information Commission was set under the leadership of intellectual property group, and Bruce Lehman, the commissioner was the convener of Patent Office. The team was responsible for holding public hearings and understood demands of different classes with the proposal of Green Paper. According to the Green Paper, all reproduction would be considered infringement, which aroused strong objection among users including providers of library network information for public writers. Surely, the Green Book achieved strong support from traditional copyright industries including publication, film, music and software, etc.[8] After the issuance of Green Paper, Lehman team held public hearings and convened representatives from traditional copyright industries

[8]Guilda Rostama, Remix Culture and Amateur Creativity: A Copyright Dilemma, WIPO Magazine, June 2015, https://www.wipo.int/wipo_magazine/en/2015/03/article_0006.html, Accessed date: 02/15/2018.

and school libraries for consultation. According to Lehman's team, traditional copyright owners would be reluctant to upload their works on the internet if their rights were not protected well, and then the communication would be weakened.[9] In addition, the international treaty cannot be directly executed in America. Instead, a certain domestic law needs to be designated by the Congress to perform obligations in the international treaty. Therefore, it is of extreme necessity to carry out requirements of international treaty for the legislation of digital copyright.

9.6 The Adaptive Development of Copyright Law in Network Age

By comparison, the development of Chinese network copyright is self-reconstruction because of external pressure. The development of network technology has brought new challenges for copyright protection, so international treaty, bilateral agreement and domestic laws in each country have all made adaptive adjustment since the 1990s; while comparatively copyright law in our country cannot only meet domestic demand under network age, but also it cannot adjust itself to international need since its "birth date". Therefore, we had two amendments for the Copyright Law in 2001 and 2010, respectively. The first amendment in 2001 was out of direct need after joining the WTO, some articles in Copyright Law, which are inconsistent with those in Intellectual Property Agreement Related to Trade of WTO, were revised and supplemented. Compared to the former two times of passive amendments because of external pressure, the third amendment launched in July 2011 was an active choice based on national conditions, which aimed to enhance the operability of law to adapt to the constantly changing network environment. On March 31, 2012, the Copyright Law of the People's Republic of China, draft amendment, was issued on the official websites of State Copyright Bureau and GAPP,[10] soliciting suggestions and proposals from all walks of life in public. It perfects protective measures for technology and rights management information system with addition of practical artistic works and "three-step test", perfects the definitions of information network broadcast right and broadcast right, defines the attribution of audiovisual works and copyright works, establishes the administrative mediation for copyright disputes as well as improves the standards for infringement compensation, etc.

It has been over 30 years since China's reform and opening up, and the Copyright Law has been issued for over 20 years. Now Chinese social economy has been developed to a brand new stage, so we should not be satisfied with the role of "world factory" anymore, especially after issuing the Outline of National Intellectual

[9]Ibid.

[10]State Administration of Press, Publication, Radio, Film and Television of People's Republic of China.

Property Strategy in 2008,[11] which elevated intellectual property issue to a national strategic high for the first time with clear goal of building an innovative country by protecting intellectual property rights. Since then, "intellectual property" entered the mainstream discourse of contemporary Chinese society. The issuance of the Outline of National Intellectual Property Strategy was not by accident. One hand, the original values and lifestyle of Chinese people changed a lot when Chinese society developed to a particular stage; on the other hand, after over 20-year communication, with the promotion of globalization and deep educational exchanges, Chinese people have accepted copyright law gradually, occurring subtle integration with traditional Chinese discourse. For example, Chinese people have changed their views on "merchants" and "interest" with the replacement of planned economy by market economy. The change of Chinese values makes it possible to recognize the property value of "works'; besides, with the development of network technology and material life, Chinese people are capable of satisfying their spiritual life, which has promoted innovation of works in various types and changed their traditional cautious attitude towards "expression" gradually, and meanwhile it is suitable for the idea of "expression" regarding copyright protection. People's knowledge about copyright system and idea has been affected subtly by a series of cases with social influences. After joining the WTO, China has had negotiations, conversations and conflicts with Western countries for many times. By propaganda, common people's awareness of protecting intellectual property has been gradually strengthened, etc. Thus, sincerely speaking, social changes in contemporary China have largely changed Chinese people's traditional way of thinking, which has gradually improved the environment for implementing copyright system. It does not mean to deny the correctness of protecting copyright in China to recognize the conflict between traditional Chinese culture and copyright culture, instead, the deep cultural element behind a series of difficulties needs to be interpreted objectively for copyright protection in contemporary China to determine copyright protection level that is suitable for Chinese current situation gradually with proposal of localization basis for Chinese copyright law. At present, domestic scholars generally consider that at the very beginning of Chinese intellectual property legislation process, it did not give full consideration to Chinese social economic development as well as traditional Chinese cultural acceptance, therefore the legislation was extremely ahead with an "over-protection" state for intellectual property so that Chinese intellectual property legislation has become a tool for some Western countries to monopoly technology and contain China's development.[12] The intellectual property system has not promoted Chinese economic and cultural development earnestly. On the contrary, it has greatly increased the developmental cost. Such idea has its rationality since it has experience and observation basis. The level of a nation's copyright protection is determined by

[11]《2008年国家知识产权战略纲要》.

[12]Bryan Mercurio, The Protection and Enforcement of Intellectual Property in China since Accession to the WTO: Progress and Retreat, China Perspectives, No.1, 2012. https://journals.openedition.org/chinaperspectives/5795?file=1, Access date:07/24th/2018.

many factors such as cultural prosperity, economic development level, traditional legal concept as well as the current international environment and so on. Take America as an example, as a big power for intellectual property in the world, the determination and improvement of copyright protection in America is gradual rather than happen in a while. It is right because America had clear knowledge about different needs of copyright in different development stage that it did not join the Berne Convention until 1989. Thus, it guaranteed the adaptability between copyright protection level and social culture, economy, legal traditions as well as international environment in particular period to most extent. However, as for the legislation and implementation phase of Chinese copyright law, the "Take-ism" and passive feature of legislation mean that it did not fully considered the factors above, especially the effect of legal and cultural differences between China and the West on copyright protection level. Therefore, legislation in China is of advancement to some extent, which leads to poor implementation effect. Moreover, during the conversation and negotiation with Western developed countries regarding intellectual property, our country has been in an awkward and passive situation usually.

Law is about the social norm with objective content though it is subjective in the form; while technology is one social norm with both objective form and content, but it can be employed by people subjectively. Few people have always mastered special technology, and those who master particular technology have always made the best use of it to its ultimate probably to damage the legitimate rights of common people who possess or master no particular technology. However, law needs to embody requirements of justice. That is to say, everyone should obtain what they deserve to obtain. No one is allowed to gain more than he deserves, and no one is allowed to gain less than he deserves as well. Therefore, law must restrain abuse of technological advantage out of needs for justice. A legal state should give top priority to its rule under the law. Within the whole social system of norms including morality, laws and technology, the role of law as the ultimate norm should not be challenged, while technology as a norm must be restrained by law; otherwise, legal state should give way to state dominated by technology, which is obviously impossible and irrational in the near future.

The law always leaves behind the development of technology. The powerful impact brought by the technical progress to the Fair Use has broken the benefit balancing mechanism in the field of traditional copyright law. It is just the claim of the public for the fair use and the demand on the development of social and cultural industry that urges us to go into the relationship between the digital rights management and the Fair Use and to coordinate the conflicts between the two by improving the relevant legal systems.

Based on the objective data and the typical cases, through the comparative study on the anti-circumvention protection and prohibition exception laws for the digital rights management at home and abroad, and through the comprehensive grasp and the latest follow-up of the essential root of interest conflict between the Technological Measure and the public and the conflict coordination theory, this paper has concluded that: 1. The legal protection of digital rights management has its necessity in existence; 2. The Fair Use also its own rationality under the environment of new digital media; 3. The key for the benefit balance between the digital right holder and the public is to coordinate the conflicts between the two with the benefit balance theory of copyright law as the foundation, and oriented by the matching of the rights and obligations. From this in-depth study, this paper has proposed a variety of scientific and practical coordination approaches from the perspective of digital technology solution, judicial practice and administrative law enforcement.[13] In addition, combined with the status quo of the construction of relevant legal systems in China, it is believed in this paper from the perspectives of the direct and indirect coordination of conflict between the digital rights management and the Fair Use that, the key to coordinate the conflict between the two is to define the effectiveness principle of the Technological Measure, to expand and refine the prohibition exceptions on circumvention, to introduce copyright validity system for the Technological Measure, to develop the protection system of personal privacy involved in the Technological Measure, and to extend the application scope of the Anti-Unfair Competition Law and the Antitrust Law.[14]

There are still many drawbacks in this paper because of limited knowledge. For example, the fair use right is constantly adjusted and improved with the technology improvement, but its reality conflicts with the digital rights management technology are countless, and the conflict coordination theories are also changing with the technology improvement. Therefore, more researches are required for the deep reason analysis and the new coordination theory of the conflict between the two. This paper is not entirely satisfactory, which not only brings many flaws and regrets for the study, but also urges me to constantly improve it in the further study.

International Intellectual Property Right has only developed for more than one hundred years. Earlier Paris Convention, Berne Convention and nowadays TRPIS are results from cooperation and game between various countries, which are definitely led by Western countries with a Western centrism-style legislative pattern. Correspondingly, international academic mainstream, such as popular Western thinking model, values and theoretical systems are widely known in International Intellectual Property Rights. From an extreme perspective of intellectual property fundamentalism, intellectual property law in developed countries is the only way to promote development, and misappropriation of intellectual property amounts to terrorism. In international discourse system communication, we have to make Chinese style declaration and voice to modify the Western centrism trend to construct a fairer and more reasonable intellectual property international order. The international protection system of intellectual property is same to other laws and provisions, which should be a global legal mechanism and internal rule which are recognized and connect various countries. Furthermore, it should be an organic solidarity of adjustment rules created by different countries based on experiences which indicates the universally historical rules of legal practice and reflects legal wisdom as well as the pursuit of rationality. It can be seen from these that the

[13]Menell [5], p. 1363.

[14]Ibid.

theoretical foundation of international intellectual property right should not focus on Western centrism or national chauvinism.[15]

The formation of intellectual property's international discourse system is based on common legal value and legal faith, which, at the same time, helps to realize interactive development of diverse legal culture and legal ideas. When referring to the achievements of legal civilization and advanced legal philosophy, Chinese intellectual property circle has to focus on local theoretical innovation and independent thought, trying tireless efforts to search for property-rights theories that are suitable for Chinese context and cultural background, including legal interpretation rules and policy use methods. The final aim is to construct a discourse system for developing countries in terms of intellectual property. To the theoretical system of International Intellectual Property Right, it is critical and constructive.

The research on theoretical system of intellectual property should not be satisfied with the academic requirement constructed by basic contents, but should revolve around intellectual property's career construction to form a Chinese pattern based on the thinking of Chinese matters, Chinese experiences and Chinese roads. Chinese matters being studied all arise from the special conditions of China. The peculiarities of Chinese matters in intellectual property right show as follows: a big rise. As an intellectual property power and major developing country, its large-scale population and industry size, economic size and society size are unprecedented, which will inevitably exceed previous rising countries and is not copying or imitation.[16] This big rise contains powerful innovation ability with unprecedented big problems and difficulties. Besides, the different recognition of different groups on intellectual property and special attention paid by Western countries make the intellectual property problem have both internal confusion and external divergence; furthermore, there are development differences.[17] An outstanding problem of Chinese economy and society is imbalance. Rural-urban differences, differences between west and middle regions as well as industrial differentiation determine the situation that the development of Chinese intellectual property right career cannot be rigid uniformity or synchronized development. Here, balance urban and rural development, regional development and economic and social development; harmonious development between human beings and nature; opening and domestic development are big issues China has to face in the course of development; furthermore, it is the leap-transition.

As an emerging industrial country, China only takes 20 years to change its intellectual property right system from low-level to high-level, completing the transition from localization to internationalization. In another word, in the new international environment of intellectual property protection, China does not experience the long preparation and transition construction period. Consequently, the governance on institutional environment is not enough and enterprises lack experiences in applying systems.

[15]Coglianese [6].

[16]Qian [7], pp. 309–310.

[17]Ibid.

9.7 Summary

There is a general cognition accepted by former Chinese scholars: at the beginning of making legislation for intellectual property right, China does not take the social economic phase and the acceptability of traditional people into consideration, which must be ahead of time. It is in a state of ultra protection, and may even used as a tool for Western countries to carry out technological monopoly and curb the development of China. Besides, it does not help to promote the cultural development and economical benefits but increases the development cost. This statement has observations with rationality. The level of a country's intellectual property right protection ability is determined by cultural prosperity, economic development level, legal attitudes and international positions.

Take America as an example, as the biggest intellectual property country, its protection ability is developed gradually. It is because of the clear recognition different development phases collected that America joined the Berne Convention in 1989. America is able to guarantee the adaption of social culture, economy, and legal traditions to the international environment in the premises of safeguarding the nation's interests. When comparing to the legislation and implementation process of Chinese copyright law, it is not hard to see the plagiarism and passiveness characteristics. It does not take above elements especially the influences of differences of Chinese legal culture and Western legal culture on copyright protection ability into consideration. Consequently, it is in a state of ultra protection to some extent. In addition, the ultra protection state leads to the so-called passable effect. By the way, China always falls into a passive position when talking about the intellectual property protection with Western countries.

The Chinese legislators really want to show the national conditions and features while implementing international treaties and referring to the legislations of other countries and they are trying their utmost to do so. However, the copyright law, because of development of human civilization, has its own rules, which have been widely accepted worldwide. Therefore, if people want to modify the copyright law based on the unique features of national conditions, they have to fully understand the legislative purpose with sufficient reasons or it cannot be easily changed. After all, Copyright Law has only experienced 30 years in China.[18] Thus, in the third revision, legislator should carefully study on and completely refer to concrete rules of developed countries in terms of copyright legislation. To sum up, in a developing country lacked of native resources of copyright law, it is hard to avoid or even has positive meaning to refer to or imitate international treaties to quickly build copyright laws in line with international norms. However, after 20 years of the publishing of this copyright law, the simple reference leads to outstanding logical contradiction; besides, it is hard to realize the legislative purpose without deepening understanding of popular international rules. This time, the task to modify the copyright law is carrying on in a relaxed international environment, which provides a good condition

[18]The First Copyright Law of People's Republic of China was enacted in 1991.

to reasonably refer to international treaties and foreign laws. It is ineluctable historical responsibility for legislators to seize this opportunity and make out logical and refined rules which are in line with the habits of Chinese expressions.[19]

References

1. Jiang M, Zhao K (2015) Managing the micro-self: governmentality of real name registration policy in Chinese microblogosphere. Inf Commun Soc 19:203, p 4
2. Adam B, Beck U, van Loon J (2000) The risk society and beyond: critical issues for social theory. SAGE Publications Ltd
3. Lash S (2000) Risk culture. In: Adam B, Beck U, van Loon J (eds) Chapter II of the risk society and beyond: critical issues for social theory. SAGE Publications Ltd
4. Giddens A (2013) The consequences of modernity. Wiley Publishing
5. Menell PS (2005) Regulating spyware: the limitations of state laboratories and the case for federal preemption of state unfair competition laws. Berkeley Technol Law J 20:1363
6. Coglianese C (2005) The internet and citizen participation in rulemaking. J Law Policy Inf Soc, vol 1. https://doi.org/10.2139/ssrn.421161. Accessed 8 Aug 2018
7. Qian W (2011) Research on copyright protection in the network environment. Law Press, China, pp 309–310

[19]Clinton, Hilary., "Internet Rights and Wrongs: Choices & Challenges in a Networked World", http://www.state.gov/secretary/20092013clinton/rm/2011/02/156619.htm. 15 February 2013.

Chapter 10
Conclusion

Technology and law exist unique, but not isolated on digital rights management regulatory model. Factors involved in the regulatory model, as discussed in chapters above, could be relevant with economic, societal, cultural and other areas. In this regard, it is firmly believed that how digital rights management regulatory model vigorously run primarily depends on how successful those elements coordinate.[1]

There is a debate currently underway in some circles about whether digital rights management regulatory model would die. Nevertheless, I think that debate is largely beside the point. Technology routinely violates the former peace in copyright world that copyright holders presume, which makes regulatory model an inevitable option. "The choices we make today will determine what the internet looks like in the future".[2] Businesses have to give careful consideration on whether and how to enter markets where digital rights management strategy hang in the balance. People have to choose how to act online, what information to share and with whom, which ideas to voice and how to voice them. Governments have to be responsible to live up to their commitments to regulate these two above.

This book offered a starting point for that vision by calling for concentrating on individual difference about digital rights management regulatory model country by country. These diversities reflect a landscape that is complex, and sure to become more so in the coming years, as billions of more people connect to the internet. Moreover, to maintain digital rights management regulatory model that delivers the greatest possible benefits to the digital world, we need to have a serious conversation about the principles that will guide us, what rules exist and should not exist and why, what mechanisms should be encouraged or discouraged and how.

[1]Ibid.

[2]Ibid.

C. Xu, *Regulatory Model for Digital Rights Management*,
https://doi.org/10.1007/978-981-15-1995-6_10